THE UNIVERSITY OF
WINCHESTER

Much attention has recently been given by scholars to the widening of the gender gap in the nineteenth century, and the concept of separate spheres. Testing such constructions, and questioning the stereotypes associated with Victorian domesticity, Monica F. Cohen offers new readings of narratives by Austen, Charlotte Brontë, Dickens, Eliot, Eden, Gaskell, Oliphant and Reade to show how domestic work, the most feminine of all activities, gained much of its social credibility by positioning itself in relation to the emergent professions. By exploring how novels cast the Victorian conception of female morality into the vocabulary of nineteenth-century professionalism, Cohen traces the ways in which women sought identity and privilege within a professionalized culture, and revises our understanding of Victorian domestic ideology.

CAMBRIDGE STUDIES IN NINETEENTH-CENTURY
LITERATURE AND CULTURE 14

PROFESSIONAL DOMESTICITY IN THE VICTORIAN NOVEL

CAMBRIDGE STUDIES IN NINETEENTH-CENTURY
LITERATURE AND CULTURE 14

General editors
Gillian Beer, *University of Cambridge*
Catherine Gallagher, *University of California, Berkeley*

Editorial board
Isobel Armstrong, *Birkbeck College, London*
Terry Eagleton, *University of Oxford*
Leonore Davidoff, *University of Essex*
D. A. Miller, *Columbia University*
J. Hillis Miller, *University of California, Irvine*
Mary Poovey, *The Johns Hopkins University*
Elain Showalter, *Princeton University*

Nineteenth-century British literature and culture have been rich fields
for interdisciplinary studies. Since the turn of the twentieth century,
scholars and critics have tracked the intersections and tensions between
Victorian literature and the visual arts, politics, social organization,
economic life, technical innovations, scientific thought – in short, culture
in its broadest sense. In recent years, theoretical challenges and
historiographical shifts have unsettled the assumptions of previous
scholarly syntheses and called into question the terms of older debates.
Whereas the tendency in much past literary critical interpretation was to
use the metaphor of culture as "background," feminist, Foucauldian,
and other analyses have employed more dynamic models that raise
questions of power and of circulation. Such developments have re-
animated the field.

This series aims to accommodate and promote the most interesting work
being undertaken on the frontiers of the field of nineteenth-century
literary studies: work which intersects fruitfully with other fields of study
such as history, or literary theory, or the history of science. Comparative
as well as interdisciplinary approaches are welcomed.

A complete list of titles published will be found at the end of the book.

PROFESSIONAL DOMESTICITY IN THE VICTORIAN NOVEL

Women, work and home

MONICA F. COHEN

CAMBRIDGE
UNIVERSITY PRESS

PUBLISHED BY THE PRESS SYNDICATE OF THE UNIVERSITY OF CAMBRIDGE
The Pitt Building, Trumpington Street, Cambridge CB2 1RP, United Kingdom

CAMBRIDGE UNIVERSITY PRESS
The Edinburgh Building, Cambridge CB2 2RU, United Kingdom
40 West 20th Street, New York, NY10011-4211, USA
10 Stamford Road, Oakleigh, Melbourne 3166, Australia

First published 1998

Printed in the United Kingdom at the Unversity Press, Cambridge

Typeset in Baskerville 11/12½ pt [VN]

A catalogue record for this book is available from the British Library

Library of Congress cataloguing in publication data

Cohen, Monica F.
Professional domesticity in the Victorian novel: women, work, and
home / Monica F. Cohen.
p.   cm. – (Cambridge studies in nineteenth-century literature
and culture; 14)
Includes bibliographical references and index.
ISBN 0 521 59141 4 (hardback)
1. Domestic fiction, English – History and criticism.   2. English
fiction – 19th century – History and criticism.   3. Women and
literature – Great Britain – History – 19th century.   4. Literature and
society – Great Britain – History – 19th century.   5. Domestic
relations in literature.   6. Occupations in literature.   7. Sex role
in literature.   8. Women in literature.   9. Home in literature.
10. Work in literature.   I. Title.   II. Series.
PR878.D65C64 1998
823'.809355 – dc21   97-11305   CIP

ISBN 0 521 59141 4 hardback

For Mary-Ellen and Harvey Feinberg, whose untiring work,
untiring patience, and untiring wakefulness are home.

Such weighing and mixing and chopping and grating, such dusting and washing and polishing, such snipping and weeding and trowelling and other small gardening, such making and mending and folding and airing, such diverse arrangements, and above all such severe study!

(Charles Dickens, *Our Mutual Friend*)

Contents

Acknowledgments

Written in quiet places and noisy ones, libraries, coffee shops, offices, airports, seminar rooms and playgrounds, this project is the work of many voices. Born as a dissertation at Columbia University, it had several caregivers to whom I am eternally grateful: Franco Moretti provided the book with its first guiding spirit by teasing out the interesting and banishing the unsubstantiated; Michael Seidel gave it a brain by protecting its close textual analyses from fashionable appropriation; and Karl Kroeber cultivated its heart by keeping the argument true to novels that I can still love even after writing a book about them.

With unparalleled intellectual generosity and that perfect balance of humor and high ideals that makes his friendship so invaluable, Jonathan Freeman has read more drafts of this project from dissertation to book than I can count. Margaret Homans' intentional support and unintentional example gave the book an intellectual identity without chaining it to adolescent politics.

The book could never have been written without the financial, emotional, intellectual and familial support of my colleagues at the California Institute of Technology: Kevin Gilmartin, Cindy Weinstein, Alison Winter, Mac Pigman and John Sutherland showed me in every variety of ways what it means to be part of a vibrant intellectual household and I could never thank them enough.

Jeffrey Cohen, editor, critic and co-gerunder, will never accept my loving gratitude for all his unhistoric acts, but I will feel it no less deeply.

Professional domesticity was partially funded by a Marjorie Hope Nicholson Fellowship and a Whiting Foundation Fellowship in the Humanities. Earlier versions of several chapters have appeared in *Novel: A Forum on Fiction*, *Victorian Literature and Culture* and *Studies in the Novel*. Other parts have been given in talks and conferences. I am grateful to these generous and helpful audiences; their comments and suggestions have played a significant role in the formulation of this project.

Introduction

Every story of Victorian domesticity must begin with John Ruskin's paean:

This is the true nature of home – it is the place of Peace; the shelter, not only from all injury, but from all terror, doubt, and division. In so far as it is not this, it is not home: so far as the anxieties of the outer life penetrate into it, and the inconsistently minded, unknown, unloved, or hostile society of the outer world is allowed by either husband or wife to cross the threshold, it ceases to be home; it is then only a part of that outer world which you have roofed over, and lighted fire in. But so far as it is a sacred place, a vestal temple, a temple of the hearth watched over by Household Gods, before whose faces none may come but those whom they can receive with love, – so far as it is this, and roof and fire are types only of a nobler shade and light, – shade as of the rock in a weary land, and light as of the Pharos in the stormy sea; so far it vindicates the name and fulfills the praise of Home.[1]

Ruskin's home conjures the set of dichotomies most characteristic of what is understood as domestic ideology: it is a place of peace and not strife, rest and not labor, confidence and not anxiety, unity and not division. As secularized holy ground, it is most distinctly a state of mind: materially indistinguishable from "a part of that outer world which you have roofed over," the home is only "true" if it can be correlated to psychological comfort. The "shelter" is a sense of shelter, the peace a peace of mind. So the great portraitists of Victorian domesticity have recorded and so the critics of its ideological structures have been informed.

In light of Ruskin's imagery, *Professional domesticity* began with the expectation that the home-bound plots of novels written by Austen, Charlotte Brontë, Dickens, Eliot, Gaskell, Oliphant and Reade would pivot on a narrative convention that used psychological interiority as a means of broadening the scope of privileges associated with individualism. Before long, however, the project had to make sense of the fact that

I

the domesticity conveyed in mid-century novelistic discourse fostered a collectivist spirit that ultimately edged out the psychoanalytic dimensions of humanist novel-craft. Whereas Ruskin's mythology of the home emerges out of his prescription for female education, something else emerges from a novelist's description of female experience; when she cannot remember, for example, which of her ninety-eight novels she happened to be working on at this biographical moment, Margaret Oliphant describes the home as something other than a holy place of peace and shelter from the workaday storm outside:

> Other matters, events even of our uneventful life, took so much more importance in life than these books – nay, it must be a kind of affectation to say that, for the writing ran through everything. But then it was also subordinate to everything, to be pushed aside for any little necessity. I had no table even to myself, much less a room to work in, but sat at the corner of the family table with my writing-book, with everything going on as if I had been making a shirt instead of writing a book. Our rooms in those days were sadly wanting in artistic arrangement. The table was in the middle of the room, the centre round which everybody sat with candles or lamp upon it. My mother sat always at needle-work of some kind, and talked to whoever might be present, and I took my share in the conversation, going on all the same with my story, the little groups of imaginary persons, thcse other talks evolving themselves quite undisturbed.[2]

By saying, "the writing ran through everything," Oliphant emphasizes that the work ran through everything and everything through it: the spheres were not at all separate. Admittedly, the passage's description of the home as a busy, noisy, chaotic place of manufacture, work and sociability is not Oliphant's central purpose. But this is nevertheless the effect: in the course of rationalizing female paid labor – that is, her own very middle-class professional writing – according to the terms of female domestic duty, Oliphant makes the home a workplace. For Oliphant, the home is a workshop of sociability not only because it was so in her experience, but because the ideological agenda she chose for her own woman writer's autobiography made it so. For part of what inspired her to write her "life," she protests, are the unsatisfactory "lives" published about her novelistic competitors, Anthony Trollope's *Autobiography* and John Cross's *George Eliot's Life as Recounted in her Letters and Journals.* In a long deflation of the professional novelist as a mystifying artistic pariah who scribbles away in the isolation of a "mental hot house," Oliphant is primarily motivated to advance the argument that writing a novel is indistinguishable from other household tasks, not an occasion for self-indulgent emotional exploration. It is a definitively social process, she avers, no different than needle-work or family chatter, a domestic activity the products of which – those "little groups of imaginary people" – only contribute to the general bustle of a family where work and play are by economic necessity intermixed.

But this representation of the home as work is also a pointed justification for why she may not have always been able to produce her "best." Oliphant defends her position as a female worker from the perspective of domestic duty, but finds herself forced to inadvertently undermine her position as a serious novelist by implying that when writing is a service one provides for others, there can be no romanticizing it as art. By thus identifying the novel as a social service rather than as an artistic form, Oliphant's portrayal of novel-writing ends up reaffirming the renunciation characteristic of the domestic woman: as a homekeeper, *she* could not abandon her children for Eliot's mental hothouse; as a homekeeper, *she* could not indulge in a Trollopian relationship to characters who were, after all, not real-life flesh and blood, as Trollope, she claims, seems to have forgotten. Rather, she had to abandon the hothouse itself; she had to renounce renunciation and live in the material world, exactly what we shall see so many domestic heroines doing in novels written throughout the period. But this renunciation of artistic life is ultimately paraleptic: for by posing her anti-aestheticism in the terms of a woman's self-sacrificial discourse, Oliphant is still able to preserve the idea of her own artistic potential, however unrealized. In other words, although she speaks of having perhaps failed to produce her best, she uses the rhetoric of female self-sacrifice to challenge any definition of "best" that would separate artwork from homework. In this sense, her preoccupation with work and the various pleasures of renunciation that it engenders not only produces a representation of the home that is quite distinct from Ruskin's idyll, but occasions a somewhat Protestant and utilitarian aesthetic theory of the novel whereby art is not created by an isolated ascetic spirit, but happens as an organic part and economic supporter of busy household life.

It is not accidental that this version of domesticity emerges out of Oliphant's defense of novel-production as a social duty. By sneering at George Eliot for her "hot house" study, she revises Ruskin's flower-like domestic women by asserting that a woman's natural duty is to support her relations by writing novels beside the family hearth. In this sense, Oliphant's metaphor of the hothouse employs a romantic discourse of the natural in order to argue in favor of a domesticity that rests on the sociability and renunciative imperatives of women's literary work. In doing so, she implicitly stresses the wisdom of experience over the information of education, a perspective that will be important in understanding both nineteenth- and twentieth-century feminism's ambivalent relationship to the professional institutions that govern economically remunerative work and the class divisions largely repressed until recently in the women's movement. Hence, the intellectual assumptions informing Oliphant's writerly construction of valuable and evaluatable women's work remain middle-class: in the final analysis, the representation of intellectual and emotional labor as a potential livelihood applies to the homekeeper, on an allowance of sorts, whose activities may include washing clothes, but not to the wage-receiving washerwoman who is paid to do only that task.

In novelistic discourse, this ambivalence toward direct remuneration takes shape in interesting ways and affects the encoding of domestic ideology. In Margaret Oliphant's *Phoebe Junior*, for example, Reginald, the older son of a widower clergyman with a large and impoverished family, refuses a "sinecure" on the grounds that it means pay without work. His sister, Ursula, the daughter saddled with the bulk of the household work and poignantly wishing that there were "sinecures for girls," argues convincingly, "They pay you for that which is not work, but they will find you plenty of work they don't pay for."[3] The sentence invokes two opposites – being paid and not being paid – and equates them through a rhythmic repetition of words (pay, work, for) in inverted syntactic parallel. Heralded by a string of evenly cadenced iambs, each clause's concluding dactyl, "is not work" and "don't pay for," suggests that the absence of work and the absence of pay still artfully inscribe work and pay in the novel's imaginative economy. The syntax implies that there is an epistemological problem inherent in the way the relationship between work and pay is culturally constructed. Because pay makes work legible, pay is often taken as a metonymic representation of work when in truth pay is only a condition that makes work recognizable. In other words, the implied metonym misleads in the sense that although work and pay may coincide, one cannot be taken as evidence of the other.

In being an object of envy for both Northcote, the Dissenting minister who has a salary but no poor people in his congregation to tend, and for Ursula, to whom a salary would provide her father with irrefutable proof of her contribution to the household he takes for granted, Reginald's vocational condition stresses the importance of work and the importance of pay without endorsing any notion of paid work. In this sense, Ursula's evocation of the sinecure as workless pay for payless work performs a strange reversal: rather than desire to work so as to have money, she seems to desire to have money so as to be free to work. Her model of domesticity does not demand pay *per se*, only the recognition that pay would confer. Such domesticity is professional in Harold Perkin's sense that it, at least overtly, eschews wage-labor in favor of service-based prestige.[4]

In representing the home as work, Oliphant is thus forced to confront one of the accuracies of Ruskin's idyll: the absence of pay, which for Ruskin and generations of materialist critics after him means the removal of capitalist work and the consequent preservation of capitalist ideology through a virtual phantasmagoria of domestic leisure. For Oliphant, however, the absence of the wage clouds the home's visibility as a workplace. She turns to the idea of domesticity as a "sinecure for girls" – as, that is, a profession – as a means of inscribing work that deserves pay but does not get it through direct conventional channels. In doing so, she depicts her very own domestic work situation, which was, as one reviewer acerbically implies, remarkably close to that of a sinecure. For Oliphant was, after all, a professional novelist. And as a novelist, one of her disgruntled reviewers comments, she had access to what was essentially workless pay:

In what other calling would she have been so fortunate? Perhaps if she had been a painter, a picture dealer might have advanced her a few guineas. But we know of no "profession" other than letters in which remuneration can be anticipated to the same amount and on the same terms. Solicitors do not finance barristers to the tune of several thousands. A struggling surgeon will probably fail to raise a five pound note on the strength of a promise to cut off the lender's leg if called upon to do so. When the countless iniquities of "the trade" are rehearsed by prosperous and well-fed authors, let not the recording angel fail to note that publishers have long done and still continue to do, what is asked and expected of no man in any other kind of business.[5]

Although the reviewer distinguishes novel-writing both from "professions" and "trades" by brackcting the terms in patronizing punctuation, his comparison of the writer to the lawyer or the surgeon and the publisher to the businessman suggests that novel-writing both is and is not a professional business. His high-minded objection, like Reginald's, is to workless pay. But Oliphant would have argued that such workless pay culminated in doing a great deal of pay-less work: she acknowledges the generosity of her publishers, but complains that they were still considered her "benefactors" even when "the balance changed" (*Autobiography* 90), thereby implying that she was often underpaid, if paid at all. Indeed, her Byzantine arrangements with publishers for future work often meant that she received in the end less than she might, had she marketed each piece individually and closer to a projected publication date, as canny strategists like Trollope often did. But Oliphant had so many extended advances going on at the same time that it is unlikely that she made the best deals per item, and this perhaps explains why she never made as much money as Trollope, despite her popularity and productivity.[6] In so far as her publisher "bankers" provided her with use of their capital "for nothing," requiring no security other than her sound mind (*Blackwood's*), her business dealings departed from conventional capitalist arrangements. Like so many other novelists of the period, she made money as a professional rather than as a laissez-faire capitalist.

Reginald's sinecure and his sister's praise for it introduce into the novel an idea of paid unpaid work. In the Anglican church, Oliphant identifies an institution that, in its practice of paying individuals to do unpaid work, provides a locus of value for the narrative generation of a courtship plot. Romance, and consequently Oliphant's success in the literary marketplace, are enabled by a financial arrangement traditionally cited as evidence of clerical corruption. That sinecures can be praised by virtue of the *de facto* social work they perform suggests that Oliphant's novel is positioned to intervene in Reform politics, albeit in a fundamentally conservative if not ironic way. Although Oliphant claims that the purpose of her novels was to entertain, not to preach, and that the purpose of her writing them was to earn a living, not to create art, the political implications of working at entertaining and entertainment as work collapse separate spheres in a slippery, however audacious, way. For when Ursula wishes for professional domesticity, for a "sinecure for girls," is she wishing for a concrete share in patriarchy or is she setting up the institution of marriage as patriarchy's false imitation? Is it patriarchy that professional domesticity questions, or only its fake? In this sense, Oliphant exemplifies some of the more complicated formal and political issues at stake in the figure of the professional home.

The sociable setting and the ethical imperative assumed by the model of work characteristic of professional domesticity lead to a vision of novelistic domesticity as somehow communitarian. I use this somewhat clumsy word to capture the sense in which the home is presented as a small community where routine work is held as the primary source of meaning in individual life. Of course, this work is generally represented as intellectual rather than physical and therefore presumes a set of associations to the middle classes that distinguishes professional domesticity from the industrialist discourse of "social problem" novels. I use "communitarian" very broadly and do not mean to suggest that this depiction of the home contained an overtly collectivist agenda that posited a small community's control over production and distribution. I should point out, however, that many advocates of women's property reform did use the value of domestic work (even if that work was presented strictly as emotional or psychological labor) as grounds for a more equitable distribution of household property, and who is to say what role novel-reading may have had in the persuasiveness of that argument.

Central to the depiction of the home represented in these novels is a notion of work that reveals ties to Protestantism in its extroverted, continuous, self-renunciative nature: consistently Victorian novels unveil domesticity as an elected vocation. In stressing the importance of devoting a cultivated knowledge of the specific to the service of others, the homecraft of these novels betrays a vocational purport that places it on the cusp of late nineteenth-century professional culture.

In seeing the home as a vocational outlet, it becomes possible to see Victorian feminism overlapping nineteenth-century professionalism in so far as both movements are concerned with the social role and value of communal principles. The assertion of women's rights as merited by a female's inalienable connection to others (whether experienced as a blessing or a curse, biologically determined or culturally mandated) precedes and in some ways foreshadows the professional's conception of his or her service as a sign of entitlement.

Like my use of the term "communitarian," I use the word "professionalism" broadly as well; both serve me more as descriptions than as definitions. The narrative of my findings developed whereby I saw the home as a place of nonpersonal sociability, as a workplace, as a vocation and then as a profession. But even if I had been able to reconstruct a nineteenth-century professional culture, as I have tried to do with the help of historians who see in Victorian England the seeds of the modern British welfare state, by which homekeeping would indeed count as a profession, being a housewife could never be quite the same as being a doctor. So even if we accept the argument that in nineteenth-century England's professional society all occupations were potential professions, we would have to allow that all professions were not potentially equal. As Mary Poovey has demonstrated, midwifery may have been professionalized, but it was nevertheless closed out from that profession called medicine, gender difference having played the operative role.[7] Hence we can only understand the gender-neutral professional domesticity presented in these novels in a prescriptive rather than a descriptive relationship to the historical moment in which they were produced.

Mary Poovey and Nancy Armstrong, among others, have demonstrated how the separate sphere doctrine of Victorian England used emotion and psychology to displace politics and to effectively elide class conflict from the collective consciousness. In this light, the domestic ideology represented by cultural products like novels can be seen as middle-class political interest masquerading as psychology. Armstrong has argued that Woman, as a figure of emotion and psychological interiority, came to lubricate the sharp contradictions of social praxis by naturalizing class conflict into the universal language of a "personal life" governed by sexual and romantic preoccupations.[8] Poovey has argued that this divorce between the personal and the political, the private and the public, provides the basis for the rise of an ideological professionalization whose exclusionary logic only replicated middle-class hegemony. The woman, according to this narrative, remains the amateur against which the professional expert is measured and empowered.

In the meantime, historians of nineteenth-century professionalism suggest that Victorian society, while being entrepreneurial and capitalistic, was also increasingly professional and at times socialistic; because English professionalism created and promoted a host of collectives and associations, communitarian structures and presumptions existed alongside capitalist incentives and institutions, which changes what can be understood by the term "middle class." I adopted this model of Victorian society in *Professional domesticity* because it helps to account for why, unlike the novels Poovey and Armstrong address, this set of novels uses the home unexpectedly as a trope for expressing hostility towards, and indeed a wish to repudiate, the psychological language of individualistic subjectivity that Poovey and Armstrong identify as characteristic of domestic ideology. In other words, the novels of *Professional domesticity* substitute occupation for preoccupation and thereby borrow easily from Protestant traditions of work. They articulate claims to prestige and economic rights (though not necessarily political rights) by virtue of properties, both material and intellectual, manufactured at home. Hence scenes of baking, mixing, chopping, dusting and waxing occur amid reading, writing, translating and corresponding (often with readers and publishers). One explanation for this strange amalgam of crafts whose relations to the capitalist market is repeatedly mystified lies in the woman writer's rebellion against the terms of domestic ideology without her sacrifice of its central symbol, one in an idea of art as both encoding and exposing a reigning ideology and one in a Bakhtinian theory of the novel by which competing discourses can flourish in a forest of untroubling irony.

The interest of this project therefore is to place alongside Armstrong's psychological discourse a professional one that represents the home as a profession, as vocational work. Although the professionalization of the home should not be confused with an identity between home and profession, the fact that these novels invent such a similitude suggests that the metaphor can be followed along several trajectories. We can speculate that professional domesticity afforded women an escape from emotional life without demanding that they abandon their putative monopoly on emotion. We can imagine that claiming expertise in ethical love might have functioned as a coping mechanism for all the Maggie Tullivers who wished to make themselves "a world outside of love, as men do."[9] We can consider how professional society, where intellectual capital began to carry political and legal benefits as it became recognized as equivalent to property, placed the idea of moral or ethical capital in a potentially more powerful role than the initial phases of a separate sphere society had allowed; the prosperity enjoyed by Dissenters and the influence Dissent had on the social organization of the Established Church altered the Puritan sequestering of the psychological from the political at the same time that an emerging marketplace of ideas changed the position intellectuals bore both to social justice and to the capitalist economy.

In this sense, the Victorian homekeeper depicted in these novels stood on common ground with the intellectual and the artist: amateurs who used the language of professionalism to represent their work as the fulfillment of a higher calling that, in answering to the collective good, merited rights and privileges, all of which extended the definition of property in a characteristically English conservative tradition. While many advocates of "civic maternalism" used a woman's moral superiority as grounds for the legal recognition of her property and even for her political enfranchisement, novelists promoted their own careers in claiming a moral higher good for their quasi-intellectual, quasi-artistic products. Professional domesticity can be seen then as a temporary means of resolving the oppositions subtending the separate-sphere doctrine: rather than saying a woman should have equal rights because a woman is like a man, professional domesticity implied that a woman should have equal rights because her innate moral property entitles her to them. That this argument is imagined in novels at a time when the profession of novel-writing was increasingly based on intellectual capital and advance payments – not unlike Reginald's sinecure – is surely not simply felicitous.

The problem remains, however, that in Protestant culture, vocational work still correlated with uncertainty: the doctrine of predestination, even in the form of a watered-down influence on Anglican intellectual reflexes, still produced a level of anxiety that reinscribed psychological categories in a professional discourse that was ostensibly poised to countermand the life of love dictated by the separate spheres. However much the professional domesticity of these novels might repress the psychological imperatives of an earlier domestic ideology, the focus on work in a Protestant context predestines the return of psychological lines of development. Hence the aesthetic emerging from these novels conveys a virtually irresolvable tension, but one that makes this fiction a peculiarly interesting fantasy.

This is only to stress that my study of professional domesticity is a study of a set of novels. For heuristic purposes, I have borrowed from Max Weber in viewing the nineteenth-century idea of home to be a "historical object." In a different context, Weber defines an "historical object" as "a complex of elements associated in historical reality which we unite into a conceptual whole from the standpoint of their cultural significance."[10] In this sense, domesticity figures as a systematized body of concepts about human life and culture. But because my primary sources are novels, and not historical artifacts whose narratives operate according to different rules of verisimilitude, my emphasis as a literary critic must be on the "complex . . . associated" rather than on the "historical reality" of the Victorian home.

This leads me only to emphasize that professional domesticity is an invention of middle-class Victorian women and men who worked at home writing novels and essays that were supposed to be as edifying as they were entertaining, which is to say, as socially useful as personally profitable. Although each of the novelists under study here subscribed to a different idea of what constituted the useful and the profitable, they all chose to publish in three-decker and serialized forms; they did not work with "pulp" presses where quicker money might have been more certain, but where a "literary reputation" would not have been possible.[11] In this choice, they can be seen as participating in an intellectual culture that was still connected to popular entertainment but which, for various reasons, stood in an ambivalent and complicated relationship to the capitalist marketplace.

CHAPTER I

Persuading the navy home:
Austen and professional domesticism

In 1839, Sarah Ellis prefaced her lengthy meditation on Victorian domesticity and the condition of English women by pronouncing a truly oceanic sentence:

it seems an ungracious task to attempt to rouse [English young ladies] from their summer dreams; and were it not that wintry days will come, and the surface of life be ruffled, and the mariner, even she who steers the smallest bark, be put upon the inquiry for what port she is really bound – were it not that the cry of utter helplessness is of no avail in rescuing from the waters of affliction, and the plea of ignorance unheard upon the far-extending and deep ocean of experience, and the question of accountability perpetually sounding, like the billows of this lower world – I would be the last to call the dreamer back to a consciousness of present things.[1]

In a periodic sentence that culminates in shameless paralepsis, the call to duty is deferred by waves of clauses – parentheticals, modifiers and participles – that wash English, and presumably female, readers away from the national shore of those "present things" that Ellis will later tell us consist of the economic hardships endemic to British capitalism. Yet even at sea in the billows of this extended metaphor, we cannot but notice that it is a she at the helm, a she who steers. If we convert the metaphor's equivalencies, it is hardly remarkable to see a woman presented at the head of her household, in charge of her own sphere. But it is interesting that Ellis should use nautical imagery as the pivotal trope in her polemical endorsement of separate spheres; for it asks how Ellis' fantasy of female empowerment can be enabled by the position of seamanship in the nineteenth-century English imagination. By using professional seafaring in this way, the passage asks us to envision what I shall call professional domesticity, and to speculate as to what is at stake in the invention of that rhetorical figure.

Although Ellis' preoccupation with the sea in her depiction of English domesticity may be merely accidental, the dramatic imagery it inspires contradicts many of the assumptions literary critics make about the representation of the home. In his Foucauldian description of England's late eighteenth-century "cultural revolution," for example, Gary Kelly explains that domesticity "included the idea of the home as a refuge from a hostile and competitive social world . . . the separation of the home from place of work."[2] But Ellis' seascape reveals nothing of the sort. *Her* domesticity involves not only work, but exposure to the devastating elements representative of a nation in crisis. *Her* domesticity calls for professional reform: even the smallest "ship" will be called to account for its destination in these national stormy seas. In this, Ellis directs our attention from the economic turmoil of early Victorian capitalism to the revolutionary period of which Kelly speaks, and to the first literary merging of the sea and the home at the beginning of the century in Jane Austen's *Persuasion*.[3]

Persuasion provides a starting-point for a discussion of Victorian professional domesticity in a variety of ways. Permeated by a single consciousness, removed from the propriety of a landed social world and deepened by a personalized marriage plot, *Persuasion* is generally seen by critics as exemplifying Austen's break from Augustan literary conventions and a presage of the more inwardly turned Victorian novel. More pertinently, it occasions an exploration of the relationship between domesticity and professionalism in so far as so much of its domestic plot is preoccupied with the professional navy and the gendered transvaluation that occurs when the sea becomes a professional English home.

For Gary Kelly, the domestic woman of this period is "a female version of the professional man, distinguished from woman as partner in the family owned business and woman as ornament in courtly upper-class life . . . [she] was to provide a moral intellectual service, ostensibly without remuneration" (*Revolutionary Feminism* 16). Produced by the professional classses whose "capital was in the first instance intellectual and moral – of the mind" (5), Kelly's woman writer is in a position to popularize the values of the professional bourgeoisie and disseminate its cultural revolution: because a woman's "property" was necessarily limited to matters of propriety and conduct, a woman's interests were indistinguishable from the interests of a class equally invested in redefining property. Thus Kelly's cultural revolution coercively inducts "woman" by giving her access to the profession of writing while subordinating her within professional bourgeois culture generally. In other words, though the professional homekeeper may be a "version of the professional man," she is a version etched in bad faith. According to this story then, professional domesticity is part of the history of the middle class's cooptive drive to cultural hegemony.

But Marilyn Butler tells another story. In identifying a "Tory women's tradition, which must also be thought of as proto-feminist,"[4] she suggests that the women writers who best inculcated the cult of domesticity were not pawns in a middle-class game of domination that would ultimately exclude them, but forerunners of a reform tradition that had as one of its main goals the public advancement of women. Tory feminism, Butler argues, is too prevalent throughout eighteenth- and nineteenth-century writing to have been merely a part of a post-French Revolution backlash (*Jane Austen* xxxiii). Aware of the gender inequalities characteristic of public life, Tory feminists insisted on the religious sanctity of women's service both to the family and to the larger community (xxii) in an effort to promote greater equality for women. Seen as a part of a Tory feminist tradition, professional domesticity is not a figure of cultural deception, but a radical means of non-revolutionary change.

As I will argue, *Persuasion*, by telling the story of how the navy is domesticated in the Napoleonic and post-Napoleonic years, also tells the story of how domesticity is professionalized: two lines of potential narrative development, the naval adventure and the domestic plot, merge. The novel thus provides an occasion for asking whether this narrative hybridization reproduces the conditions of professional bourgeois culture thereby contributing to Kelly's cultural revolution, or whether the novel's peroration on the idea of the naval home contributes to the creation of Butler's Tory feminist tradition. The answer, I believe, can be found in property: who loses it and who gets it. That Mrs. Smith will prove the only character of the novel to acquire ownership of property, and that she does so without possessing the propriety that conventionally marks Austen's upwardly mobile heroines, is indeed the radical *tour de force* buried in an ostensibly incidental subplot.

Mrs. Smith's property is neither a landed estate nor the manners associated to one in a fictive age of equipoise. Rather, it is the legal right to assets attached to colonial land sequestered from her deceased husband's estate. Mrs. Smith finally comes to own this property only when a professional man acts on her behalf, and only when the discourse of professionalism succeeds in controlling the romantic destiny of the courtship plot. In this sense, Mrs. Smith's property is a professionalism that is itself fictive: borrowed from the naval heroes Austen sketches, it displaces one avatar of domesticity only to author another. Although the conclusion's coy conflation of "national importance" and "domestic virtues" (254) gestures towards a more fluid sense of sexual difference, Mrs. Smith's material gain, and indeed Anne's, remain predicated on the ennobling sacrifices and sufferings professed in the novel as peculiar to women.

INGENIOUS PROPERTIES

Persuasion concludes with a homeless heroine: Anne Elliot, like so many of Austen's other heroines, has little income and "no family to receive and esteem" her spouse properly (253); unlike her predecessors, however, there is no literal home awaiting her post-nuptial arrival – no landed estate house like Pemberley, Northanger Abbey, Donwell Abbey, the Parsonage at Mansfield Park, or Delaford House. When Elizabeth Bennet tours Pemberley, the narrative whispers her desires: "to be mistress of Pemberley might be something!"[5] All this could have been hers. The narrative objective in *Persuasion*, however, looks quite different: for when Anne Elliot muses over her missed marriage opportunity, the "this" is the company of Wentworth's "brother officers" and the scene a boarding-house they inhabit (119). Company substitutes for property; rented rooms stand in for a manor house:

> they all went indoors with their new friends, and found rooms so small as none but those who invite from the heart could think capable of accommodating so many. Anne had a moment's astonishment on the subject herself; but it was soon lost in the pleasanter feelings which sprang from the sight of all the ingenious contrivances and nice arrangements of Captain Harville, to turn the actual space to the best possible account, to supply the deficiencies of lodging-house furniture, and defend the windows and door against the winter storms to be expected. (119)

As the landscape of Pemberley speaks to Elizabeth Bennet, the Harville home is what has voice for Anne Elliot. But the values conveyed are different. Whereas the landscape prospect of *Pride and Prejudice* is distinguished in its evocation of generational continuity, historical order and what can be understood as ownership or mastery – over the servants who praise Darcy, the fish Mr. Gardiner is invited to catch and the trees that compose the park – the seascape home in Lyme impresses by virtue of its "ingenious contrivances." In its strange mixture of romantic inspiration and utilitarian purport, or what Butler observes as a potential overlapping in Austen's late fiction of evangelicalism and utilitarianism (*Jane Austen* 284), the very phrase is precocious, a pleonasm that implies a shift: a contrivance that is not ingenious would perhaps connote the social plottings and theatrical artifice deployed and critiqued in a comedy of manners like *Mansfield Park*; the ingenious contrivance here, however, is linked to handiwork. It refers to Harville's faculty for something like interior design, a skill that mixes dexterity with intellect.

It is important that Harville is accorded respect for labor that is not often represented in Austen's fiction. But whereas Darcy's prestige derives directly from his land, we cannot say that Harville's prestige derives from the literal work he does. It is connected rather to his ingenuity. In this scene we can see the courtship plot deflected from a social hierarchy organized around landed property and towards one centered on ingenuity. This repudiation of land as property in favor of some intellectual equivalent is established early on when Anne, however admiring of the happy Musgroves at Uppercross, is saved from envying them by not wanting to give up "her own more elegant and cultivated mind" (*Persuasion* 67). Although we can see the same kind of independent spirit in Elizabeth Bennet, the landed world of Pemberley is ultimately tagged the more elegant and better-cultivated property. Indeed not only does Elizabeth seem to recognize the land as the precondition for maintaining that independent mind, however relative the final independence, but her intellectual gifts find their equivalence in the real property of Darcy's estate. For Anne Elliot, however, there is no such possibility offered among the traditionally propertied or conventionally moneyed classes. "Mind" itself surfaces as the desirable property and ingenuity an ascendant value.

As the passage continues, it becomes clear that Harville is so handy in these otherwise impersonal rented rooms because he is a sailor:

The varieties in the fitting-up of the rooms, where the common necessaries provided by the owner, in the common indifferent plight, were contrasted with some few articles of a rare species of wood, excellently worked up, and with something curious and valuable from all the distant countries Captain Harville had visited, were more than amusing to Anne: connected as it all was with his profession, the fruit of its labours, the effect of its influence on his habits, the picture of repose and domestic happiness it presented, made it to her a something more, or less, than gratification. (120)

At first blush, the scene recalls a Vermeer interior where maps and Oriental rugs bear witness to the comings and goings characteristic of a merchant marine culture. Here even more so, the "personality" that stamps the room is of an entirely vocational significance. Connected to his profession, the souvenirs militate against that "common indifferent plight" of faceless owners and transient tenants. A testimony to his profession, the souvenirs are not strictly the signs of bourgeois consumption; for their professional significance produces a sense of the scene as situated within an artisan-based, rather than a commodity-based, culture. The passage stresses that the "fruit of his labour," the consequences of his job, do not consist exclusively of the material objects he brings back; his vocation has an "influence on his habits" that allows him to "fit up" a home, much like he would fit out a ship, contriving to use the tight quarters of a frigate or man-of-war most efficiently and most comfortably.

NAVAL CONTRIVANCES

Harville's fittings-up can be understood in the context of the innovations happening in the British navy during the years of the Napoleonic Wars. Writing a slim history of the British navy during its "classical age," C. Northcote Parkinson provides a plot for the British naval defeats in the early years of the war by attributing them to the "change in professional attitude."[6] Rather than finding themselves engaged in an earlier aristocratic-type battle that culminated in some arrangement that allowed the members of each fleet essentially to shake hands and go their own ways, Parkinson maintains, the English were astonished to find the newly democratized French navy battling to the death. The English response was to reform naval practice, especially management at sea, but later the Admiralty administration and the dockyards as well: the "pressure for reform," which took the form of a "heightened sense of professionalism and desire for efficiency," was in this sense "institutionalized."[7]

That the Napoleonic Wars were won at sea before they were won on land seems to be a favorite claim of British naval historians.[8] Parkinson's argument colors in this assertion by stressing that the British, and the rest of anti-Bonaparte Europe, owed their success not only to Lord Nelson and his brilliant tactics, but to the behind-the-scenes man, Sir John Jervis, later known as Lord Saint Vincent. Famous for imposing a strict economy whereby bookkeeping was prioritized, expenditure rationalized and ship garbage recycled (Parkinson, *Britannia Rules* 23), Jervis attended to the quotidian life of a naval fleet. He bickered with doctors over whether his men should wear warm flannel or a cotton weave that could be kept cleaner. He improved each ship's ventilation and windsails. He instituted a schedule of regular fumigation. And he was the first admiral to order soap for his fleet (Pope, *Life in Nelson's Navy* 147–8). By inventing a procedure for refitting at sea rather than in port, Jervis initiated a division of labor among the ships belonging to a fleet which gave them greater mobility and speed. Rather than rely on sick-bays, Jervis kept a hospital ship with each fleet. Rather than rely on the resources of ports whose allegiance during the height of the Continental system was unreliable, he kept store-ships traveling with each group (Parkinson, *Britannia Rules* 24). These specialized seacrafts, alongside fire ships, prison ships and repair ships, marked the beginning of what would later become the Auxiliary Navy.[9]

In Parkinson's story, Jervis is responsible for moving the British navy away from its dependence on charismatic tacticians and personalities like Sir Francis Drake and Lord Nelson, and toward an organizational principle: specialization. The endeavor catalyzed, albeit gradually, the British navy's own democratization in a way quite different from the democratization characterizing the French "National" fleet, which regrouped under the ideological principles of the French Revolution. The English response to the "change in professional attitude" among the French nationals can be seen then as a different kind of professionalization, one that was implicated in that nationalism associated to the new French *Nation*. The democratization of the French force, whereby its professional attitude (that is, its spirit) dismantled the international aristocratic confraternity that had kept battle a relatively amateur competition between equals, provoked a response within the British navy that changed the nature of the profession as an institution (that is, the institution of the English navy): for in countering the French fighting *esprit*, the English turned towards expertise.[10]

Later in the nineteenth century as Harold Perkin, among others, has argued, English "professional culture" will be marked by its stress on trained expertise, institutional affiliation and an ethic of social good – all of which enable professional service to command a high price in a national marketplace.[11] In the revamping of the navy of the earlier part of the century, we can see the signs of this type of professionalism: Jervis' installation of labor divisions produced specialized ships as well as naval specialists, men who concentrated on performing only specialized tasks; the navy as an institution was already a formally recognized association increasingly less concerned with its traditional class-based "gatekeeping" duties and more vigilant about providing officer training; the ethic of social good is putatively self-evident in a military association serving a nation at war. In terms of the national marketplace, it is important to recall the extent to which the Napoleonic Wars at sea were significantly commercial. Captains and admirals got rich mostly by seizing ships – French as well as others caught without a "permit" issued from a British port – and auctioning their cargoes (Parkinson, *Britannia Rules* 107). Although these sailing officers were not paid more for their services, their services provided them indirectly with rewards that made that service more attractive. Although they were making money, they did not make money like capitalists. It is important that the first of England's four professions to open to ambitious young men was the navy of these years. The century began with an infusion of wealth made by professionals in service to their nation, men whose relationship to the economy was neither aristocratic nor capitalistic, but professional.

Unlike the charismatic Nelson who inspires his fleet by the force of his personality, Jervis is Parkinson's sleeper hero. Dismissing the brilliance of Nelson's battle strategies and martial intuition, Parkinson marvels at Jervis' ingenuity ("all this [ships repaired and freshly painted] without a pause in the fleet's movement") and at the ethic of care his activities seem to illustrate:

It was he [Jervis] who had done so much for the fleet's hygiene and diet that there was not a man sick when the day of battle came. Nor could Nelson have created the fleet he led. Superb as he was as leader and tactician, he had no comparable gifts as an administrator. (65)

The cartoon informing this picture of Jervis the naval hero discloses both an imperial idea of his administration as well as an ethical image of his cleaning and feeding the men. In this, there is a touch of the heroine about Jervis.

SHIP-SHAPE HOMES

In light of the domestic management narrative that emerges from *Britannia Rules*, we can return to Harville's household and see the navy's "influence on his habits" (*Persuasion* 120). His imperial acquisitions, curiosities implicitly valuable for their foreignness, coincide with his knowing how to make small and temporary spaces comfortable – as if his tenure aboard seacraft had trained him for homecraft. Lest we assume that only small spaces are improved through such naval arts, we can see the same sort of household measures taken at Kellynch-hall, where Admiral Croft moves the umbrellas from the butler's room to a more accessible place by the front entryway, repairs the laundry door and gets his wife to help him move the mirror out of the master bedroom: "and now I am quite snug, with my little shaving glass in one corner, and another great thing that I never go near" (142–3). The fact that Anne confesses she cannot but feel that the house is in better hands suggests that the hands-on, do-it-yourself spirit of the Crofts is good because it is more practical. Why practical people should be more deserving of a manor house is not explicitly stated, as if utility's morality is self-evident, which perhaps it is.

The vision of the Crofts doing all these things themselves in a large estate house appears deliberately lovable. Equally deliberate is the Admiral's small shaving set-up: tucked into the corner of a grandiose bedroom, he participates in an aesthetic of the charming. The naval trappings informing these at-home scenes suggest that the diminutive aesthetic that will eventually characterize key sites in domestic novels take their cues from the influence of the navy on domestic habits. As professional sailors, Harville, Benwick and Croft know how to make the best use of small spaces – and even how to create small spaces out of larger ones. Naval narrative metonymies process the cramped into the cozy. In this sense, the novel displays the effect of the navy's homecoming on the courtship plot in the tropes of diminution it borrows. Indeed, many of the homes idealized in domestic novels are, like the Harville rooms, tiny but ingeniously fitted out: Wemmick's castle of *Great Expectations*, Bella Wilfer's kitchen in *Our Mutual Friend*, the Meyrick parlour of *Daniel Deronda*, Lucy Snowe's final schoolroom in *Villette* – all materialize in a "small, but . . . " idiom. Why these domestic spaces must be small is never really explained. If we read *Persuasion* as a nostos that tells the story of how navy men are reintegrated into a home country no longer at war, we can perhaps locate the origins of the premium placed on small spaces in domestic narratives as a revisit to the tight quarters characteristic of a British frigate. *Persuasion* documents an early instance of the idealized small, impermanent, home, and shows its likeness to naval quarters. The implication is that the home when it is represented in fiction can assume the national significance of the navy when it is at war.

In returning to the Harville home scene, we can see that unlike the men in many Vermeers, the sailor-homemakers of Austen's setpiece are not about to leave. Harville is lame. Benwick is bereaved. Admiral Croft is retired. And most importantly, the war is over. Though the novel is set during the Hundred Days War, Austen may not have completed it until after Waterloo and arguably after it became obvious that finding something to occupy the navy during a peace was a national concern. We can see in *Persuasion* its prestige – its influence – changing from one being based on martial deed to one predicated on domestic utility: sailors are good to have around the house because they're so good with their hands.

The Harville home as a "picture of repose" is so fraught with the significance of the navy's presence that the "repose" is less relaxation than a reposing, or repositioning. Through the nineteenth century, "repose" designated "to place" or "to put confidence or trust in a person or thing," and "to place or leave something in the management of another" (*OED*, first edition) A "picture of repose," the scene in this light depicts delegation. It is a scene in which authority is delegated, which is not the same as a scene in which people relax. Surely we must allow the possibility of this *double-entendre* when Austen expands the scene in a series of complicated moves:

Captain Harville was no reader; but he had contrived excellent accommodations, and fashioned very pretty shelves, for a tolerable collection of well-bound volumes, the property of Captain Benwick. His lameness prevented him from taking much exercise; but a mind of usefulness and ingenuity seemed to furnish him with constant employment within. (120)

At first, it would seem that because Harville owns a useful and ingenious mind, his "employment within" refers to a contemplative posture. Although we know that he is not a great reader, the passage situates his invalidism amid books. As the agent of book-accommodating and shelf-fashioning, Harville is associated with intellectual culture. His ingenuity links him to activities that look like literary appreciation, or at least an appreciation of books. The sedentary life consequently seems to entail some intellectual preoccupation: his mind the agent of "furnish[ing]," Harville's "within" would seem to designate a psychological interior that is anticipated in the literature references that precede him.

The next sentence, however, clarifies what Harville's "employment" actually is:

He drew, he varnished, he carpented, he glued; he made toys for the children, he fashioned new netting-needles and pins with improvements; and if every thing else was done, sat down to his large fishing-net at one corner of the room. (120)

Not only is this "picture of repose" a scene of activity, but the labor presumably involved in the activity is modulated by the setting "within." Borrowed from the bookshelves and their contents, the contemplative associations Harville's work carries with it make it seem less like labor and more like what the later nineteenth century will call craft.[12] In other words, the scene's leisure is animated by a labor that is itself modified by a metonymic association to intellectual products. The scene of repose enacts a scene in which the authority associated to the leisure classes is delegated to – is *reposed in* – a professional who, however busy, is, nonetheless, at leisure.

PAYING FOR UNPAID WORK: THE SINECURE REVISITED

Harville's labor in the scene is further mediated by his being unpaid: sort of. As a war veteran, he presumably receives a stipend for his past service. Unlike a salary, his pension is paid by virtue of his having been a sailor. In other words, he is paid for being a member of a respected profession, rather than directly for an expenditure of labor. That his naval tenure influences his expending quite a lot of labor around the house suggests that there is indeed a connection between his pay and his domestic work: his household labor is essentially paid for by the nation.

Recall Oliphant's *Phoebe Junior* in this context: both Reginald's sinecure and Harville's pension introduce into their respective novels this figure of paid unpaid work. Whereas Austen uses the navy and Oliphant the Anglican Church, they both identify an institution that will generate narrative action and romantic closure by virtue of its practice of paying individuals to do unpaid work. Ursula's work, and consequently her place in a romance plot that threatens to jilt her, becomes readable through the glass of the sinecure paradigm much as, several decades earlier, the navy's claim to a domestic place of honor becomes legible in the rewriting of Wentworth's initial jilt. *Phoebe Junior* and *Persuasion* can both be seen as novels preoccupied with investigating the narrative possibilities housed in the marriage plot: the former opens with a discussion as to whether Ursula will marry, the latter with why Anne did not. Ursula and Anne do indeed come to marry only once Ursula's future spouse comes to recognize the value of a sinecure and only once Anne's social world comes to recognize the value of the navy on a pension at home. That a clerical sinecure or a military pension should occur as central citation-points in these recognition sequences suggests that the efficacy of the courtship plot relies on a peculiarly domestic conceptualization of the relationship between work and pay. We will see this tension played out in different ways in *Villette, Great Expectations, Little*

Dorrit, Felix Holt and *Daniel Deronda*, as well as in other domestic novels.

Historically, the uncomfortable relationship between work and pay seems to have been a problem for middle-class women for a variety of reasons ranging from Puritan objections concerning any capitalist accumulation to a patriarchal protectiveness that need not be exclusive to nineteenth-century England. Jane Lewis, for example, illustrates the problem as especially apparent to "intellectual" women: recounting the anecdote of Jex Blake, she remarks with bemusement, the protective father was thrilled that his daughter had won a prestigious job teaching mathematics at Queen's College, but when he heard that she would be paid, he was so distressed that he offered to provide her with an equal "allowance" if she would decline the salary.[13] He did not object to her job, only to her salary. But although Lewis emphasizes that gender was the root of this tension between work and pay, her selected anecdote reveals that the tension may have been aggravated by the intellectual nature of the work itself.

This perhaps explains why an uncomfortable relationship between women's work and pay is replicated repeatedly by those intellectual workers known as novelists. Negotiating pay appears to require not only elaborate euphemisms in extra-paginal spheres, but double-jointed plot acrobatics within a novel's pages as well. In her correspondence with John Blackwood, for example, George Eliot declines his bid to renew the copyright of her novels by taking refuge in domestic figures of speech that dress her in maternal robes of care and concern for her "progeny": "but no one will understand better than you that I incline to keep up a sort of active parental relation to those grown-up children."[14] That this issue can resonate structurally within a novel's pages as well surfaces in governess narratives like Charlotte Brontë's *Jane Eyre* and Elizabeth Gaskell's *Wives and Daughters,* whose domesticity seems poised to confront the *Pamela*-driven maxim that a female household employee is nothing but a husband-hunter. The transition between paid governess and kept wife comes to a head in *Jane Eyre* over the question of her financial status. Indeed, the wedding ceremony is interrupted by Jane's own hand in so far as she is the one responsible for informing Mason of Rochester's pending nuptials when she writes to her Uncle John in Madeira. Although the novel had hitherto refused to provide Jane with any financial resources, her wealthy uncle suddenly materializes in answer to her wish for "ever so small an independency"[15] to make Mr. Rochester's spending money on her more bearable. This is to say that the courtship plot is suspended by the novel's incapacity to invent a form of financial "independency" for Jane the Wife once the wages belonging to Jane the Governess disintegrate.

Returning to *Persuasion*, Harville's pensioned position is conditioned by his membership in the navy, that is, by his belonging to a profession, by his being in this sense a professional. That his pension in the context of the homey scene above enables, but does not pay for, his domestic labors allows us to abstract the profession and to see it as a conceptual model for how home-working comes to be a viable culmination of the marriage plot, a means of reinventing it precisely because it finesses that gnarled issue of how and why to pay a woman.

But it is important here to recall that the narrative conflation of marriage and homekeeping is not predetermined. Not every novel that ends in a marriage detours through scenes that glorify home work. Moreover Anne, again like Ursula, will have taxing domestic duties whether she marries or not. Why these duties could figure as something like a career in marriage and not in spinsterhood does not necessarily turn on the obvious sexual and emotional differences between the two states. As an aesthetic matter, the question does not have a simple answer in recourse to the "real life" of a reader, writer or character. In articulating Anne's marriage to Wentworth as her "belonging to that profession" (254), *Persuasion* implies that there is a professional difference between managing Wentworth's domestic affairs and managing a father's, though the tasks themselves are virtually the same. The difference emerges in the line of development invoked and rejected in the reappearance of Mr. Elliot. Putting aside, for the moment, the potentially incestuous implications of, as Anne puts it, "having the precious name of Lady Elliot" (172) and, of equal importance, the family property, by marrying her father's heir, what is at stake in the villainization of the heir is the choice between property and profession. In the ideological world of *Persuasion*, marriage (in addition to representing a host of other attributes, of course) is an instrument whereby the choice between property and profession can be made. And the professed alternation underlines their fictive and perhaps fictional equivalence.

AT HOME IN THE NAVY

At home with prestige but no pay, Harville is presented as if he were a homemaker. Indeed, that we see Harville connected to implements traditionally associated to female work – needles and pins – suggests a gendered transvaluation implicit in the language used to describe the influence these sailors have both in the home and on it. That is, given navy men's influence (the prestige they enjoy at home), their influence on the household routine (their assumption of domestic tasks like sewing) changes the significance both of navy men's work and of domestic women's work.

The relevance of gender to naval professions emerges when Anne and Harville discuss the difference between men and women in coping with the loss of a loved one. Harville is angry that Benwick engaged himself to marry another woman only months after his previous fiancée had died. A woman, he is certain, would never be so changeable. Anne responds in terms that conflate changeable emotions with changeable places, a psychological mobility she admires and wishes to own. She is not only the most vigilant champion of the scheme of retrenchment, which would require a physical move to achieve its financial objective, but hopes that developing a faculty for integrating into every "social commonwealth" would ease her unhappiness when she finds herself shut out from the place-specific "matters of discourse" preoccupying the Musgroves (69). Whether or not we accept her praise of psychological mobility as sincere, its relevance to the novel's story-line surfaces when Anne warns Harville that emotional fidelity is nothing but a symptom of physical immobility:

"We live at home, quiet, confined, and our feelings prey upon us. You are forced on exertion. You have always a profession, pursuits, business of some sort or other, to take you back into the world immediately and continual occupation and change soon weaken impressions."

"Granting your assertion that the world does all this so soon for men (which, however, I do not think I shall grant), it does not apply to Benwick. He has not been forced upon any exertion. The peace turned him on shore at the very moment, and he has been living with us in our little family-circle ever since."

"True," said Anne, "very true; I did not recollect; but what shall we say now, Captain Harville? If the change be not from outward circumstances, it must be from within; it must be nature, man's nature, which has done the business for Captain Benwick." (236)

The conversation continues with Captain Harville's insisting that, as there is no natural difference between men and women, Benwick must be judged according to a universal standard that will find him wanting in feeling; and with Anne countering that because women are indeed different by virtue of the role emotion plays in their daily lives, Benwick is to be judged only according to the conduct expected in a man. What is important here is that the essentialist question – is there a natural difference between the sexes or not? – occurs only because there is a peace that has placed Benwick, and presumably other sailors like him, back at home with nothing to do but domestic work. In other words, the war that provided mainly nonpropertied men with a profession turned into a peace that put these newly professionalized men back at home. Returning to a higher place in the socio-economic hierarchy than that which they occupied before the war, these men still had no active means of exercising their professions. They each may have a profession, but they literally do not have employment. Nothing to do, that is, other than housework. Hence the Harville home's activity can be called a picture of repose because Harville himself is not active at sea, at his job. He is, officially speaking, at his leisure. But his profession not only makes him adept at handiwork, but lends professional prestige to improving pins and mending nets.

Harville's conversation with Anne calls our attention to this new equation between the sailor and the homekeeper. That the conversation begins by raising questions about the relationship between emotion – or more precisely emotional suffering – and professional activities, but finds an essentialist course once the occupational difference is historically removed, suggests that it is the navy's return that is somehow implicated in a construction of gender that both invokes and mystifies professional distinctions. This is important because whereas Anne begins by expressing something like a wish for a career that will take her out of herself (give her a means of coping with emotions that can find no outlet), she ends by expressing a wish to be something like a man, mention of the navy's homecoming having meanwhile intervened.

Just as she finishes an eloquent depiction of the self-sacrifice women perform by doing all the feeling, however, she and Harville are interrupted by a slight noise coming from Wentworth's sphere of the room: "nothing more than that his pen had fallen down" (237). It is unclear whether Wentworth has dropped his pen because he is moved by Anne's indication that she is still unwavering in her love for him or because he is absorbed in her moving representation of his heroism: "'You are always labouring and toiling, exposed to every risk and hardship. Your home, country, friends, all quitted. Neither time, nor health, nor life, to be called your own'" (237). What is clear though is that when Harville and Anne resume their debate, they agree to dismiss the authority of literature that represents women as fickle on the grounds that it is written by men – "'the pen has been in their hands.'" That the pen has fallen out of male hands, whether out of Wentworth's or that of the song and proverb writers to whom Anne and Harville refer, seems to be relevant in that the rest of the conversation involves Anne and Harville in a battle of the sexes for the dominion of emotion: Harville asserts on behalf of men that the seafaring life sensitizes them to the emotional turmoil of constant leave-takings and homecomings; Anne asserts that women love more because they continue to love even without an object. Like an elected soul of Weberian Protestantism, he who works for the sake of work rather than for personal aggrandizement, Anne's woman loves without object or objective. As Nancy Armstrong has argued, feeling – that which in modern times can make a man a mensch – is historically constructed as "natural" to a woman. So even if navy men do indeed feel, as Harville insists, the woman still wins as her feelings derive from a sexual condition that is prior to the sailor's professional one. But what is lost or won? A monopoly on emotional suffering is a strange object of desire.

As all but the novel's denouement makes clear, love for love's sake is no day at the beach. Like the "comprehensive retrenchment" (43) that Anne champions at the story's beginning, "the severe degree of self denial, which her own conscience prompted" (43) registers the novel's psychological line of development alongside its economic one: for the repression of material needs that the scheme of retrenchment poses correlates to Anne's repression of her love for Wentworth. If love is the vocation that a woman as a woman comes to, there can be no romanticizing it. And indeed, *Persuasion* presents loving without an object as painful work in that it requires the continual repression of self in communal duties and services. In her debate with Harville, love becomes work and sacrifice; though Anne might win by a stricter application of Protestant doctrine, the high cost of her heroic election does not go unquestioned.

That women's love should be distinguished in this context – as the standard that emerges in connection to maritime careers – makes women's love into something like a profession comparable to the navy. In answer to Wentworth's apologies about delaying their exit, it is no accident that Harville invents a metaphor that impresses naval idiolect into the service of domestic sociability: "'There is no hurry on my side ... I am in very good anchorage here,' (smiling at Anne) 'well supplied, and want for nothing. – No hurry for signal at all – '" (237). The moment marks the beginning of Anne's apotheosis, her improved looks, her recovery of Wentworth. And the scene's two successive images are powerful: in the course of her articulation of male naval heroism and female emotional pain, a pen is dropped and ships stay at bay. In equating Anne with good anchorage, Harville's metaphor translates her appeal into professional dialect, conveys her influence through naval lingua franca. As good anchorage, Anne is both naturalized and professionalized: she designates gentle weather as well as a well-tended port, the latter being one of the primary objectives of reforms at the Admiralty (Parkinson, *Britannia Rules* 92–7). As Nina Auerbach has pointed out, *Persuasion* marks "the new importance of productive labor as fulfillment itself" whereby Wentworth's fortuitous naval career can be seen as "labor in harmony with nature."[16] For Auerbach, labor in harmony with nature is utopianism. But it can also be seen in *Persuasion* as that which links professionalism and feminism: labor in harmony with nature is not only the goal of the Admiralty reforms that make possible Wentworth's professional and social success, but a strategy for defining women's work. For the feminists of Butler's Tory tradition, familial and community service was religiously sanctioned because it was a natural extension of a woman's natural role.

As Denise Riley has pointed out, the notion of women as improvers was nothing new in Enlightenment and post-Enlightenment discourse.[17] What is new here, however, is the representation of a natural sociality that, already saturated by eighteenth-century concepts of femininity, cleared new terrain for public action: "If women's sphere was to be the domestic, then let the social world become a great arena for domestic interventions" (48) runs Riley's representation of what will become the nineteenth-century feminist argument. According to Riley, this new production of the social provided some women with occasions to work for the improvement of other, generally less fortunate, women. And it marked the beginning of a systematized formalization of the goodness of women under the auspices of the social sciences (53–4). It follows then that this new conception of the social should allow in fiction for the emergence of a professional woman who is both the agent and the object of her work.

In light of her bid for the superiority of female emotion, this combination of nature and profession conjures the vocation of care Anne exhibits at the novel's climactic moment. When Louisa falls off the wall and out of the running for Wentworth's affections, it is Anne who manages the scene:

Anne, attending with all the strength and zeal, and thought which instinct supplied, to Henrietta, still tried at intervals to suggest comfort to the others, tried to quiet Mary, to animate Charles, to assuage the feelings of Captain Wentworth. Both seemed to look to her for directions. (130–1)

Transitive, active-voice verbs all attest to Anne's command. Yet the specific work of attending, comforting, animating and assuaging is elided. How emotional work gets done is mystified at the same time that it is recognized as crucial to the well-being of this "little commonwealth." Like a nineteenth-century professional, Anne is distinguished by virtue of her instinct's utility: the "thought which instinct supplied" presents her feeling intellect as expert in the management of caring for others.

THE CONSEQUENCES

The application of naval metaphors and measures to life at home contributes to a playful idiolect that presses an equation between sealife and homelife. That we should come to view naval officers as the rightful tenants of manor houses and the most sought-after guests at dinner parties results from a complex series of home–navy tropes. The application of a naval frame of reference makes naval officers look like a particular class of people: they are "responsible tenants" due to the fact that so many of them had made fortunes in the war (47); they are reliable as evident when the Crofts take possession of Kellynch-hall "with true naval alertness" (74); and they have an aesthetic appreciation of lay "realism," as Admiral Croft displays when critiqueing a print-shop picture that depicts an unseaworthy ship in which he "would not venture over a horsepond" (179). The novel invents an idiom for identifying what can be seen as a naval culture and a narrative line that can absorb it.

It would seem that the significance of the navy at home has formal implications as well. For the scene of repose at Harville's home entails accommodating the narrative structures characteristic of a career whereby deed and consequence follow in a chain of events to a synchronic medium governed by the imperfect tense of quotidian life. The problems this project encounters emerge in the novel's first paragraph, which focuses on the grammatical resonances contained in the word "there." We are reminded that "there" is an adverb. Despite its spatial, and ostensibly static designation, it describes a verb; it orients the expression of an action. The disequilibrium that initiates *Persuasion* occurs as a chain of "theres," adverbs that refer to Sir Walter's favorite book, the Baronetage:

there he found occupation for an idle hour and consolation in a distressed one: *there* his faculties were roused . . . *there* any unwelcome sensations arising from domestic affairs, changed naturally into pity and contempt, as he turned over the almost endless creations of the last century – and *there* . . . he could read his own history with an interest which never failed. (1) (my emphasis)

What has presumably in this moment driven Sir Walter there, to seek solace in the national record that distinguishes him, is his family's financial trouble. But the genealogical narrative seems to have fallen silent. The genre has nothing to say, no marriages to record or deaths to acknowledge. In particular, it can provide no solution for the immediate lack: the baronet's incapacity to answer "the claims of creditors" (43). The novel makes it clear that the "state" of Sir Walter's property is threatened by claims that emerged because of the family's loss of the "method, moderation, and economy" that its deceased mother, Lady Elliot, had imposed. The book's story is threatened by the father's inability to fill the mother's shoes.

When the silence of the Baronetage collapses into the family's need to raise enough cash to satisfy "the claims of creditors," the antidote adopted is a "scheme of retrenchment" that poses an entirely new plot sequence and a new set of sociological valuations. For it becomes immediately apparent that the economic claims of creditors can be deflected by honoring the ethical claims of the navy, the nation's newly returned war heroes: " 'The navy, who have done so much for us,' " Anne adds to Mr. Shepherd's description of rich admirals' making the best tenants, " 'have at least an equal claim with any other set of men, for all the comforts and all the privileges which any home can give' " (49). It is not just that these navy men have ready cash, but that they seem to carry a prestige that Sir Walter cannot override by pointing out, however accurately, the extent to which they disrupt the traditional social order. Although he concedes that "the profession has its utility," he objects to the navy as "the means of bringing persons of obscure birth into undue distinction, and raising men to honours which their fathers and grand-fathers never dreamt of" (49). But by replying to the claims of creditors with the possibility of recognizing the claims of the navy, the novel turns towards that upstart profession as both a legitimate financial and ethical resource. Although changing and exchanging homes is common in Austen's fiction, here the presence of the navy and the inception of a debt-driven economy usher in a new kind of narrative line.

The scheme of retrenchment is formulated around several uses of the word "consequence." The retrenchment is initially discussed in two parts, both of which concern the formation of social status and its relationship to the kind of narrative generation that falters when the Baronetage fails. In the first, the family decides to relocate to Bath, because in Bath Sir Walter will not lose any "consequence" (45), by which we can assume Austen means that he will not lose any "importance in rank and position, social distinction" (*OED*). This sense of "consequence" emphasizes the potential fluidity characteristic of social distinction and its reliance on public opinion, however much that sense of public might expand or contract: so it is that from the Renaissance through the end of the nineteenth century the English senses of "consequence" illustrate the extent to which social status stood in a complicated and variable relationship to economic and political power. That men in 1603 "had made use of his Lordship's name . . . to make themselves men of consequence" displays a willful cultivation of prestige; that in 1770 "Brutus now felt his consequence lie heavy upon him" reveals a sense of responsibility attendant on deed; that it is necessary in 1879 to say "No form of property gives to its owners so much consequence as land" attests to variable kinds of consequence-yielding property. By articulating that the objective for the retrenchment scheme should be retaining "consequence," Sir Walter's words apprehend a world where influencing public opinion is comparable to owning property. And I might remark here that a world in which influencing public opinion is equivalent to owning property is a good world in which to write a novel.

The second part of the retrenchment entails renting the house, a proposal the cunning lawyer Mr. Shepherd frames for Sir Walter in the following way:

I presume to observe, Sir Walter, that, in the way of business, gentlemen of the navy are well to deal with . . . Therefore, Sir Walter, what I would take leave to suggest is, that if in *consequence* of any rumours getting abroad of your intention [to leave the house] – which must be contemplated as a possible thing, because we know how difficult it is to keep the actions and designs of one part of the world from the notice and curiosity of the other, – *consequence* – has its tax – I, John Shepherd, might conceal any family-matters that I chose, for nobody would think it worth their while to observe me, but Sir Walter Elliot has eyes upon him which it may be very difficult to elude – therefore, . . . if, with all our caution, some rumour of the truth should get abroad – in the supposition of which, as I was going to observe, since applications will unquestionably follow, I should think any from our wealthy naval commanders particularly worth attending to . . . (47) (my emphasis)

Rather than assert the ethical claims that Anne articulates for the navy "who have done so much for us," Mr. Shepherd lures Sir Walter away from belief in inherited class distinction by different means. Initiating a defense of the navy's merits, Mr. Shepherd interrupts himself with a set of parenthetical ruminations on the meaning of consequence, which culminates in his return to the navy's claims as if they were the self-evident conclusion to an argument of which they were really the premise. Although Mr. Shepherd's treatment of "consequence" semantically has nothing to do with making householders out of naval officers, formally it produces such an effect. For Shepherd, "consequence" is the conclusion of his syllogism, of that which follows logically or can be deduced or inferred. In other words, the consequence – as in the "thing or circumstance which follows as an effect or result from something preceding" (*OED*) – of Sir Walter's consequence – as in his social status-is honoring the navy's "equal claim" to a home: acknowledging *their* consequence.

By interrupting his naval housing advocacy, Shepherd's playful re-minder that "consequence has its tax" suggests the sense in which social systems that operate according to principles of prestige make prestige a transferable property. Put simply, the phrase simply explains how rumors get out, how prestigious people cannot expect to veil their personal habits from the community's stare. But the word "tax" as in "compulsory contribution to the support of the government" *(OED)* equates "consequence" with the property according to which tax payments are levied. The figure not only emphasizes an unavoidable communal exposure (of the kind which *Pride and Prejudice* finesses by directing a reading of Pemberley that preserves at least Darcy's right to privacy if not his actual privacy), but broadens the notion of property by connect-ing it to public opinion. For in the idea that a tax can be levied on consequence is the idea that public opinion can be owned.

Besides inflecting the scheme of retrenchment, this play of conse-quence punctuates the novel's courtship plot by stressing the narratabil-ity of Wentworth's martial adventures: unlucky in love, Wentworth leaves "the country in consequence" (56); rising in his profession, he is "made a commander in consequence of the action off St Domingo" (55). As the "relation of a result or effect to its cause or antecedent" (*OED*), consequence for Wentworth means action and result, deeds which can be narrated. And he is the life of the party at the Musgroves for precisely this reason: the navy has made him into a great storyteller. As Went-worth regales the company with "the little narratives or descriptions which conversation called forth," the novel explains, "His profession qualified him, his disposition led him, to talk" (88). Wentworth's profes-sional qualifications emerge here as authorizing: the navy has given him a subject as well as an audience. The consequence here is a new source of story.

The narrative potential attendant on this new kind of consequence refers us to the *OED*'s final sense of the term: "Consequence" designates a "round game, in which a narrative of the meeting of a lady and a gentleman, their conversation and the ensuing 'consequences' is concocted by the contribution of a name or fact by each of the players, in ignorance of what has been contributed by others." In other words, "consequence" designates a courtship plot. That the citation documenting the game of consequences refers to *Sense and Sensibility* suggests that it is not accidental that *Persuasion*'s play on "consequence" places the consequence of the navy as domestic men of consequence in a complicated relationship to narrative invention.

I want to hypothesize here that Austen's depiction of story-making as a group project suggests a communitarian conception of intellectual property that was compatible with late eighteenth- and early nineteenth-century judicial interpretation of married women's property. According to Susan Staves, the period 1660–1833 was marked by a high degree of judicial experimentation in the interpretation of married women's property law. As new forms of wealth like stock and bank annuities replaced land, equity practices in particular devised ways of providing married women with new forms of ownership – many of which had as their primary objective the protection of a wife and her children from a financially troubled husband.[18] One of these measures was "sequestration" by which equity courts sought to protect assets belonging to the household from creditors preying on the husband.[19] Although not an express critique of the doctrine of coverture by which a wife's legal status was "covered by" her husband's thereby precluding her from owning property, sequestering had an erosive effect as it became more common to view the household's property as separate from the husband's. In this light, reform of married women's property law can be seen as a limitation on laissez-faire capitalism in so far as it limited a creditor's rights so as to preserve a woman's. Or, to put it another way, treating the wife like a creditor could preserve the household property without doctrinally limiting the husband's liability.

That assets sequestered in the name of the household could inscribe married women as *de jure* creditors in contractual arrangements that had as their object the preservation of the household collective often meant that sequestered assets could become *de facto* married women's separate property. This suggests that the first inroads in married women's property reform relied on a communitarian notion of household property that, at least in practice, equated the woman with the group. Read as the story of how the navy wins national consequence, *Persuasion* thus incorporates in the form of the game "consequence" a communitarian definition of property that in the period's legal discourses carried gendered applications.

Wentworth's newly found role as *raconteur* reveals the gendered slant of his professionalism. In its martial context, Wentworth's naval profession would presumably produce an adventure story. Interestingly enough, however, Wentworth describes only one real "adventure": his "touch with the Great Nation," that is, his capture of a treasure-rich French frigate (90). And the plot of this adventure hardly allows for any action drama, pivoting as it does on his luck in *avoiding* a storm at sea. Everyone shudders when he bids them to imagine what would have happened if he had not reached port before the storm began. Everyone shivers when he commands them to imagine him as a "gallant Captain Wentworth, in a small paragraph at one corner of the newspapers" (90), as if burial in a tabloid were as spine-chilling as death at sea. Regardless as to whether Wentworth raises questions here as to the fitness of deed and genre, his substitution of newspaper burial for a funeral at sea evinces a domestic and a literary perspective: like Anne's speculations as to his financial status – she has "navy lists and newspapers for her authority" (58) – Wentworth's deed, such as it is, is represented, not as it is experienced at sea, but as it is read about at home.

This calls our attention to what it is precisely that he talks about at the Musgroves when they profess interest in "naval matters":

he was very much questioned . . . as to the manner of living on board, daily regulations, food hours etc. . . . the degree of accommodation and arrangement which was practicable . . . [and their surprise] drew from him some pleasant ridicule, which reminded Anne of the early days when she too had been ignorant, and she too had been accused of supposing sailors to be living on board without anything to eat or any cook to dress it if there were, or any servant to wait, or any knife and fork to use. (89)

Rather than narrating heroic tales of triumph and defeat, struggle and sacrifice, Wentworth entertains his audience with information about quotidian life. In place of Sir Walter's Baronetage, the novel offers the Musgrove's navy-list as the viable book. But what comes into focus as each of Wentworth's ships are located, looked at, and discussed is Wentworth's faculty for describing them in domestic terms: a ship is no different from a home, he seems to reiterate, only a little smaller. And not only are cooks, servants and silverware present, but Wentworth seems to take a great deal of pride in their assembly. Well he should, for a captain once assigned a ship was responsible for all its fittings-out, from staff to stores, including even the hire of a schoolmaster for the midshipmen (Padfield, *Rule Britannia* 19–20). And it seems that Wentworth was a rather fastidious shipkeeper in being, as Dick Musgrove wrote to his parents while serving on Wentworth's ship, "'two perticular about the school-master'" (78). Like a good domestic manager whose merits cannot be distinguished in the monotypic terms of battles won and ships captured, Wentworth oversees Dick's conduct, making sure that he writes home without asking for money. Wentworth is glimpsed here cultivating, not only good manners, but affection between parents and the son they had half-hoped to get rid of by enlisting in the navy. Although their infanticide fantasy is realized, so is their more sentimental fantasy: for Wentworth's role in overseeing Dick's studies (instruction that would otherwise have taken place at home) and his initial place subsequently in the Musgrove home as Dick's surrogate care provider depict the navy as implicated in preserving a fiction of familial affection. He is, in this context as a fiction-maker, a literal homemaker.

THE WORTH OF VOLUMES

This hypothesis emerges: *Persuasion* wants us to see structural affinities between the nineteenth century's incipient professionalism and a domesticity aimed at expanding the woman's sphere by defining it as social and ethical expertise. In other words, what emerges in the navy's literary homecoming here is a model of professional work that allows us to see the domesticity practiced by many novelists later on in the nineteenth century as an early form of professionalism, one that used an ethic of social good as an intellectual property that could potentially carry the same rights and privileges as other forms of property.

This becomes clearest in the Mrs. Smith subplot. Apparently incidental, Anne's renewed acquaintance with Mrs. Smith comes at a key moment in the villainization of Mr. Elliot, a plot sequence some have seen as evidence of the novel's ultimate incoherence. But such incoherence yields an important alternative narrative even if it disrupts the decorum of romantic closure. We may recall that Mrs. Smith owes her poverty to her spendthrift husband who died without making provisions for his widow. But Mrs. Smith would have been better off, she tells

Anne, had Mr. Elliot acted on her behalf when he found himself executor of Mr. Smith's will. Specifically, Mrs. Smith's main complaint is that Elliot refused to look into some colonial property that had been "under a sort of sequestration" (215) and thereby refused to protect it from the creditors who engulfed the rest of her husband's estate.

Mrs. Smith first contacts Anne in the hope of securing a man to act as her agent in reclaiming this sequestered property or, what would have been more likely, rights to some of the assets attached to it. That Elliot would not do it and that Wentworth eventually does not only suggests that the choice of Wentworth over Elliot in the courtship narrative is the choice of profession over property in a Barthesian referential code, but that there is something about professionalism that can restore – or indeed invent – a married women's property rights.

How then does the novel use professional culture to construct a definition of property that benefited married women? Although the income from Smith's sequestered household assets is actually not enough to fully support her, it is enough to subsidise her other activity: knitting "little thread-cases, pin-cushions and card racks" (167) that her nurse, Mrs. Rooke, sells to her patients' relatives. Nurse Rooke is so effective a saleswoman because "Everybody's heart is open, you know, when they have recently escaped from severe pain, or are recovering the blessing of health" (168), which is to say that the merchandise's status as a commodity is determined by the professional context in which the sale is made. This then is a market that operates according to rules that make its transactions look more like charity than actual sale, not unlike the game-like tea enterprise that is set up for Miss Matty in Gaskell's *Cranford*, a very real business that relies on everyone's maintaining the genteel fiction that it is not a shop.

Besides acting as agent for an all-female economic support group that trades in handicrafts, Nurse Rooke is important in another way. She is for Mrs. Smith an indefatigable source of story, not the kind produced by "the best education in the world," but the kind "that makes one know one's species better" (168). Nurse Rooke is a good storyteller also by virtue of her profession: "Hers is a line for seeing human nature" (168), which leads Anne to a somewhat romantic rumination on nursing as a profession:

What instances must pass before them of ardent, disinterested, self-denying attachment, of heroism, fortitude, patience, resignation – of all the conflicts and all the sacrifices that ennoble us most. A sick chamber may often furnish the worth of volumes. (168)

We know from Mary Poovey's work that before Florence Nightingale's reform campaign, nursing held a subordinate position throughout the century as other branches of medicine and health care became increasingly professionalized (*Uneven Developments* 173–9). Nurse Rooke's role in *Persuasion*, however it might or might not represent an early defense of nursing, conjures an idea of women's professional work as polytypic and ethical. The actual work itself is neither illustrated nor applauded and indeed, Mrs. Smith denies that a real sickroom holds any of the attractions Anne imagines. But the manual and intellectual sidelines of such work, marketing handicrafts and telling good stories, are both described and praised. As a nurse in a novel, Rooke thus becomes the site for the construction of a new market, one in which middle-class women trade stories and goods for money under the somewhat disingenuous aegis of "all the sacrifices that ennoble us most." In this sense, women's work is rationalized in the same terms that reading fiction is: understanding one's species better is "entertaining and profitable;" it is worth and worthy of volumes in both a moral and an economic sense.

LITERARY CONSEQUENCE AND SEMI-DETACHMENT

It might now be possible to speculate that Austen's deliberate and ironic pairing of female unsalaried domestic work with male professional naval endeavor serves as preface to the emergence of the housekeeper heroine in later Victorian fiction. Emily Eden's 1859 "bestseller" novel, *The Semi-detached House*, provides an interesting case study.[20] Eden, a famous Whig hostess living in India at the time of the novel's publication, and serving as surrogate wife to her brother, Lord Auckland, India's Governor-General, already enjoyed the kind of public and political career available sometimes to women of her class when she became a famous novelist as well.

When *The Semi-detached House* became such a success, Eden was immediately compared to Jane Austen. Her writing was praised for its witty and womanly representation of English society, and her literary talents were thereby registered in terms of her gender and her nationality: above all, Eden's writing was successful in conveying a sense of femaleness and a sense of Englishness. That reviewers should adduce Austen as Eden's model goes beyond superficial likenesses between the two authors, for it raises interesting questions about the role of authorship in the forging of a female career at the threshold between Victorian notions of private and public. In other words, despite the differences between Eden's work and Austen's, the brief success of The *Semi-detached House* affords a glimpse at what kinds of cultural fantasies informed the construction of a female authorship that used Jane Austen as its figurehead. In particular, this perceived affinity between Eden and Austen during the first half of the nineteenth century attests to the national popularity of narratives that depicted an uncanny resemblance between the homecraft of domestic life and the seamanship of life in the British navy.

The plot of *Semi-detached* follows how Lady Blanche, a wealthy and powerful member of the aristocracy, overcomes her prejudice against the middle classes, figured in the shape of a housewife who "'will be immensely fat, wear mittens – thick heavy mittens – and contrive to know what I have for dinner every day'" (14–15) – a housewife who appeared not unlike the model housewife that the critic Margaret Homans describes as one of Queen Victoria's favorite guises. When Blanche's "interesting state of health" (18) – that is, her pregnancy – and her husband's mystified naval mission to Berlin (15) require her to rent a "semi-detached house" in the suburbs, she is thrown into a semi-communal living arrangement with the Hopkinson family. Although Mrs. Hopkinson is, in fact, a fat mitten-wearer, she is also marked early on as the novel's sleeper heroine. Indeed, the novel quickly turns into a recounting of the romance these aristocrats have with the solid, law-abiding, hard-working, down-home Hopkinsons, a relationship that culminates in a host of well-paid professional appointments procured for them by Lady Blanche's well-connected family. Importantly, none of the Hopkinsons save and scrimp, start businesses or invest in industry. Although they have serious financial concerns about how to marry off their fortuneless daughters, they seem utterly uninterested in money. Their upward mobility happens only when Lady Blanche's father makes Captain Hopkinson Duke's Agent for a busy pier and harbor, and when his son-in-law is appointed rector to a local wealthy parish. In this sense, the navy and the church – that is, professional institutions – provide the conduit for the transfer of wealth as well as for the novel's happy ending.

The domestic woman responsible for her family's good fortune is not the angelic emotional spirit championed by Ruskin and common in other fiction of the period (such as Dickens' Little Dorrit or Eliot's Dorothea), but a fat housewife with questionable taste in curtains and upholstery. The rotund Mrs. Hopkinson, shown managing her spick-and-span household like a business whose time-clock is regulated by punctual afternoon tea, describes herself looking "like a respectable housekeeper" (112), while she plays a variety of salvational roles: a sanctuarianne who provides timely shelter for residents exposed to the consequences of a defective slue; an adjunct domestic manager who organizes the servants of local *nouveau riche*; most importantly, a midwife who calmly delivers the Duchess' son. It is Mrs. Hopkinson who generates what energy the novel has. It is a housewife who forges the pivotal lucrative friendship with *Semi-detached's* true aristocrats, having been naturally capable of distinguishing them from the town's *arriviste* Jews.

Though she may not intend it, the care she provides results in direct financial and arguably ideological gains. Through her influence, her husband and sons-in-law are promoted to prestigious professional places, in the clergy and the navy. In presenting this influence as deriving from the polytypic job of housewifery, the narrative strains to link the idea of domestic work to the idea of professions like the navy and the clergy, professions that also happen to be institutions invested in by the English nation-state.

We can see then in the plot of Eden's novel a metonymic connection between domestic work and a professional ascension that neutralizes class differences by translating those markers (such as sensible mittens and afternoon tea) into a universal utilitarian grammar: although Blanche predicts disparagingly that Mrs. Hopkinson will "'contrive to know what I have for dinner,'" such "contriving" proves extraordinarily useful, for the communal living situation imposed by the house's "semi-detachment" allows Mrs. Hopkinson's housekeeping expertise to shine when she fixes Blanche's slue and delivers her baby.

In terms of plot, Mrs. Hopkinson's activities can be seen as the cause of her family's professional promotions. In making the housewife the heroine, the novel uses domesticity to repudiate more overtly capitalist forms of social mobility – in the shape of Jewish speculators and bankers – by favoring a professional career that relies on appointments by fiat and on the successful persuasion that a service is of vital importance to the household community and, given the preeminence of Blanche's family, perhaps even to the nation. In this sense, Eden's world can be seen as participating in a "professional" society.

It is important to establish here what it means to locate Eden's domesticity in professional society. Historians characterize nineteenth-century professionalism as a culture organized according to three criteria: (1) expertise or specialization, often in an esoteric or abstract form of knowledge; (2) associations and institutions that "gate keep" by conferring and/or recognizing the training or education necessary and sufficient for such specialization; (3) an ethic of social good attendant on the performance of that expertise (although not necessarily on an efficacious performance) by which society is persuaded of a professional's right to resources and rewards. This social-good imperative has led historians like Harold Perkin to depict English nineteenth-century professionalism as a necessary precondition for the formation of the British welfare state in the next century. As class conflict peaks and industrialism slows, Perkin sees emerging throughout the nineteenth century a new principle of organization: human capital trained into expertise. Whereas the "entrepreneurial ideal" characteristic of high capitalism was based on competition and active capital, the "professional ideal" of post-industrial Britain stressed human capital as it emerges in a meritocracy after training and certification have been completed. For Perkin, English professionalism is successful in the dialectic it enacts between capitalists and labor because its organizational principles are potentially applicable to every job, every member of the nation. And in this regard it fosters a quiet sort of nationalism. Professionalism cuts across economic class differences without doing away with an idea of privilege and prestige at the same time as it cultivates a sense of national participation.

It should be noted, however, that "professional culture" designates the sum of invariants historians have noticed as characteristic of the institutional reforms happening throughout the nineteenth century in England's four traditional "great professions" (clergy, law, military, politics) as well as in other incipient and often unrecognized "professions," such as medicine, the civil service, science, architecture, engineering and teaching. When historians talk about professionalism, there is a sense in which they are trying to account for various signs of institutionalization. What they see is a host of institutions emerging in association with different kinds of employment: sometimes these were qualifying bodies that corresponded with education or training, as in the four Inns of Court for barristers, the two Royal Colleges and the Society for Apothecaries for medical doctors, and the Institute of Chartered Accountants (Perkin, *Rise of Professional Society* 20); and sometimes they were nonqualifying organizations, as is the case with trade and Civil Service unions, the London Ethical Society, the Society for Promoting the Employment of Women and the London Association for Opposing Early Closing (of shops) (146). In describing how clubs and other informal groups transformed into more formal organizations, Davidoff and

Hall identify four categories: philanthropic, such as Sunday schools, charity schools, hospitals, organizations devoted to alleviating poverty and illness, and organizations devoted to specific causes (like the conversion of the Jews and bringing religion to the working classes); cultural, such as assembly rooms, libraries, book clubs, subscriber concerts, literary and philosophical societies, and botanical and horticultural societies; business- and property-related, such as farmers' clubs, agricultural societies, doctors' and lawyers' organizations, the Association of Ironmasters, and the Chamber of Manufacturers (which later turned into the Chamber of Commerce); political, such as anti-slavery societies, political unions, and the Anti-Corn Law League.[21] But whether a labor union, a training school, an appreciation society, or a lobbying group, the proliferation of organizations that represented potential vocations and that produced literature articulating a corresponding vocational ethos (charters that outlined a scientist's social purpose or an accountant's field of responsibility, for example) has led many historians to characterize Victorian England as an emergent professional society.

Much has been written about the relationship between intellectual culture and professional society. Intellectual culture – where we might place novelists and artists – can be seen as developing on the cusp of professional society, its capital being less obvious than the services of a doctor or a lawyer, but theoretically no less important to the community as a whole. Although art and literature can be described more rightly as synthesizing forms than they can be called fields of specialization, it is still possible to see artists and writers of the period being affected by, and perhaps having an effect on, Victorian England's increasingly professionalized society. Whether in Eliot's intensive research of Renaissance Florence or in the exhaustive consultations Trollope pursued with legal scholars familiar with the laws governing heirloom inheritance, we can see novelists of the period infected with a kind of expertise fever unknown to Sterne or Richardson. Surely this drive to exhibit expertise in the production of fiction at this time raises interesting questions as to the influence of professional society on intellectual culture. As Perkin points out, although we might want to differentiate the intellectual classes ("men of letters," "men of science," university teachers, painters, sculptors, musicians, and actors) as people who organized themselves for "cultural rather than professional purposes," many intellectuals began to harbor aspirations characteristic of professionals and organized accordingly: in 1883 the Society of Authors was founded; in 1847 the Royal Society restricted its membership to practicing scientists; in 1872 and

1874 the laboratories at Oxford and Cambridge were instituted; in the 1850s and 1870s the Royal Commissions reformed and secularized Oxford and Cambridge, producing for the first time a "career-oriented" intellectual elite who felt it incumbent on them to reshape and reorganize society (Perkin, *Rise of Professional Society* 85–6).

If *Semi-detached* is read in this context, strange structural affinities emerge. That Mrs. Hopkinson's particular brand of domesticity stands in a complicated relationship to nineteenth-century professionalism emerges in that the "semi-detachment" that makes her work legible to powerful outsiders is conditioned by a pregnancy and a naval mission: the novel's action is precipitated by Blanche's pregnancy coinciding with her husband's naval mission abroad. This almost archetypal representation of women's biological work and men's martial work suggests that in the economy of the novel the two can be traded against each other. They are presented, that is, as if they were equivalent. But it would seem that this equivalence relies on the martial work referring specifically to a naval career. For the moment in which Blanche's tepid gratitude toward Mrs. Hopkinson's good will turns into wild enthusiasm for her good offices is the moment in which she discovers that it was Mrs. Hopkinson's husband, the jovial and stalwart Captain Hopkinson, who nursed her husband Arthur back to life when he fell ill while training aboard Captain Hopkinson's ship (*Semi-detached* 61). However impressive Mrs. Hopkinson's obstetrics, the great equalizer between these two classes seems to be Captain Hopkinson's nursing. Though Mrs. Hopkinson delivers Lady Blanche, her work is preceded by Arthur's rebirth at Captain Hopkinson's hands. The navy appears center-stage in this novel not only as an increasingly respectable profession, but as a profession whose claims are again implicated in an ethic of care traditionally associated with women's work.

As *Persuasion* has indicated, that navy men should learn how to do women's work in a maritime setting is a logical consequence of the itinerancy of their profession; unlike an army on land, a navy at sea had to rely on its own resources in the management of its living space. The navy's mobility can be seen as involving a portable domesticity that other kinds of itinerant occupations did not. But this calls attention to the sense in which *Semi-detached*'s story of geographic mobility is strangely unmotivated: no attempts are made to explain either the purpose of Arthur's trip to Berlin or the need to remove Blanche from London. Indeed, the national importance of their move is conveyed more through "Arthur's" and "Blanche's" onomastic reference to British legend than to any narrative rationalization.

In this sense, the plot begins by reverting to paradigmatic organizational principles: Arthur's and Blanche's potential status as English figureheads directs us to a discourse outside the text by which the move might make sense. Their need to move invokes what Michael McKeon calls a "qualitative standard of completion" whereby the story is rationalized along a vertical axis.[22] That the movements of this English knight and his pregnant "white" lady should figure as the narrative frame for recognizing the significance of domestic work performed both at home and at sea raises two important questions: what is at stake in the equation of male professional work at sea with female domestic work at home? And how does this equation bear on the fact that the home-centered plots of *Villette, Great Expectations, Little Dorrit, The Cloister and the Hearth, Felix Holt* and *Daniel Deronda* turn on a geographic mobility that is either unmotivated or mystified in the terms of each novel's ruling narrative grammar? In other words, is it possible to see Victorian domesticity as a varying and often contested discourse about the portability of national identity?

CHAPTER 2

Homesick: the domestic interiors of Villette

NONPERSONAL SOCIABILITY

With romance and marriage relegated to the Polly Home subplot, *Villette*'s unattractive and acerbic heroine unhappily resigns herself to a solitary life – a life spent out of wedlock, a homeless life:

But, afterwards, is there nothing more for me in life – no true home – nothing to be dearer to me than myself and by its paramount preciousness, to draw from me better things than I care to culture for myself only? Nothing at whose feet I can willingly lay down the whole burden of human egotism, and gloriously take up the nobler charge of labouring and living for others? I suppose, Lucy Snowe, the orb of your life is not to be so rounded; for you the crescent phase must suffice.[1]

By threatening Lucy Snowe with spinsterhood, *Villette* displays here a peculiar rhetoric of renunciation. The moment records Lucy's decision to redirect her desires: instead of wishing for a "true home" of her own, she will wish for a school of her own; instead of wanting to establish herself in the institution of marriage, she will construct a surrogate establishment. Despite the passage's subtext of desire, Lucy's paean to home does not represent marriage as a pleasure, or as a means of emotional gratification or even as a personal or private relationship shared with one other person; on the contrary, Lucy presents the institution of marriage as a noble and ennobling space, a "rounded" place populated by anonymous "others" for whom she would have laboured and lived selflessly. In giving up the true home, however, Lucy will have to resign herself to the "conditions of denial and privation" (451) that constitute "independence," stoically enduring this "too selfish" an object (450) that is a life of solitude. Thus Lucy's renunciation of true home turns into a surrender of self-sacrifice – and in fact, makes self-sacrifice into the desirable.

By presenting True Home in the context of a disjunction – either Lucy will desire a self-sacrificing marital establishment *or* she will desire a

44

self-serving educational one – *Villette* throws the home into a complicated and seemingly oppositional relationship with what is called the self. It is therefore not surprising that critics like Tony Tanner mistakenly attribute the superanimated quality of the novel's material details specifically to the failure of domestic metaphors to represent a self; because Tanner takes "domesticity" as a metaphor that uses a house and its accouterments to articulate "consciousness," he can conclude that *Villette*'s domesticity "offers an inadequate spatial model for the complete self."[2] Tanner assumes here that home and home metaphors are about houses, as opposed to being about an ideal of social life, and that home is about the personal in so far as we understand the personal to be synonymous with some psychologically delineated selfhood.

What emerges then out of Lucy's renunciation of marriage as her personal and narrative objective is the question as to where home figures on a continuum that has at one pole a life devoted to the self and, at the other, something that opposes such a life, let us say, one centered on an anonymous community of "others." The demarcation points on such a continuum[3] are difficult to determine because we tend to assume certain imbrications that *Villette* does not – particularly that marriage presumes romance and romance overlaps desire and desire aligns with the sexual and the sexual with the private, the private with the personal and the personal with the psychological. This puts an interpreter on a slippery slope where the home, presumably a consequence of marriage and sexual engagement, seems part of a psychoanalytic line of development even when the novel's domestic discourse suggests otherwise. Lucy, for example, avoids mentioning in her representation of a true home that the marriage that would ostensibly secure her such a home would require entering into a relationship with a lover; she skirts the assumption that a home is a connubial household founded on sexual love. To rationalize Lucy's choice of words here, Mark Lilly makes an understandable mistake in commenting that Lucy, by substituting words like "nothing" for "nobody" and "others" for "him" instead of directly naming M. Paul, provides "an extremely good example of nineteenth-century reserve in the face of intimate personal relations."[4] Rather than attribute this grammatical anomaly to Victorian reserve, or even to some quasi-Freudian repression of the sexual, it is important to recognize that by erasing the figure of the lover from the home scene, Lucy reveals that the domestic ideal ultimately has nothing to do with romance, or the egocentric concerns that sexual engagement would entail, but has at its roots something more communitarian.

Lucy's obfuscation of the sexual in the marital household bespeaks her exclusion from the home of what I will provisionally call the category of the personal. But it is an exclusion complicated by the logistics of her chosen narrative form. In formal terms, the passage simultaneously invokes the operational principles of psychological narratives as well as more extroverted genres: in presenting Lucy's departure from the home ideal, the passage harnesses the punctuation of dialogue to the task of representing interior monologue; monopolizing both voices of a dialogue that would otherwise signal the presence of others, Lucy invokes a basic *conversation-with-the-self* convention which, at the same time that it translates a psychologically delineated self to a reading public, denies the presence of any potential husband to make the marriage plot realizable and the home attainable. Thus M. Paul can figure as nothing more than a nothing with feet, important only as a prop in the representation of Lucy engaged in worship. It would seem then that interiority itself requires a peculiar idiom when it articulates home: that home would enable Lucy to labour "gloriously" for others emphasizes the ironically egotistical implications of proclaimed self-sacrifice regardless of where it occurs – in the home where a woman renounces herself for others, or outside the home where a woman renounces the pleasures of renouncing herself. In this sense, the passage suggests that novelistic interiority, by making "home" discursive – a matter now of conscious choice and no longer merely the narrative's bourne – not only renders self-denial impossible, but entangles a once impersonally oriented home in the workings of personal desire. By presenting home in a grammar that makes self-sacrifice a privilege and self-engendered pursuit a liability, *Villette*'s rhetoric of renunciation is thus double-edged: the passage implies that although home and marriage themselves may be definitively unconcerned with issues that have to do with desire or the self, a narrative that makes marriage its "bourne," what George Eliot calls the "home epic,"[5] will have to wrestle uncomfortably with the burden of justifying selfhood. Why a home epic should have the duty of justifying a self rather than justifying a happy home remains a question.

So as to organize the relationship between the self and the communal, I want to invoke Richard Sennett's distinction between the private and the public, dehistoricize it and add a tertiary term.[6] *In The Fall of Public Man*, Sennett stops the socio-historical clock in the eighteenth century when, according to his etymological model, there existed a clear division between public and private life: the city, an economically, nationally and vocationally diverse territory, afforded the average citizen with the privilege of participating in a variety of emotionally satisfying impersonal exchanges with a collection of people to whom he is not committed by "ties of family or intimate association" (3). Juxtaposed to the city, the family (Sennett does not say which kind – nuclear, extended or household)[7] provides an arena for "family members" and their close friends to interact personally with "warmth, trust, and open expression of feeling" (5). Although Sennett grossly overestimates the heterogeneity of daily civic life,[8] his notion of emotionally satisfying "impersonal" sociability provides the terminal category that will make home localizable on a conceptual continuum. What to place on the other end, however, remains a problem throughout any discussion of nineteenth-century domesticity in that social historians and sociologists alike, Sennett as exemplary, do not see private life as synonymous with individual psychic life; for Sennett, the private sphere is not a spatial representation of selfhood or consciousness, but an arena of social interactions that are "personal," a term he never fully stabilizes. As a result, his distinction between public or impersonal social transactions and private or personal social transactions breaks down. To call impersonal social interaction, for instance, "emotionally satisfying" without also calling it "personal" raises some problems, to say the least.

The tautological trap of aligning the private sphere with the personal and the psychoanalytically resonant offers a cautionary tale relevant to reading *Villette*, for it emerges out of inadequate consideration paid to the psychological and is perhaps due to the difficulties involved in bracketing the psychological as a category that we can isolate from the other categories that constitute an individual life. So, at least heuristically, I want to do the following: (1) place at one end of the continuum "nonpersonal" sociability in which routine, business-like transactions that happen regularly and according to understood patterns of conduct provide emotional satisfaction,[9] (2) set aside any notion of "personal" sociability and instead (3) extend the continuum beyond the category of sociability entirely and onto a psychological plane that culminates in the self-analysis characteristic of Freudian psychoanalysis. With this extension, I aim at identifying more precisely a category of social interaction (no matter what kind – whether between merchants or between lovers) that is significant exclusively by virtue of its psychic resonances. Moreover, I want to make it possible to classify an instance of sociability according to the activity performed and not the relationship characterizing the performers.[10]

In addition, I prefer using a model of eighteenth- and nineteenth-century family life which, besides providing a historically plausible alternative to Sennett's, helps dilate some of the values at stake in *Villette*'s use of domestic discourse. Much current socio-historic evidence documents that the typical English household, regardless of class and independent of geographic location (although this shifts periodically throughout both centuries), rarely consisted of exclusively immediate family members; on the contrary, educational, vocational and medical conditions subjected aristocratic, bourgeois and working households alike to the comings and goings of an army of virtual strangers – extended relations, surrogate relations, servants, servants' relations and a host of others who, in regularly crossing any given home's threshold, can be said to have comprised the home as well as set the tone for the kind of sociability that transpired there. In this sense, home surfaces in current social history looking like a community no different in composition or operation from other communities (except maybe in terms of scale or setting).[11] That homes generally functioned very much like publicly run houses, like institutions in fact, makes it historically plausible to locate Sennett's category of emotionally satisfying "impersonal" sociability not on the street, but in the home.

Despite this historical evidence, the question as to where *Villette*'s own home is placed on the continuum spanning nonpersonal sociability and psychological self-scrutiny is complicated by the novel's formal constraints. Because *Villette* emerges as a hybrid novel, the product of an ostensibly unholy marriage between home epic and psychodrama, the borders separating what belongs to a community of others from what belongs to a self that is engaged in representing itself to a community of readers get blurred. There are then two paths of approach to *Villette*'s domesticity: home within the terms of the novel's plot does make an arena of nonpersonal sociability available; but the novel's discourse, the grammar in which it presents the plot, reveals that home, no matter how tidy, has been traumatized by a transplanting to the psychological plane, disarrayed by the imposition of a "registering consciousness"[12] and the messy consequences that the introduction of an individual's desire has for plot construction.

HOME SWEET HOME

At times, *Villette*'s plot seems to take the shape of an allegorical journey in which Lucy is tested by having to choose from among false and true homes. She rejects the notion that true home is a place of origin (she never tells us about her parental home), or where she resides (such as at the Rue Fossette); she denies that it consists of family, whether her own or the mock familial figures of the Catholic Church. But after having concluded volume I by passing out, Lucy opens volume II by awakening in "Auld Lang Syne," an oneiric domain which Lucy embraces as domestic perfection.

Villette presents the La Terrasse home as an idyllic space, a fairy-tale place where Lucy's childhood playmate and god-brother playfully banters with a mother he nicknames "Titania" across a blazing hearth:

> a tall door, standing open, gave admission into the blue damask room. How pleasant it was in its air of perfect domestic comfort! How warm in its amber lamp-light and vermilion fire-flush! To render the picture perfect, tea stood ready on the table – an English-tea, whereof the whole shining service glanced at me familiarly; from the solid silver urn, of antique pattern, and the massive pot of the same metal to the thin porcelain cups, dark with purple and gilding. I knew the very seed-cake of peculiar form baked in a peculiar mould, which always had a place on the tea-table at Bretton. Graham liked it, and there it was of yore – set before Graham's plate with the silver knife and fork beside it. (245–6)

Operating to the timeless pulse of routines organized around the hero's comings and goings, the Bretton home is marked by the regularity of its rituals: having tea at the same time every day, eating the family's traditional seedcake, pretending to argue over the best chair, falling asleep while reading the daily paper. In its timelessness, La Terrasse is a place where no matter what the winter weather dictates, a sense of summer reigns inside. It is a place where, regardless of the season, its "family" snuggles around the fireplace to "have a Christmas wassail-cup, and toast Old England" (362–3). A place made holy specifically through its secular staples: "In its Christmas-like fire alone," Lucy raptures, "there was a clear and crimson splendour which quite dazzled me" (357). Though there is a constant gale outside, "the dash of its fiercest breakers could sound down in this submarine home, only like murmurs and a lullaby" (255).

But there is something suspect about a home that Lucy enters only by waking out of a solitude-induced delirium, that she finds not by crossing the front door's threshold, but by descending from the bedroom:

> And here my eye fell on an easy chair covered with blue damask. Other seats, cushioned to match, dawned on me by degrees; and at last I took in the complete fact of a pleasant parlour, with a woodfire on a clear-shining hearth, a

carpet where arabesques of bright blue relieved a ground of shaded fawn; pale walls over which a slight but endless garland of azure forget-me-nots ran mazed and bewildered amongst myriad gold leaves and tendrils A gilded mirror filled up the space between two windows, curtained amply with blue damask. In this mirror I saw myself laid, not in bed, but on a sofa. I looked spectral . . . as I gazed at the blue arm-chair, it appeared to grow familiar; so did a certain scroll-couch, and not less so the round centre-table with a blue covering, bordered with autumn-tinted foliage; and, above all, two little footstools with worked covers and a small ebony-framed chair . . . old acquaintance were about me, and 'auld lang syne' smiled out of every nook. (238)

Instead of encountering the still basins and stationary ewer stands of the *pensionnat*, Lucy greets objects whose quickened affect refuses to lie dormant, whose status refuses to remain that of object. Even a toilette table appears "dressed like a lady for a ball, in a white robe over a pink skirt" (241). Lucy's eye must contend with a quivering superanimated room whose vibrant, anthropomorphized objects intrude on her consciousness, aggressively monopolizing the active verbal agency of the passage: while Lucy's eye passively *falls*, seats *dawn* on her, wallpaper *runs*, the blue arm-chair *grows*. All these objects, she protests, she "was obliged to know . . . compelled to recognize and hail" (241).

That the happy home's rooms are a bustle of seemingly human activity suggested that it is a place distinguished by its sociability. But what kind of sociability? What kind of companionship crouches in the damask chair or figures in the arabesque carpeting? Nineteenth-century social historians tend to limit their definitions of domestic sociability to what pertains to "family life." Witold Rybczynski, for example, describes the eighteenth century's "privatization" of domestic space – the spatial reorganization that transformed a house of multipurpose rooms arranged *en fillade* into a home distinguished by a more complex array of specialized dining rooms, drawing rooms, salons, boudoirs and bedchambers – as reliant on a "growing sense of intimacy, of identifying the house exclusively with family life."[13] But if we look at who occupies *Villette*'s happy home, only two of its inhabitants (Mrs. Bretton and her son) are related by blood: Lucy is a step-relative; Mr. Home is either a friend or (when identified as M. Bassompierre) an acquaintance; Polly is really just a guest. In fact, the "family" appears as a collage of already broken families, the absence of Mr. Bretton, Mrs. Home, and all of Lucy's blood relatives throwing the group into a variety of surrogate relationships to each other. Hence La Terrasse even allows a degree of diversity in the roles available to each person: in the same way that, according to Sennett (*Fall of Public Man*), a variety of civic exchanges allowed people to change roles in relation to each other, La Terrasse's composite family structure allows for a variety of substitutions. Polly, for example, plays Graham's daughter in her adoration, sister in her teasing, mother in her cutting his food for him and eventually wife in her loving him. Moreover, these virtual strangers are incorporated into the household as a result of men engaged in impersonally pursuing their vocations: Polly and her father enter only when she requires medical care at the theatre; Lucy gets in only after Pere Silas, ministering first to her spiritual health and then to her physical health, delivers her unconscious body to Dr. John's house, a hospital-like asylum where this self-starved Spartan, despite her usual recoil from physical contact with others, joyfully accepts food from Mrs. Bretton's hand (253). "Family life" appears, then, not only to be composed of primarily nonfamily and even non-intimate others, but is starting to look a lot like a site for Sennett's emotionally fulfilling impersonal sociability.

Indeed, nearly all social historians stress that the nineteenth-century home was designed to facilitate a social interaction that on closer scrutiny resembles the kind of businesslike transactions that Sennett describes as proper to the civic life of eighteenth-century streets. Rybczynski, for example, sketches the importance of domestic life – and therefore what he assumes is a new kind of sociability – in his late eighteenth-century-drawing room, which shows its furniture pulled away from the walls and organized around a conversation center, its windows positioned and sized according to the demands of the house's various interior activities (119). But even though he documents the centrality of indoor leisure activities, he ignores the fact that such a variety of parlour pastimes – backgammon, cards, charades, music recitals or even reading aloud – would suggest that time spent at home often entailed following the rules of nonpersonal games rather than indulging in any heart-to-heart-laying-bare-of-the-soul. Instead he inappropriately invokes Mario Praz's notion of "*stimmung*" as a "sense of intimacy created by a room and its furnishings" that mirrors the owner's soul (Rybcyznski, *Home* 43). In Rybcyznski's discussion, the privacy proper to family life slips into the personal of psychic life. The furnishings that once represented family life now represent the owner's self:

Domesticity has to do with family intimacy, and a devotion to the home, as well as with a sense of the house as embodying – not only harboring – these sentiments . . . the rooms, and the objects that they contained, now required a life of their own. This life was not, of course, autonomous, but existed in the imagination of their owners, and so, paradoxically, homely domesticity depended on a rich interior awareness . . . (75)

Read in context, Rybczynski's discussion of "interior awareness" begins as a documentation of how homeowners in the eighteenth and nineteenth centuries lavished more attention on interior design, but quickly jumps to the assumption that "people" consequently possessed more complex imaginative faculties. Having undergone psychological translation, the intimacy of a space shared with a close few is abstracted into a psychological interiority shared with no one.

There is then in socio-historical literature the same problematic pattern of imbricating terms that recurs both in Sennet's work and in *Villette*: the sociability of family life that is intimate (if only perhaps because it is indoors) is confused with the solitude of interior life that is exclusively personal. Although La Terrasse, given its piecemeal composition of surrogate family members and its hospital-like function, calls up the possibility of engaging in nonpersonal social interaction, Lucy never participates in it in an emotionally gratifying way. Why not? How is Lucy excluded from this home's happiness? In his essay, "The Uncanny," Freud identifies the uncanny as the recurrence of the familiar outside its usual context, the return of what belongs to the house in some dehoused form. The uncanny, according to this definition, marks therefore that which is "secretly familiar [*heimlich-heimisch*]."[14] But what does it mean exactly for a room to be "secretly familiar"? For a person to find an unoccupied room uncannily homelike means that it is filled with personal associations – associations he has to the people who once occupied it. Embedded in the furnishings that represent Auld Lang Syne is thus not only the spirit of the people who once used such housewares, but more particularly Lucy's memory of her own participation in these past moments. That Lucy enters the parlor eagerly but only through the bedroom illustrates that there is written into her story a tension between the social and the personal and that her confrontation with domestic ideals is problematized by a narrative interiority that strives to represent nothing more than psychological selfhood. It is therefore crucial to note that *Villette* presents return, and the identification of the home, in terms of memory.

Although casting the associative properties of descriptive scenes in human terms may seem like stating the obvious, it is Lucy's incapacity to admit the interpersonal dimension of her psychodrama that produces the heightened quality of the Auld Lang Syne scene. That she so conspicuously elides her past interactions with the people depicted in the miniatures hanging over the mantelpiece, representing their humanness only through the synechdochal designations of "pearls" and "velvets" (*Villette* 238), certainly suggests that Lucy wants to avoid acknowledging that this home is animated by human figures. That Lucy knows the pictures, however, "by heart" (238–9) – not only through rote memorization, but by means of her emotional faculties, her heart – not only attests to her emotional investment, but predicates the importance of material objects exclusively on the significance they have in her psychic life.

Thus, Auld Lang Syne is itself a place delineated through the temporal auxiliaries, "old long since," – in other words, a place composed of parts of speech that do not as a rule stand independently. Auld Lang Syne comes to mean not just old times, but Lucy's sense of her own very personal history. Finding herself amidst a community of household accessories, Lucy "finds herself," in the contemporary sense of the expression; the moment of recognition comes when she identifies her godmother's monogram on a cushion, but pleated into her godmother's name, Lucy's own appellation betrays itself as parenthetical at the same time as it is central: Louisa *Lucy* Bretton. Thus recognition, so often a novelistic staple, appears in *Villette* as emplotted in self-discovery.

Begging the question as to whether it is Lucy who haunts home or home that haunts Lucy, the novel at this point shows most clearly that it occupies a threshold – undecided as to whether to be a psychodrama or a marriage plot. Although *Villette* is a novel that won't let its love story out of the closet until well into the third volume, Lucy Snowe never lets us forget that she is a self-scrutinizing solitary woman. Now, however, she becomes recognizable as a type: the Old Maid. Famililess and almost penniless, Lucy finds herself not only vested with the requisite spinsterly monikers, "old Crusty," "old Diogenes," "Mother Wisdom," "dear old Tim," and "dear grandmother," but also haunted, literally and figuratively, by an archetype of virginity, a nun. It is not surprising then that while Paulina chooses to sing one of Schiller's ballads about love, Lucy selects his "Des Madchens Klage" (389) instead, thereby voicing a strangely theatrical willingness to die now that she has loved unrequitedly.

Whether Lucy's solitude functions to expand her psychological interiority or to transmit her to her readers as a type relies on how *Villette* incorporates her physiologically. How solitude performs the paradoxical task of communicating itself throws the grammar of psychodrama and that of home epic into another battle in the dialogic war that is this novel. At first the novel limits itself to isolated pictorials. Perhaps most visceral in Lucy's psychedelic array of solitary self-portraits is the starvation collection. Here *Villette* presents its human population as potential meals that, though Lucy is famished, she nonetheless finds herself prevented from eating.[15] So when Ginevra has become tiresome, Lucy calls her "small beer" that had "turned insufferably acid" (353). When Graham refers to his childhood indifference to Lucy, Brontë words his apology, " 'quiet Lucy Snowe tasted nothing of my glance' " (403). When Lucy droolingly receives a letter from Graham, she "feast(s)" her eyes on its seal, but leaves the treasure "untasted" (319). And when she pines for the human contact that a letter from Bretton's hearth might bring her, she describes her excruciating isolation as seven weeks of "gnaw[ing] on a file to satisfy hunger" and drinking "brine to quench thirst" (349). Comparing herself to a starved animal confined in a cage, she hungers for the next Bretton installment, hoarding what letters she has previously received as if it were possible to make a nourishing feast out of a "crust" (350). Nor does Brontë resist making the equation between gastronomic and social engagement explicit: "The world can understand well enough the process of perishing for want of food: perhaps few persons can enter into or follow out that of going mad from solitary confinement" (356).

Significantly, the consequences of this supposedly metaphorical starvation are quite material. Ghostly pale and imposingly thin as she repeatedly describes herself, we begin not even to notice such details as Lucy's habit of avoiding windy weather for fear of the exertion it would require. What is important in such details is that Lucy visually registers herself in the novel through a vocabulary of malnutrition which, given its roots in her longing for and incapacity to achieve a gastronomic engagement that itself stands for human engagement, and especially romantic engagement, predictably develops into a discourse of psychic illness, specifically what Graham diagnoses as "hypochondria," or what we would call depression. In its grafting of physical and mental categories, the word hypochondria reveals that creased into the illness metaphor is an equation of the material and psychological whereby the diseased is no different than the ill at ease. It suggests in this sense a continuity between what a character knows himself to feel and what others, including a reader, can see.

The medical discourse according to whose sanction Lucy narratologically materializes reveals, however, that Lucy's solitude can work in two ways. On the one hand, illness can work as an alibi that keeps Lucy's inner life unavailable, chaste, private to the point of seeming nonexistent. Thus Brontë explains that the inhabitants at the Rue Fossette "bapti[zed]" Lucy's fevered lovesickness for M. Paul an "illness – a headache" because, as Lucy thankfully realizes, her "whole inner life for the last six months was still [hers] only . . . " (545–6). But given the love interest of the novel, we as readers know that Lucy is supposed to be "lovesick." In terms of plot, illness provides the psychological Lucy with a material register that casts her inwardly turned novel into the currency of romance. Thus Graham describes keeping Lucy healthy as "keeping away the nun" (335), essentially attributing her illness to her spinster-hood and implicitly prescribing marriage as the remedy. Hypochondria not only enables Lucy to penetrate the La Terrasse home where she must confront her childhood beloved, but the physical manifestation of homesickness brings her into intimate conversation with the novel's other prospective husband, M. Paul: noticing Lucy's debilitated appear-ance shortly after her return from visiting with the Brettons, M. Paul asks her if she is "home-sick" (452). What is important to note here is that hypochondria propels Lucy into romance only by presenting her as needy, as someone in need of institutionalization.

INSTITUTIONAL HOME

I do not mean this jokingly. An institution, as the *OED* designates, can be "an establishment, organization, or association instituted for the promotion of some object, especially of a public or general utility, religious, charitable, educational . . . " and, I would add, medical. Lucy, as a homeless woman, certainly counts as belonging to the category of the needy. Given the psychosomatic nature of her affliction, however, it is difficult to say whether the institution that will remedy her solitude is a hospital or a home. And the equation for Victorians is salient in so far as Brontë writes during a period when the domestication of institutional life was in vogue among social reformers: public institutions of all sorts – hospitals, sanitariums, schools, workhouses, orphanages – were increas-ingly reorganized in imitation of domestic space.[16] It follows then that "home" acquires its institutional sense at mid-century: "an institution providing refuge or rest for the destitute, the afflicted, the infirm . . . or for those who have no home of their own or are obliged by their vocations to live at a distance from the home of their family" (*OED*). But there is also another way in which Lucy as a psychological subject is in want of an institution; for the first listing of "institution" in its active sense is "the giving of form or order to a thing . . . the established order by which anything is regulated . . . a system . . . a constitution" (*OED*). To institutionalize Lucy in this sense would mean to process her psyche into a form, a regularity, a constitution that would no longer be so private as to be unrecognizable – to process her, in a sense, the way a novel would.

But at the time that Lucy's homesickness surfaces, she has of course already been institutionalized; she has already made the *Pensionnat de Demoiselles* her home. At this point the distinction between houses and homes becomes significant in so far as Lucy features Mme. Beck's establishment as decidedly not home, whereas the novel shows its striking resemblance to the La Terrasse establishment. Situated at the very center of an international, cosmopolitan city, this "demi-convent" (163) of narrow passages, inner cabinets and nun's cell dormitories operates according to the cyclical time of schools – classes, and breaks, and religious holidays – but rarely does it record the linear historical time of life outside its purlieu: rarely does anyone speak of the school's past, nor is it until the onset of the romance segment of volume III that we learn about the pasts of any of the school's residents.

Besides recording its isolation in terms of time, *Villette* also limns it in terms of gender. Not only does the *pensionnat's* address on Rue "Fossette" translate into both a feminine dimple as well as the diminutive of a pit or a grave but, as an institution, the Rue Fossette admits entrance only to those men possessing the proper professional passport: as teachers, M. Paul and his college examiners cross its threshold; as a physician, Dr. John freely comes and goes; and as eligible suitors, an elite of bachelors ceremoniously receive invitations to a fête. But even Dr. John is not excused from playing the transgressor: Lucy trembles that even though Dr. John speaks softly, "the hum of his man's voice pervaded . . . the whole conventual ground" (182). And when Dr. John invades the school's secluded garden with its adjacent *allée défendue* in search of a billet doux, Lucy recoils: "It was sacrilege – the intrusion of a man into that spot, at that hour; . . . he was lost in the shrubs, trampling flowers and breaking branches in his search – he penetrated at last the 'forbidden walk'" (179–80), thus rendering in bald English the drastic significance of his breaking in to her French-veiled *allée défendue*.

And yet, however fortified Mme. Beck appears against the intrusion of men, it is not the institution of marriage that it forbids, but unprocessed sexuality; Dr. John is invasive only when he is playing a seducer, an Isidore, and not an approved suitor. Thus the only change the school records is when the composition of its population alters due to one of its inhabitants marrying. Although the school demands that the men who pass through its portals belong to the "right" category – the proper vocation, whether medical, educational or religious – once such conditions are met it operates much like a grand marriage-broker, the ebb and flow of its members corresponding directly to transactions going on in the marriage market. Thus all the establishment's females, whether students or teachers, dream or know or speak of a "prospective bridegroom" (177). Like a good bourgeois family, the school invites the proper prospective husband to the appropriate dinner, but forbids entry to the seducer.

But what Lucy appears to find particularly objectionable about the house she must call a home is its institutional status. By referring to the school's residents as those unfortunates "who live in retirement, whose lives have fallen amid the seclusion of the schools of other walled-in and guarded dwellings" (348), Brontë suggests that the protection institutional homes offer consists of a seclusion that is synonymous with exclusion; thus depending on whether one is inside or outside, "guarded" can mean protection from intrusion as well as prevention of escape. What is wrong with such institutions seems to be the very fact that they are institutions, that they are places that can only imitate homes with residents who can only pretend to be a family. In other words, they are not authentic; they are not "true."

And what exactly is untrue about the Rue Fossette establishment turns out to be the systematic principles that govern its operation. Thus Lucy scathingly criticizes the autocratic system that organizes the Rue Fossette school: it is not only that the house operates in compliance with a strict regimen, but that its organizational principle can acknowledge only categories of people and not individuals. Brontë's most explicit critique of what sociologists would call bureaucratization surfaces when she discloses the ironic inhumaneness of what she entitles Mme. Beck's "sufficiency of rational benevolence" whereby the directrice exemplifies the distinction between charity and mercy by donating funds to classes rather than to individuals (137). What is wrong with the sociability of Mme. Beck's institution is that it is nonpersonal; it deals with categories and not individual psyches. For all its seclusion, it is not private because it does not acknowledge individuals, a failure which consequently defines privacy as proper to an individual and not to a group.[17] In this sense, authentic homes seem to emerge, in contrast to their institutional forgeries, as invested in a notion of the individual, and consequently in the sanctity of private life only in so far as an individual experiences it personally.

But can we really say that La Terrasse, or any other of *Villette*'s spaces for that matter, provides an example of such concern for the individual? How "emotionally fulfilled" is Lucy ever, even when at La Terrasse? For if we divorce Lucy from her Auld Lang Syne memory, the household she maintains as home is actually a very nonpersonal place. After all, Lucy, whether in the role of indigent stranger or needy godchild, only gets into the home due to Mrs. Bretton's benevolence – out of charity. And as a type, as one who belongs to a category, she does not always receive the attention she craves, but is often forgotten. Nor can we distinguish the Bretton household as Lucy's place of origin; on the contrary, whether La Terrasse or its Bretton original, neither home ever figures as anything more than a surrogate home housing a surrogate family. In its surrogate status, each functions primarily according to its capacity to invoke a sense of the homelike, an idea of home – does in fact, precisely what institutional homes do.

Are there then any material differences between Mme. Beck's and Mrs. Bretton's? Although it is true that the *pensionnat* is a workplace, rarely do we see anyone engaged in work other than the same drawing, sewing, letter-writing and meal-taking that happen at La Terrasse. Although the *pensionnat* is a school for girls, La Terrasse is not exactly a mixer. And even though the original Bretton home is not literally a school, Graham and Polly, like so many children of their time, take their lessons there. Moreover, both places operate to the same principles of time: whereas a bell signals the interruption of lesson-writing for meals at the Rue Fossette, La Terrasse's striking clock signals that tea-time will offer a respite from letter-writing. Nor is attire any more or less formal; whereas Lucy dresses to descend to the salon at her godmother's, Mme. Beck shuffles through the school in her bedclothes and slippers. Thus, regularly reading the newspaper, pouring Graham's tea or bantering over a chair, when removed from the status of memory and hence from the psychological plane, are no more personal than regularly writing a lesson, sharing a breakfast roll with Ginevra or arguing with M. Paul. From the kinship between these two spaces, one good and one bad, it is possible to conclude therefore that a home, regardless of such relative valuation, not only provides an arena for nonpersonal social exchanges, but is instituted specifically to promote only such exchanges. To expect more would mean asking a home to be more than a home.

THE RHETORIC

If La Terrasse is virtually indistinguishable from Rue Fossette, perhaps the real question is not what makes Rue Fossette false, but what makes true home, as embodied in Auld Lang Syne, so true? In other words, the question is not what makes home home, but what makes the true true. The simple answer is Lucy Snowe makes it so. For ultimately the true home cannot be located anywhere other than in the language Lucy calls on as guide: Lucy is able to distinguish true homes from false houses only because she is armed with such a virulent rhetoric of domesticity – a mode of speaking that uses domestic metaphors momentarily detached from any particular site called "home." Having experienced, for example, the warmth of sitting around an open coal fire, Lucy inherits an English nineteenth-century pattern of images metonymically rooted in the hearth. In order to explain what she means by "a sense of comfort," Lucy finds the homey simile, " . . . as in England we like a fireside" (309). In order to demonstrate her attraction to the Brettons, she describes a carriage trip with them as being "warm and as snug as at a fireside" (303). In order to tag Graham Bretton as the novel's hero – as desirable – Lucy praises him for demonstrating, despite an audience's panic during a fire at a theatre, "that same repose of firmness that I have seen in him when sitting at his side amid the secure peace of his mother's hearth" (243). In order to prove her good taste in art, she castigates a colossal portrait of a nude Cleopatra for depicting nothing but a bad housekeeper who lounges on a sofa at noon while "pots and pans – perhaps I ought to say vases and goblets – were rolled here and there" (276). In expressing her social vision, she sketches an allegory of Human Justice as another slovenly housekeeper who beats the members of her confused and chaotic household with a hearth brush (495). In this sense, Lucy uses domestic metaphor as a compass by which she locates what she wants – what is like Graham, what is like the Brettons, what is like England, what is like art, what is like justice, what is truly home.

But *Villette* does not borrow from the hearth only in order to identify what Lucy desires, but uses domesticity's adjectival function to pass off what it calls "good" as absolute Good. This becomes most clear when questions of truthfulness emerge alongside the desirable and the good, and all under the aegis of the homey. When Lucy, for example, chooses false flattery in order to soothe Ginevra Fanshawe's wounded ego, she discloses, "this must be done in language of which the fidelity and homeliness might challenge comparison with the compliments of a John Knox to a Mary Stuart" (408). When Lucy reasserts her preference for penetrating "to the real truth" (564), she promises to "be honest, and cut, as heretofore, from the homely web of truth" (563). When Paulina asks Lucy about Graham's personality, she words her request, "'You know his home-side. You have seen him with his mother; speak of him as a son'" (462). All these instances dilate the homelike into a mode of speaking, an idiom which promises to sibilate the answer to that ever so gossipy *but-what-is-he-really-like* question, as if seeing someone at home provides a window onto some fundamental truth about his or her moral construction. So it is not surprising that Lucy articulates her English patriotism by faulting "foreigners" for possessing "the art of appearing graceful in public" when the fireside picture shows them to be clumsy domestic companions, as if to say that when you get these beautiful creatures home, you'll find they're not very comfortable. In order to lay bare their grace, Lucy challenges them with distinctly domestic objects: "however blunt and boisterous these every-day home movements connected with peignoir and papillotes, there is a slide, a bend . . . kept nicely in reserve for gala use" (286). Thus she elevates household accouterments like the peignoir and papillotes to the status of moral talismans, indicating that the homey is plainsaying, unembellished, "truthful" speech – a linguistic tool ostensibly shaped for measuring ethical values.

In this sense, domesticity as a rhetoric operates as a remarkably athletic language of evaluation – a language that locates the category of the homegrown on an axiologically polarized landscape whereby it provides a vocabulary for conflating the good and the desirable – for representing what one lonely Lucy wants in ethically absolute terms. What is telling, then, about *Villette*'s domesticity is not the set of values evoked in making home teleologically central, but that its rhetoric of domesticity provides the novel with a moral economy ostensibly independent of the marriage plot it negotiates and yet actually subtending it, thereby forcing the good and the desirable into necessary collusion. The secret it hides is that La Terrasse is good – is true home – because and only because the dreamy memory that Lucy experiences of it is pleasurable to her.

And this is where the collateral damage of grafting a psychodrama onto a home epic shows up. For as the renunciation passage that I began with indicates, the introduction of psychological planes coincides with an ethical agenda focused on making consciousness itself, that which is inwardly bent, morally justifiable. Whether Lucy will *have to* selfishly pursue an independent career in an institution or will *get to* "gloriously" work for others in a home, she still winds up having to justify herself even if it means justifying the act of justifying herself.[18] But moral justification of anything is impossible for a text predicated on the workings of a single psyche; because such an autocratic registering consciousness curtails a text's ability to provide a reader with multiple sites of sympathy, the good becomes indistinguishable from what a particular self wants. The result therefore of transferring the home epic to a psychological bailiwick is to introduce an ethical agenda already enfeebled by the demise of the absolutes that would make the true and the good independent of the desired.

Moreover this privileging of the interior view in *Villette* relies on certain narrative conventions. Graham, for example, has two sides or two "views – the public and the private – the out-door and the in-door view" (273). From the outside, Graham appears noble and philanthropic; but the "fireside picture" confers on Lucy the authority to add that he "is also vain and sometimes insensitive." Although she claims that both versions are "correct," implicit in her homegrown supplement is an embrace of the epistemological and ultimately moral perspective that household words somehow furnish; as the perspective that contributes additional information, the insider glimpse gets closer to "truth" through the act of embellishing what is already known. In this sense, the sequence by which the novel presents the view from within as that which follows the view from without, thereby improving it by glossing it, suggests that private knowledge is not privileged by any virtue proper to itself but derives its value from its relationship to what has already been seen from the outside. In terms of truth, there is nothing necessarily more intrinsically authoritative about the private other than its placement in the order by which a novel chooses to disseminate information. In this sense domesticity's moral edge emerges as reliant on the narrative convention of retrospection according to which a narrator knows more because he has already been processed through the plot. Of course, retrospection is very shaky ground for making absolute moral claims. But by conflating the good and the desired, the rhetoric of domesticity conceals its relativism at the same time that it operates to translate a personal psychodrama into a grammar of romantic plotting. In addition to being the site of selfless work, Home must appear as the good, because otherwise getting into it would look like nothing but wish-fulfillment.

ROMANTIC PROCESSING

Nevertheless, *Villette*'s domestic rhetoric finally fails to resolve the tension between the novel's psychically bound concerns and the demands of a romantic plot that must end in the nonpersonal sociability of True Home. This becomes particularly clear in terms of the narrative function Graham fills. Lucy's experience of institutional life, whether at Mme. Beck's or Mrs. Bretton's, forces her to confront a conventional romance plot specifically in the figure of Dr. John. The terms of the romance that Dr. John represents become clear when Lucy encounters him at La Terrasse and must explain that she had already recognized him as Graham Bretton several episodes earlier when they had had a misunderstanding in the window recess at the Rue Fossette. From the way in which *Villette* presents it, the spatial arrangement of the Rue Fossette establishment allows Lucy her privacy in the shape of the forbidden walk behind the garden. The garden itself, usually surfacing as a place where Lucy spends much of her time by herself ducking *billets doux* and dodging disguised lovers, can be seen only from a particular household spot that, like the novel it occupies, weds interior and exterior scenes but only through a stationary, single vantage point. The "window recess" functions both as a place of personal and of scenic contemplation: set off from the activity of the room's center, the recess offers a preserve for individual meditation, psychological probing, self-examination; overlooking the social activities of the garden, the window contextualizes the interactions of a human community exclusively in terms of self-exploration.

When the window recess surfaces as a reference point several episodes later, it is when Lucy explains that she had previously recognized Graham when, glancing at the recess's mirror, she finds him catching her stare (163). Taking her look as lewd, Dr. John obtusely reads Lucy as if she is part of a traditional romantic storyline, rebukingly accusing her of harboring an unavowed attraction to him. In this sense, Graham functions as the agent of romance, insinuating institutionalized marriage plots into Lucy's psychic space. But the marriage plot he represents, despite all of Lucy's sexual longings, is distinctly asexual. As the novel's ubiquitoid, Graham seems at first to play the roles of virtually every eligible bachelor in the entire city, eclipsing the effete de Hamal and the Napoleonic M. Paul alike, wooing a gamut of the Rue Fossette residents from Rosine Matou to Mme. Beck herself. And yet despite, or perhaps due to, his label as hero and hence husband-to-be, his representation of romance is strangely desexualized; Lucy often marvels over his coolness, his characteristically British lack of passion – he only glances as the voluptuous Cleopatra, he is unmoved by Vashti.

The moment in which Lucy recognizes Dr. John as Graham Bretton, or, more accurately, the moment in which she discloses the recognition that had taken place several scenes earlier, functions in two significant ways. On the one hand, Graham the representative of romance (the presence of romantic plotting) forces the novel to acknowledge the affinity between the two homes, each one – the true and the ersatz – seeming to orbit around this man. Getting into a home in fact requires entering into a privileged relationship to Graham, requires being his mother, or his wife, or his patient, or his patron, or even his coach companion: after all, it is Graham who, masked as a knight with a British accent, first leads Lucy through the fog to Mme. Beck's doorstep. By both representing romance as nonpersonal sociability and by highlighting the kinship of the novel's two homes, Graham functions to implicate romantic plotting in the institutional life of homes.

Moreover, it is only through encountering Graham again that Lucy must reveal her real secret – not that she lusts for him, but that she has already recognized him. Knowledge appears now for Lucy a question of privacy. This has devastating significance for the novel, since in order for *Villette* to represent a psychologically fleshed-out Lucy, what Lucy knows – what is personal to her – must be kept unavailable on a narrative level, unnarratable and unreadable. Graham's presence in this sense explodes the psychological and therefore private Lucy. Graham, the agent of romance, processes Lucy's thoughts, such as recognition, into scenes – into plot episodes. In his invasion of the psychic space of the window recess, Graham represents an encroachment of romance and plot that threatens this novel's right to privacy. Romantic plotting surfaces then as a process that produces a true home only at the cost of invading the privacy that designates psychic life.

THE NOVEL AS INSTITUTION

If romantic plots evince themselves as institutionally bound, what then of novels that encode such plots? Alongside such an institutionalizing of romance, *Villette*'s narrative mechanics similarly refuse to articulate Lucy in a psychological idiom, preferring to sketch her instead as a storyteller engaged in playing a game. Instead of officially representing Lucy's historical home and her journey into adulthood by adhering to the narrative conventions in which characters like Robinson Crusoe or even Pamela Andrews tell their lives, *Villette* seems to consist of primarily static leitmotifs, seems, in fact, like the timeless La Terrasse, compositionally resistant to historical time. Description, for example, often works metaleptically: instead of presenting a sequence of causes and effects, *Villette* fixates on the effects first, as if they were the true ignitors of the action. Instead of saying, "One day Polly's father returned," Lucy outlines the following scenario: One day, Polly's expression changes; "it is," Lucy hears her say; as Lucy is about to turn and tell Mrs. Bretton that "the child was run out mad, and ought instantly to be pursued, [she sees] her caught up, and rapt at once from my cool observation, and from the wondering stare of the passengers. A gentleman had done this good turn ..." (70). What is important is that Lucy postpones, not merely disclosing the "gentleman['s]" identity as Polly's father, but the very agent of the catching to the last possible moment. A simple reunion between father and daughter takes on increased significance because Lucy's narrating eye omits the presence of a gentleman on the street; at the moment that Polly is "caught up," we have no real idea as to what being "caught up" means because the agent of the action is, unbeknown to us, missing.

This syncchdochal representation of even the most ordinary of satellite details grows increasingly obtrusive. The moment of Lucy's encounter with M. Paul at the gallery thus runs in scarcely bearable slow motion: sitting on a couch gazing at the Cleopatra, Lucy breathes, "Suddenly a light tap visited my shoulder. Starting, turning, I met a face bent to encounter mine . . . 'Que faites vous ici?' said a voice . . . [more dialogue] . . . M. Paul Emanuel (it was he) returned from Rome . . . " (226). By not only deferring M. Paul's naming and, what for a reader constitutes his recognizability, to the very last possible moment, but by creasing an entire human being (M. Paul himself) into a "tap," now capable of no less than a visitation, *Villette* implicates the moment, freighting it with deeper significance. In this way, a simple gesture, because its owner appears anachronistically, calls attention to the narrative mechanism that represents it and makes the mechanics of telling seem primary.

Names work to a similar purpose. By changing all the names of the Bretton denizens, the novel is able to withhold information essential to a story that might include characters other than the narrator. And because we as readers cannot recognize the Brettons and the Homes under the guise of a John and a Bassompierre, we cannot avoid but feel excluded – as if the novel itself were too private to let even us in. Finding ourselves kept out in so many ways, we begin to suspect that the true plot of the novel pivots on a plot in the malicious sense – a plot hidden in the discourse that has as its main characters the reader and the text.[19] Before we realize it, the game is afoot and we are active participants, even if in the role of the text's opponent.

If we recall that an institution can mean the giving of form or order to something (something like the relationship between a text and a reader), then we can think of *Villette* as a novel which institutes the reader–text relationship as a game: although the obtrusiveness of its narrational mechanisms forces the reader, in his exclusion, to feel self-conscious, it is a self-consciousness that works to make the whole process of reading game-like – and hence a kind of work or play as nonpersonal as the light sewing and bridge sets of nineteenth-century home life. This under-standing of the novel as a nonpersonal game played self-consciously moves toward synthesizing the opposition between self-consciousness and self-denial (between the self-reference of psychodrama and the self-immolation of domestic endings) by prioritizing what happens on a hermeneutical plane.[20] And if we remember that institutions, whether "educational" or "domestic," provide arenas of emotionally fulfilling nonpersonal social exchanges, we might be able to think of *Villette*, in its gesture toward such a hermeneutics, as aspiring to institutional status.

M. PAUL

Romance, marriage, home: what happens to them in the prison of a psychodrama? For certainly romance, in its processing of thoughts into plot episodes, is precisely what *Villette* seems poised to avoid, and perhaps explains why the novel, when it appoints Graham to the Home subplot, seems to banish home in the same gesture that it banishes romance. And although *Villette*'s domestic rhetoric elides the overriding presence of a psychological self by setting up the ethical agenda that presents questions of desire as questions of truth, the tension between the novel's psychically bound concerns and the demands of romantic plottings never appear negotiated with enough regularity for *Villette* to compose itself as an institution. Thus it is clear that the novel's romance is irrepressible when volume III starts to look like a repetition of the syndrome; for despite its love-requited thematics, the M. Paul segment never promises anything beyond what the institution of romance can yield. Not only does romance again unveil itself as being about a community rather than merely two people, but the degree to which the marriage plot charts how deeply psychic life is wedded to institutional structures materializes as quite gruesome in Lucy's discovery of the Roman Catholic plot to abort her own self-seeking one.

By entering into a relationship with one man, Lucy finds herself engaged to a whole social network; loving M. Paul is more than merely a matter of finding her reflection in his eyes, but of joining for better or for worse the community to which he belongs. Hence Lucy breaks the code that had kept M. Paul's unexpected coldness a "Sphynx riddle" when she realizes that "the conjunction of those two names, Pere Silas and Paul Emanuel, gave the key to all" (508). No longer living plotlessly, Lucy finds her own personal destiny folded into a relationship seemingly irrelevant to her life; once her individual story becomes a type of marriage plot, she must find herself in relation to a veritable host of other people who inhabit what George Eliot calls the web of human life. Thus Lucy, having ridiculed one of her students for giving so public a display of grief over M. Paul's departure, waits until they are alone and then unprecedentedly embraces her (536). By replacing her habitual frosty conduct with such uncharacteristic physical demonstrativeness, Lucy displays how a romantic relationship with M. Paul brings her into a more active, and even physical, relationship with the community in which she lives. And so it is emblematically Lucy who is responsible for Ginevra's elopement with de Hamal when she accidentally leaves "a certain great door" unlocked (572). In her delirious midnight search for M. Paul, Lucy actively though inadvertently generates a marriage not her own.

Nor does the novel allow M. Paul any more sexuality than it allotted to Graham, but processes his erotic potential so as to be publicly digestible. Thus volume III presents him in asexual male roles: a son or a father, but never a lover. Either he resembles a little boy in his filial devotion to Mother Church, or he strikes a paternal figure in being especially noted not only as a public man, but as a great domestic manager: having conducted the school to the country for breakfast, he presides over a great symphony of knives, plates, fresh butter, coffee, chocolate, cream, new-laid eggs and baskets of rolls from his dais at the farm kitchen hearth and tenderly arranges for transportation home, thereby prompting Lucy to exclaim, "here, with good management, room was found for all" (475).

Nevertheless, M. Paul, as a continental, and especially as a continental with a "French" heritage, is coded in British nineteenth-century stereospeak as "sexual." This is why, when M. Paul asks Lucy to signal that she has forgiven him by calling him either "mon ami" or "my friend," Lucy explains her rather predictable choice of the English sobriquet over the French one:

> Now "my friend" had rather another sound and significance than *"mon ami,"* it did not breathe the same sense of domestic and intimate affection: *"mon ami,"* I could not say to M. Paul; "my friend," I could and did say without difficulty. (407)

And yet despite her choice here of the more "modest" English expression, Lucy reveals elsewhere that much of her discourse with M. Paul takes place in French. *Villette* disguises this fact in its generally arbitrary use of translation: because the novel often includes lengthy French passages (sometimes translated parenthetically, sometimes not), we assume that when English is used to report a conversation between Lucy and M. Paul, English had been spoken. We are disabused, however, when Lucy describes one of their intimate conversations during which she expresses how painful her separation from him had been: "'All these weary days,' said he, repeating my words, with a gentle, kindly mimicry of my voice and foreign accent . . ." (582). Although she has transcribed the conversation in English, M. Paul's teasing reveals that it occurred in French. Most important, though, is the fact that the phrase which finally bespeaks Lucy's desire not only bodies forth in an eroticized language, but becomes, though a series of translations and transliterating recordings, strangely community property: uttered by Lucy to M. Paul in faulty French (her thinking in English requiring an initial translation), conveyed by the novel to us in English, repeated by M. Paul to Lucy in mock English-accented French, and then again reechoed in the novel's transcription back into English of M. Paul's already echoing voice, the phrase stands as a kind of aural pastiche composed of a series of finally nonpersonal social interactions, both real and readerly. Whereas the text might have taken advantage of the presence of French here as a sign of private property – as the sign of the withheld, of the true interior – it chooses instead to call attention to an instance of forced translation, insistent publicization. In yielding to the demands of institutional romance, Lucy's desire and M. Paul's sexuality disclose themselves publicly and legibly.

"HOME SWEET HOME"

But can the M. Paul romance, readable and communal as it is, provide the home, not one that the demands of a marriage plot require, but the home that will satisfy the personal desires belonging to Lucy's psychological agenda? What to make of the little establishment in the Faubourg Clotilde? Is it True Home? Is it Happy Ending? As idyllic as Auld Lang Syne, the space that is Lucy's final home appears in self-consciously precious trappings: hence the imperatively diminutive "nut-shell," with its little kitchen, its tiny parlor, and its miniature *classe* banks on the charm of the depopulated picturesque: "its vista closed a French window with vines trained about the panes, tendrils and green leaves kissing the glass" (584).[21] But does this wish-fulfillment look any more like truth than the axiomatic mottos Victorian housewives hung up as kitchen decor?[22] After all, such a home looks hardly able to provide a resident with emotional satisfaction of any stamp, whether psychological or nonpersonal.

And yet to say that this final home is not a happy ending is not only impossible, but irrelevant. Indeed, Lucy gets the home that, as the "crescent phase" passage that I began with suggests, she both desired and renounced – a place where she lives and labors for others. Not only is the Faubourg Clotilde establishment Lucy's very own home as well as a scholastic institution where girls are processed through nonpersonal social interaction, but her happiness in working this home is unqualified. Thus she minces no words when she describes the three years of M. Paul's absence in a strange echo of Jane Eyre's famous Reader-I-married-him: "Reader, they were the three happiest years of my life" (593).

But how, I have now asked myself time and again, can the likely death of the hero who isn't even yet a legitimate spouse allow this home to constitute a happy ending for any novel, whether home epic or psychodrama? And here is precisely where all the wrong questions are asked. For the ending of *Villette* does not represent a *what-is-it-really-like-when-you-get-inside* Truth about home (it's really just an institution) or about novelistic endings (they really just unravel); nor should it generate questions as to what it is Lucy really wants, or how it comments on women trapped in Victorian families, or even whether M. Paul really dies. For what is important in this novel that does after all have home, if not marriage, as its bourne as well as its albatross is that it concludes by relocating: no longer does it seem to be about Lucy and M. Paul, but about the text and its readers: "Here pause: pause at once. There is enough said . . . Let it be theirs to conceive the delight of joy born again fresh out of great terror . . . Let them picture union and a happy succeeding life" (596).

Is this, we might ask, a promise or a threat? It is almost impossible, I think, not to see in *Villette*'s conclusion a throwing down of the gauntlet. For *Villette*'s final words demonstrate, especially in their antagonistic yanking, what I want to claim ultimately forms the definitive property of domesticity; the essential relation, the one that its final words make ineluctably central, is the one hidden in the exchange between the novel and us – a discourse that the text continuously reminds us is no more than a nonpersonal game, even if played self-consciously. In resisting the reader's desire to lose himself in the play of a reading and in putting him to work self-consciously at reconstructing plot sequences, *Villette* proffers the nonpersonal sociability of true home life. It doesn't matter what the Final Home or the Home Finale looks like; what matters is that it provocatively continues playing with us the game of reading home. This is not to say, however, that all novels are really about the relationship between the reader and the text, only that this is Brontë's way of using the novel form to emplot nonpersonal sociability.

CHAPTER 3

Dickens 1: Great Expectations *and vocational domesticity*

Domesticity, the idea of home as a personal ideal and narrative objective, emerges in *Great Expectations* in the shape of Wemmick's Castle.[1] Compared with Harville's ingenious apartment and Lucy's schoolroom cottage, the "Pleasant Home" that this dutiful clerk sequesters plays on Ruskin's idea of the home as a shelter from the "anxieties of the outer life . . . the inconsistently-minded, unknown, unloved, or hostile society of the outer world" (*Sesame and Lilies* 85). But at the same time that *Great Expectations* makes fun of the idea that a home can be successfully sequestered from the world of business, the opposition is endorsed as an immensely happy fiction. Although the presence of a Pleasant Home would seem to be what makes Wemmick and Jaggers different, it is home as an ideal that they share:

"What's all this?" said Mr. Jaggers. "You with an old father, and you with pleasant and playful ways?"
   "Well!" returned Wemmick. "If I don't bring 'em here, what does it matter?" . . .
   "You with a pleasant home?" said Jaggers.
   "Since it don't interfere with business," returned Wemmick, "let it be so. Now, I look at you, sir, I shouldn't wonder if you might be planning and contriving to have a pleasant home of your own one of these days, when you're tired of all this work."
   Mr. Jaggers nodded his head retrospectively two or three times, and actually drew a sigh. (*Great Expectations* 424)

In puzzling over what Mr. Jaggers would look like while he nodded his head "retrospectively," we should note that mention of the pleasant home signals the introduction of a temporal order different from that governing the narrative's main action: Mr. Jaggers' memory, a psychological line of development. We can assume that Mr. Jaggers remembers here a personal life whose privacy the novel has temporarily deferred invading. His private memory, or what D.A. Miller might call his open secret,[2] is maintained by the impossible figure of a retrospective nod. That the pleasant home should cause the mystifying retrospective nod while presumably alluding to the contents of the memory suggests the extent to which the fiction of its privacy is in the public domain.

THE OPPOSITION EXAMINED

The Victorians talked incessantly about the meaning of the home. Sociological and political thought generally lauded the "home" and "family" for being "the highest form of social organization" (Laslett, *Household and Family*). Feminist and reform literature often debunked it as a form of archaic imprisonment.[3] Despite this divide, the period's growing mass media records the home's popular apotheosis in kitchen wall maxims and childhood rhymes, advertising jingles and decorative household curiosities: even commercial landscapers promoted ornamental urns "replete with inscriptions of domestic harmony."[4] The home emerges as an occasion for serious and often divisive discussions about how society should be organized, managed and reformed at the same time that it provides lucrative material for England's burgeoning entertainment industry.

Much historical literature seems dazzled by a dichotomy that may have had a less monolithic significance for the consumers of the mass culture in which it was so consistently replicated. The most cherished notion of what the French called the "family craze" (Perrot, "The Family Triumphant," 134) is that the home offered a refuge from an increasingly industrialized city where men went to work, every day battling with such inhumane forces as money, dirt, greed and immorality, while women stayed at home, angelically presiding over a preserve of leisure, cleanliness and ethical love. A standard history text, for example, will devote a chapter to "Victorian morality" and explain that "the praises of domestic family ties came to be sung more loudly than ever before in British history" *because* "it was the home ... that was felt to be the center of moral virtue and a refuge against the barbarism of the outside world."[5] Asa Briggs writes of "'Home! Sweet Home!' as a continuing theme of the period" in which the home "was hailed as a refuge, too, from the often fierce competitiveness of business life" and cites Ruskin's description of the home as "the place of Peace; the shelter, not only from all injury but from all terror, doubt and division" (*A Social*

History of England 240). Alexander Welsh describes the antithesis between the hearth and the city as so widely discussed and so obviously logical that exploring it is almost embarrassing.[6] And even in one of his more descriptive socio-historical sketches, Peter Laslett registers this division of human experience as centered on the home: "the domestic group," he explains, is in many instances "the family which the suburban worker leaves when he catches his bus in the morning and returns to in the evening" (Laslett, *Household and Family* 24); the sentence's spatial and social conflation (the "family" here is as much a place as it is a group), and the point of view its transportational details impose (though "family" is not the subject pronoun of the verb, it provides the vantage point whence such routine leave-takings and returns are perceived) attest to the centrality of the home in what comes to be talked about in the twentieth century as a commuter's life.

What is common throughout such literature is not only that home is spoken about as ideal or idealized at the same time that it is spoken about as a place apart, as if there were some intuitive connection between ideal spaces and secluded ones, but that the seclusion is invariably envisioned as the exclusion of "work." Under Adorno's influence, Walter Benjamin records the attention paid to the home specifically in terms of a division between working and living spaces – a division he sets up as necessary for conferring on the latter an antidotal power. In describing the world of Paris under Louis-Philippe, he writes:

For the private person, living space becomes, for the first time, antithetical to the place of work. The former is constituted by the interior; the office is its complement. The private person who squares his accounts with reality in his office demands that the interior be maintained in his illusions. This need is all the more pressing since he has no intention of extending his commercial considerations into social ones.[7]

That Benjamin had during this phase of his career begun a tortured flirtation with communist politics despite his sojourn in burgeoning fascist circles suggests that the definition of private life as that which does not include work is, in part, born of twentieth-century intellectual anomie. The problem here is that the logic conflating the home's idealization with a vision of human experience as starkly polar takes something for granted: once it is recognized that a culture values some structure or practice like the Home, any evaluation of the system of oppositions subtending such a value is vulnerable to the binaries according to which the system operates. For in rejecting the validity of the claim that the home was considered good because it was private, it becomes tempting to say that there was nothing absolutely good about the home independent of its participation in an antithesis. Rather than ask, why are home and privacy listed by historians of the nineteenth century as the goods of bourgeois individualism, maybe it is time to ask why the homes described by novelists of the nineteenth-century are good but not private.

And maybe it is time as well to reevaluate the formal force of the religious subtext informing so much of domesticity's rhetoric,[8] a set of themes and stylistic devices that those who live in a more secular intellectual climate often overlook. When not occurring in the evangelical treatises that seized on the home as a moral preserve for a religious life that the secular business world of competitive capitalism seemed to threaten (Hall, "The Sweet Delights of Home," 74), domesticity traded on a religious currency of an ecumenical stamp. Hall, in a typical example, cites William Cobbett's *Cottage Economy*: "What could please God more than the picture of 'the labourer, after his return from the toils of a cold winter day, sitting with his wife and children round a cheerful fire, while the wind whistles in the chimney and the rain pelts the roof'?" (84). Both Hall and Cobbett place the "separation of the space where men work and the household where they love" in a divinely sanctioned context regardless of any particular religious sect and almost regardless of belief in God. More recently, Witold Rybczynski continues the tradition by turning from an ecumenical rendering of religious belief to an anthropological one: in answer to his question as to whether "we work to rest or rest to work?" Rybczynski speculates that the modern focus on balancing work done in public and play done at home is merely a secular enactment of an ancient need to divide human life into the sacred and the profane, although he leaves unclear which is sacred and which profane, the work or the rest.[9] It would seem then that domesticity invites the same treatment that religion does: when not predicated on the notion of God or on the social good, it is explained as an ancient "need," anachronistic in our own enlightened time.

Domesticity's coinciding with a representation of human experience as neatly divided between personal and professional life is a legacy of a discursive history that invites a line-up of coordinate oppositions that are tautological in being more descriptive than substantive. In other words, because the home is discussed as a haven from the industrialized world, it becomes a place of Christian charity rather than of mercantile greed, pastoral scenes rather than urban scapes, sentimental interaction rather

than perfunctory duty, personal contemplation rather than public performance, character rather than deed. The list could go on, for the effect
of lining up such oppositions is difficult to resist, but not, however, very
helpful in getting at what is really at stake in dividing up human life so
sharply and with such apparent *gravitas*. Because English domesticity
occurs, to quote Wemmick, as a principle of fortification that entails such
a division between working and "living" spaces, it is precisely the
fictionalization of this division that demands closer scrutiny.

THE PSYCHOLOGICAL AGAINST THE DOMESTIC

If nineteenth-century English culture perpetuated an idea of the home
as a warm and protected depository of familial affection and leisured
personability perversely divorced from the cold world of work done
among strangers, Wemmick certainly serves to represent the stereotype.
Wemmick's home, located in a more "pastoral" setting outside the fog
and grease of London's city limits, emerges as a place crucially distinguished by its status as an alternative to Wemmick's place of work – Mr.
Jaggers' office. Located in different settings (one urban and one suburban), housing different types of relationship (a boss and a managerial
association as opposed to a father and a familial alliance), and therefore
facilitating different brands of interaction (one demonstrably affection-
ate and one unaffectedly impersonal), the two places are so radically
different that traversing the distance between them involves nothing
short of a translation from one culture into another. So when Pip has
dinner with Mr. Jaggers and Wemmick, he is surprised to find no traces
of the man he had seen in his home: unable to even catch "his eye now
and then in a friendly way," Pip finds Wemmick "as dry and distant to
me as if there were twin Wemmicks and this was the wrong one" (401).
And when Pip observes that during the journey from the Castle back to
Little Britain, Wemmick appears "dryer and harder" and that his
mouth resumes its "post office" shape – the mechanical smile that marks
his clerkship at Mr. Jaggers' establishment – he realizes that his friend
has transformed into another person entirely: "At last, when we got to
his place of business and he pulled out his key from his coat-collar, he
looked as unconscious of his Walworth property as if the Castle and the
fountain and the Aged had all been blown into space . . . " (232).

By depicting home and office as polar sites, the graphics of Wemmick's commute present mobility itself as an expression of character
transformation, but simultaneously empty the notion of character of

anything really personal – that is, of anything having to do with a psychologically individuated self. Wemmick does not quite become another person, but he does exchange the signs of a personal life – the signs of his Walworth sentiments – for the signs of a professional life. That his personality occurs as a collection of place-specific traits suggests that in order to represent the division of home from office space, the novel must subordinate other categories such as emotional or psychological life to such spatial and hence such material concerns. Wemmick is understood, not as a person whose distinctness exists prior to his socialized personality, but as a family man or a law clerk. In this sense, the Dickensian world constructs personality out of an occupational vocabulary. It would appear than that there is something so absorbing about the division of human life into these particular two spheres that a novel organized according to its precepts pays the price in constructing what some would call an aesthetically impoverished rendering of human experience. The work–home antithesis, as it plays out in the Wemmick storyline, thus emerges as a detail, but a detail with extremely high stakes and an extremely profound reach.

What surfaces through Pip's involvement in Wemmick's Pleasant Home is that the novel has built into its plot two ostensibly overlapping but ultimately irreconcilable discourses: what I would call a psychological one and a domestic one.[10] In terms of the former, I mean a set of motivational drives – those that precipitate Pip's leaving home, for example – that register in the novel as being psychological: rather than leave home in order to make his way in the world, Pip leaves home in Freudian family romance fashion. In "Family Romance" Freud describes that while growing up, children often discover that their own homes, in comparison to other homes, are less than they originally had assumed.[11] To rationalize their disillusionment, they often fantasize an orphanhood for themselves whereby either one or both biological parents is of magical or royal or aristocratic status and their own true legacy only waiting in the wings. Indeed, once Pip meets Estelle and is humiliated by her rejection, he imagines such a familial realignment,[12] the adoption fantasy thereby serving to articulate the novel's motivational drive in terms of personal, definitively psychological, wish-fulfillment:

She had adopted Estella, she had as good as adopted me . . . She had reserved it for me to restore the desolate house, admit the sunshine into the dark rooms, set the clocks a going and the cold hearths a blazing, tear down the cobwebs, destroy the vermin – in short, do all the shining deeds of the young knight of romance, and marry the Princess. I had stopped to look at the house as I passed and its red brick walls, blocked windows, and strong green ivy clasping even the stacks of the chimneys with its twigs and tendons, as if with sinewy, old arms, had made a rich attractive mystery, of which I was the hero. (253)

The unsubtly named Satis House emerges as the narrative's bourne because the novel's psychological grammar places it there; there is very little to find appealing about a dilapidated mansion, a bratty girl and a crotchety old maid independent of Pip's personal fantasies. Indeed, leave-taking itself occurs as a psychological drive that is too private to be shared in so far as a stranger would be hard put to make a case for the desirability of the objects and activities belonging to Pip's fantasy life: cleaning and sweeping away cobwebs and vermin. Like *Villette*'s rhetoric of domesticity whereby the identification of "true home" relies on an ethical language that conflates the good and the desired, *Great Expectations*' psychological discourse makes it quite clear that the home waiting at the end of its supposed marriage plot is suspiciously reliant on Pip's personal fantasies.

But what is left muted in the wish is that being adopted by Miss Havisham would mean Pip's release from being a working-class boy. The psychologized vocabulary in which the Satis House adoption fantasy presents the target home obfuscates the economic nature of the wish. That Pip ceases to "believe" in his home at the same time that he stops believing "in the forge as the flowing road to manhood and independence" (134) suggests that the insinuation of a psychological discourse makes the relationship between home and work an incompatibility in need of negotiation. Not only does Pip present Satis House as the agent under whose influence he "continued at heart to hate [his] trade and be ashamed of home" (152), but the onset of his shame coincides with his apprenticeship to Joe. Like the hearths characteristic of a Joseph Wright of Derby painting, the forge at which he must work eventually transforms into the forge of home fire nostalgia in Pip's recollection. But at the moment of his humiliation and dawning self-consciousness, the novel makes it clear that Pip's childhood home is also a place of work. As the original surrogate father–son relationship between Pip and Joe turns into a business arrangement once Pip is of age (Pip becomes a laborer, Joe his manager), so does the original Hearth, the dear old forge of auld lang syne, emerge as an economic resource. It would seem here that creased into the psychological fabric of the narrative is a virulent uneasiness about work and about money – a discontent that such a psychologized idiom seems precipitously poised to assuage. In the psychological fantasy of Satis House, where Pip would presumably be released from working-class life, is a return of the repressed in the shape of housework: rather than envisioning himself killing dragons and fighting infidels, Pip sees knighthood in the above passage as cleaning away cobwebs and vermin. What implodes Pip's fantastic release from working-class labor is the labor of housework.

Whereas the novel's grammar of wish-fulfillment betrays its ulterior economic agenda, domestic discourse emerges as an alternative line of development. The novel appears to place a premium on establishing and maintaining the distinction between home and work in order to mark good homes, like the Castle, from the flawed homes scattered about the rest of the novel's terrain. The Pocket household, for example, is both a workplace and a living space, its "family" functioning as a working unit composed both of biologically related and vocationally related members: as a scholar and tutor, Mr. Pocket boards his students, Startop and Drummle; Miss Coiler, a host of domestic servants and a cook do the manual labor of maintaining the house; Flopsom and Millers care for the several young children; and Mrs. Pocket plays the stereotypical bourgeois female role of representing leisure by doing nothing at all. But even though the novel generates a great deal of affection for the Pockets, it nonetheless discounts their home as unsatisfactory: a chaotic house of mismanagement, its children are not brought up, but are found "tumbling up" (mostly due to a footstool's inexplicable placement under Mrs. Pocket's skirts), its alcoholic cook routinely found comatose on the kitchen floor, its baby nurse sleeping around with the Foot Guards and its paternal head continuously trying to pick himself up by the hair – all despite the fact that he has built his career – his business – on lecturing about domestic management. Or perhaps due to it. For it would seem that it is the lack of distinction between work and home that is somehow implicated in the disarray of the Pocket household.

In this sense domestic discourse uses the business–home distinction as a kind of litmus test for distinguishing true homes from their Duessa lookalikes, a test capable of laying bare the Satis House fantasy as a fake. On the surface, Satis House seems to have refined itself away from its economic origins: although the brewery that originally supplied the fortune for building the house still stands on the estate land, it no longer functions as a working plant. Adoption into Satis House would therefore mean acquisition of a home devoid of work. That the desired and expected Satis House retains the vestiges of its economic origins, even if only as a kind of ornament similar to the decorative "ruins" in vogue among the period's domestic landscapers, suggests however that it is not necessarily what it pretends to be. As the sign of having improperly managed the work–home distinction, the very presence of the brewery, operating or not, gives Satis House away as a mirage.[13]

In this way, the novel marks what is desirable twice: psychologically, the desirable home is the one Pip wants; but novelistically it is the one that fulfills the precepts of the home–work polarity. By tagging the desirable home through a line of valuation that lies beyond any psychological discourse, *Great Expectations*' discourse of domesticity articulates the novel's formal drives rather than those belonging to its primary psychological subject; aspiring to identify the good in more absolute terms, novelistic domesticity seems to battle it out with the psychological priorities of character development. It would seem significant then that the implements that Pip steals for the convict and that ultimately buy him what turns out to be his true surrogate parent – the nightmare adoption rather than the fantasized one – consist of a pie from the kitchen and a file from the shop – symbols perhaps of a less fraught relationship between home and work in the prelapserian scenes that take place before Pip as a psychological subject begins desiring Satis House and before he begins having expectations. In this way, it is a visual reference to the uncertain boundary between work and home (as manifest in the novel's pairing of a pie with a file) that plays a kind of repressed ghost; for the ghost not only links home and work in Pip's initial encounter with Magwitch, but returns – ultimately in the shape of the adopting father himself – in order to unmask the gentler "expectation" of the family romance adoption fantasy and the psychological idiom that bolsters it as a complex but ultimately ineffectual circumlocution for money and for the social status that money can or cannot buy. Once Magwitch returns and the truth about the wish itself emerges, it is unavoidable that Pip's great expectations are nothing more than the purse of money he is now loath to touch. And his new life of gentlemanly credit nothing more than a series of money transactions no longer susceptible to the mystifications of wish-fulfillment formulae. The psychological discourse of the adoption fantasy having thus failed, money and work remain in need of management.

THE TAUTOLOGICAL PROBLEM

By functioning as a detector of flawed homes, the home–office distinction directs the narrative away from the wish-fulfillment of its psychological drives and establishes in its stead a domestic line of valuation whereby the home is categorically and not psychologically desirable. Perhaps this is why Wemmick's Pleasant Home appears in *Great Expectations'* subplot – a subplot whose ideal space will ultimately elude Pip. Pip, as the novel's registering consciousness, and as the representative of an introverted form, is in the end barred from achieving that Pleasant Home in any idiom other than the absent presence of nostalgia.

But for a moment the novel makes much of Wemmick's decompartmentalized life: as the consummate home, the Castle includes no bald signs of office life – no signs of work in so far as work is understood as the exertion of effort for money payment. Although Wemmick and his father sometimes eat a vegetable from the garden, the garden itself serves more as a source of entertainment than of subsistence. Although the Aged gets to do various household tasks, it is only due to Wemmick's "pretending to employ" him (232). And although Miss Skiffins does wash the tea things, it is only "in a trifling lady-like amateur manner that compromised none of us" (315). If any work does happen in the Pleasant Home, it happens as play. And as play, work occurs here as something other than the tasks constituting it.

In this sense, Wemmick's workplace includes no signs of what might be construed as unprofessional, that is, emotional. When a client explains that he is teary-eyed over his daughter's arrest because "A man can't help his feelings," Wemmick and Jaggers respond in form: "'His what?' demanded Wemmick, quite savagely . . . 'Now, look here my man,' said Jaggers, advancing a step, and pointing to the door. 'Get out of this office. I'll have no feelings here. Get out'" (426–7). What is apparently wrong with bringing feelings to the office is not merely that emotions are forbidden there, but that the signs of human relations that are called personal – that belong to another place – must be out of place at the office. It is for this reason, as Wemmick explains, that no one is supposed to know what to make of Mr. Jaggers' manner because "'it's not personal; it's professional: only professional'" (221). Mr. Jaggers, as a paragon of the professional, owns a "private" and "personal" home that only replicates his office: "In the corner," Pip remarks, "was a little table of papers with a shaded lamp, so that he seemed to bring the office home with him in that respect too, and to wheel it out every evening and fall to work" (234). His bookcases are filled exclusively with law books, his "official look[ing]" furniture lacks any ornamentation, and the carved garlands of his walls look like the loops of a hangman's rope (233–4) – all in testimony to a homogeneity of signs: everything belonging to Wemmick's office boss must signal office.

In this respect, the way in which *Great Expectations* exaggerates the boundary dividing home from work produces a sense that the distinction itself is more complex and more meaningful than merely a difference in location or in activity. That Pip first records the home–office tension in terms of a physiological transformation he witnesses in his friend (Wemmick's facial and bodily contortions) turns a change of scene into a more viscerally moving event, even if comically presented (232). Moreover, the fact that Pip can refer to Wemmick's "Walworth sentiments" and can ask for advice and even favors in the name of the Pleasant Home indicates that the home–office distinction engenders an idiolect, a whole linguistic code and presumably a whole system of values.

That Pip wishes Mr. Jaggers had a Pleasant Home of his own to make him a more amiable dinner companion (311) suggests, however, that Pip understands and (as he is the novel's registering consciousness) also presents the distinction between home life and office life as inconsequential, nothing more than one of Wemmick's idiosyncrasies. That he would think at all of catching Wemmick's eye while at dinner with Mr. Jaggers implies that he understands the boundary as a kind of game that can be abandoned once it gets tiresome. In this way, the novel sets up a tension between our impression that the novel's home–office distinction is arbitrary and a nagging sense that it carries hidden significance.

The impression of arbitrariness derives more directly from the fact that whereas Wemmick bandies about the term "professional" quite a bit, the novel nonetheless leaves inchoate the substantive values of the professional as a category, and consequently elides the terms according to which home life might represent an alternative. Although this vagueness itself does not interfere with the novel's presentation of the antithesis as of dire importance, it allows the concreteness of spatial distinctions (the fact that the terms home and office are so available to the realist imagination) to pass for concepts that remain shadowy at best. Wemmick, for example, remarks to Pip in a staccato-speak directive that Mr. Jaggers has " 'Never seen it [the Castle] . . . Never heard of it. Never seen the Aged. Never heard of him. No, the office is one thing and the private life is another. When I go into the office, I leave the Castle behind me . . . I don't wish it professionally spoken about' " (231). Cast in the tightly organized repetitive rhythms of fragments whose abbreviated and constricted phrasing carries a quality of imperative-ness, the category of what is professional nonetheless emerges in Wem-mick's evenly divided and balanced syntax as participating in a system of alliances organized according to spatial requirements, rather than to more meaningful valuations.

But because *Great Expectations*, however one looks at it, traces how a young man comes to trade in his romantic dreams of a new family and an estate home for a career in business, surely the significance of what is professional – so important here in its relationship to the domestic – would extend beyond qualities metonymically distillable from their literal reference to the space of an office. According to the *OED*, not until the very latter part of the nineteenth century is the word "profes-sional" used as indicating a livelihood or calling socially superior to a trade or handicraft, and throughout the greater part of the century it usually pertained to a vocation that did not necessarily require training or special skills, or even payment, as the term would suggest today.[14] In other words, the literal sense of "professional" as that which refers to one's job remains for this novel and often for this period tautologically constructed. This is especially true given that there are few signs of "professionalism" among the professionals in the novel: although Mr. Jaggers has talent and has presumably attended law school, and al-though Wemmick demonstrates vocational devotion, neither one ever exhibits or mentions any special training or education – the common hallmarks that identify the later senses of the professional as connoting an authorization and an election that a mere job would lack.[15]

The ambiguity continues. For example, as a workplace the office demands "dry" conduct – impersonal, unanimated. But saying that the office is impersonal is not the same thing as saying the office has nothing to do with personal lives – that is, with relations forged outside its purlieu. For Mr. Jaggers' establishment, as the paradigmatic Office, operates more as part adoption agency, part therapeutic clinic than as a law firm. Not only do people come to Mr. Jaggers with deeply personal issues – often on behalf of a daughter, a father, a beloved who is in trouble, but this "Guardian" manages all personal familial affairs from securing fiduciary inheritances to actually reconstructing patchwork families and surrogate homes. In fact, the case that "makes" Mr. Jaggers' professional career, the one that establishes his business, is one in which he intercedes in a "deviant" family unit (the Magwitch–Molly–Estelle family – a secret family sprouting out of adultery and murder), thereby securing Estelle's adoption and providing occupational solace for Miss Havisham; all extremely personal matters. As a kind of office of social work *avant la lettre*, Mr. Jaggers' establishment demonstrates what is at stake: finding meaning for the terms "professional office" and "personal home" beyond their spatial designations entails a frustrating series of tautologies.

Casting the distinction into a psychological grammar only exacerbates its circularity. On the one hand, we can say that behavior in the office must consist of signs that are use-referential: all of Wemmick's mannerisms must refer only to his function in the office and not indicate any personality trait or betray any psychological state of mind. In this sense, the office Wemmick seems reminiscent of Richard Sennett's ideal civic world. On the other hand, we have seen how "personality" for Wemmick pretty much amounts to a collection of signs referring to his role at the Castle, a place distinguished as merely non-office. We cannot say that Wemmick's home, despite his personality, ever functions as a place of psychic or even individual exploration. In the absence of a psychological framework, personal living space becomes that much more difficult to differentiate from working space. Although the Castle looks like a world of playful pastimes enjoyed deliberately as leisure, its customs and rituals are no less structured and require no less work than those at the office. The mechanical letter-writing, hand-washing, candle-snuffing and safe-locking that closes the business day at the office have their counterparts in the routines that govern life at the Castle: Sunday tea-making, evening news-reading, ritual Stinger-discharging and customary Miss Skiffins-squeezing all background the Aged's declaration, " 'He is very regular in his walks, is my son. Very regular in everything, is my son' " (311). In terms of substantiating the spatial antithesis, we are back to where we began.

In this sense, the personal customs that serve as distinguishing characteristics of the Pleasant Home are actually not very personalized: both the logical routines that facilitate communal living (such as Miss Skiffins' doing the dishes after tea) as well as the illogical customs (such as using a drawbridge to step over a foot of water) are material enough to identify and easy enough to learn so that any stranger can, in principle, be assimilated into the Castle's fold. One might ask here, is this systematized structural openness any different from training a new employee at an office? Despite its personal status and even its fortifications, the home appears in *Great Expectations* as a space available to anyone willing to adopt its customs, because its customs appear as unmeaningful as doing the filing or reviewing the account books. In this sense, home starts to look professional. And, as the *OED* points out, one of the nineteenth-century uses of "professional" designates a set of activities pursued seriously and expertly, though during one's leisure and without pay (as in professional sailing or professional cardplaying). There is therefore a certain sense in which the Pleasant Home emerges as a kind of professional home – an unpaid engagement of serious importance that requires a degree of skillful mastery.

AMATEUR PROFESSIONALISM

Bleak House offers here a complementary gloss for the term "professional." One of the permanent features of the original Bleak House home is Mr. Skimpole, an older man whom Mr. Jarndyce calls the Perfect Child, not owing to his age but to his "simplicity, and freshness, and enthusiasm and a fine guileless inaptitude for all worldly affairs."[16] This Perfect Child, Mr. Jarndyce explains, is an "Amateur" who might have been a "Professional," that is, he pursues his talents with the devotion and expertise of one who might get paid for them, but who does not. And indeed Mr. Skimpole prides himself on having no idea of money. It is therefore not surprising that in the next scene he is arrested for debt. Revealingly, he informs the arresting officer: "'Don't be ruffled by your occupation. We can separate you from your office; we can separate the individual from the pursuit. We are not so prejudiced as to suppose that in private life you are otherwise than a very estimable man . . .'" (125–6). What we can infer here from Skimpole's epithet (the Amateur Who Might Have Been A Professional), and from his function as Bleak House's household debtor, is that the category of the professional is linked to money exchanges, to the spaces in which money exchanges can happen and, more importantly, to a particular type of human relation that is conditioned by the terms according to which money changes hands. Because Skimpole is "not a Professional" – or rather is only amateurly professional in the nineteenth-century sense of pursuing an unpaid activity devotedly and skillfully – he pretends to have nothing to do with money. That he is not immune from being arrested for debt suggests, however, that the category of the "not professional" is not at all protected from the claims of moneyed relationships, but merely represents a conception of economic life different from that which is shaped at a workplace. As everyone in the scene knows, the officer ultimately cannot be separated from his office: responsibilities, particularly economic ones, cannot be escaped by changing one's spatial (and hence, in this case, social) status. Skimpole is arrested because he is only a phony amateur professional who misunderstands the economic imperatives of communal life. A true amateur professional, emerges in the figure of Esther Summerson, *Bleak House*'s diminutive housekeeper. Never in debt, Esther pursues her unpaid work devotedly and skillfully. It is consequently Esther who, because her rational domestic management keeps the home's account books clean, saves Bleak House. Although Dickens links the categories of the professional and the amateur in the foppish Skimpole with dismissive humor, he links them in Wemmick's Castle with a great deal of affection. The domestic space figured in Wemmick's Castle emerges then as an appropriate vehicle for the representation of what is amateurly professional.

The complex of financial references subtending the distinction between the professional world of the office and the amateurly professional home bears out in the workings of Wemmick's Castle. On the surface, *Great Expectations* presents the home–office division as one of Wemmick's eccentricities and therefore as a kind of game, unmeaningful beyond the logic of its inner organization. But, eccentric as it may appear, it is precisely as a game – with rules and a method of execution – that the Pleasant Home can function as a process. Occupying one of those quizzical, amusement park corners that Dickens erects in his novels' more manic moments, the Castle is virtually a literalization of domesticity's most popular metaphor that "a man's home is his castle" (*à chacun chez soi*), and hence the acting out of a kitchen wall maxim. In this sense, the Castle stands literally as the implementation of a principle – what Wemmick more specifically calls the principle of fortification – the principle, in other words, of maintaining a sharp boundary line between the home and the office: Wemmick keeps the farm animals and the garden behind the Castle, he explains, "'so as not to impede the idea of fortifications, for it is a principle with me, if you have an idea, carry it out and keep it up'" (311). From looking at how the Castle functions, though, it would appear that what is important is not so much that the principle has a purpose, but that it represents a methodology that is self-justifying: everything at the Castle is subordinated to "keeping up" the principle, everything rationalized according to its tenet.[17]

Methodically living out a principle produces a curious space: despite its divorce from the business world, the Pleasant Home nonetheless bears the signs of the office – in fact is actually built out of material that derives from the office. What they eat for dinner at the Castle, for example, literally consists of a form of payment Wemmick receives at work: the fowl, he explains to Pip, will be very tender, since he procured it from a butcher juryman whom they might have kept in the box longer (227). And even though Pip seems offended when he notices at the office that all of Wemmick's personal jewelry – mourning rings, brooches and seals – "was derived from like sources" (224) – that is, from executed criminals, and flinches while Wemmick walks through Newgate extracting various material goods from the would-be-hanged, the same objects appear in a different light at the Castle:

> The interval between that time and supper, Wemmick devoted to showing me his collection of curiosities. They were mostly of a felonious character; comprising the pen with which a celebrated forgery had been committed, a distinguished razor or two, some locks of hair, and several manuscript confessions written under condemnation . . . These were agreeably dispersed among small specimens of china and glass, various neat trifles made by the proprietor of the museum, and some tobacco-stoppers carved by the Aged. (231–2)

Having changed the notion of a felony into an adjective, the Castle surfaces in the passage as a place that processes the signs of work into play and the signs of payment into curiosities. Doing business resurfaces as a collection of curiosities that are at least apparently cleansed of any traces indicating their original status – their function as items of exchange. In other words, the method animating the Castle seems to obfuscate the fact that these curiosities were at one time payment for services rendered. But are they really? Although they are connected to Wemmick's job, the objects are less payment for a service than they are special favors and momentoes given in remembrance of special cases. In light of Oliphant's sinecure (*Phoebe Junior*), the work-related objects that find their way into Wemmick's home suggest an extravagant relationship between work and compensation. Though innovatively participating in relations that are no less economically based than getting paid for work, the Pleasant Home performs precisely the negotiation that Skimpole, the failed amateur professional, neglects. By processing them specifically into curiosities, the Pleasant Home makes the signs of work look like the material of compensation.

This raises the question about the relationship of the Pleasant Home to the transfer of money. For besides the principle of fortifications, Wemmick's other hallmark trait is his belief in the sanctity of "portable property" – a characteristically Wemmickian euphemism for money, although sometimes a stand-in for anything that might count as an easily liquidated economic asset.[18] At first the "portable property" principle seems to belong to the Office Wemmick for it is during Pip's first meeting with Wemmick at the office that he announces his "guiding star is 'Get hold of portable property'" (224). Hence it is standing on London Bridge, itself a transitional space, in his office persona that Wemmick instructs Pip to throw his money into the Thames rather than help a friend with it, his mail-box mouth widening enough to "have posted a newspaper in [it]" (310), certainly not surprising advice from a clerk in charge of an office's cash flow. The sentiment in its official form seems to prescribe obeying the decrees of self-interest, thereby evincing an ethos according to which a self's material interests take priority over other concerns. But if looked at in terms of how it functions in the novel rather than in terms of what it claims, the portable property principle aims more at a regimented accumulation of goods than at any unleashing of sheer greed:[19] even though Wemmick admits that his mourning rings may not be worth much, he asserts that they are nonetheless "portable and property" (224), his drive to acquire them thus ironically independent of their monetary value. Specifically in connection to furnishing the castle with either decor or comestibles, getting hold of property looks more like a method than an objective, the getting hold process more important than the specific value of what is gotten.

Moreover it would seem that when it comes to portable property, maintaining the distinction between the home and the office becomes particularly critical, as if to suggest that the property principle is intricately woven into the Pleasant Home's *raison d'être*. When Pip asks Wemmick, for example, about how he might help Herbert Pocket get Capital, Wemmick mechanically responds, never invest portable property in a friend. But when Pip asks if that is his "deliberate opinion," Wemmick chains the sentiment to his place of trade and reiterates the home–office distinction, as if the distinction itself were tailored specifically to managing such interpersonal fiduciary matters:

Walworth is one place, and this office is another. Much as the Aged is one person and Mr. Jaggers is another. They must not be confounded together. My Walworth sentiments must be taken at Walworth; none but my official sentiments can be taken in this office . . . You will be welcome there, in a private and personal capacity. (310)

The reason that Wemmick's advice here relies so heavily on spatial contingencies is that this is no ordinary transfer of money; for it is not that Pip wants to leave his property to an heir – to a member of his family – but he that wants to transfer money along non-official, that is nonfamilial, lines.

It is of course no wonder that official lines – lines that plot proper fiduciary transfers and lines that designate spatial properties called homes – are intricately and immanently related. One might speculate that as a cultural issue the transfer of money, when occurring outside of a work situation, requires some sort of legitimization, some sort of official processing, and that the family or the home, however defined, provides a means of making non-office financial transfers (unearned procurement of money) officially rightful and maybe even righteous. Whereas an owner may pay a worker and a customer may pay a merchant, the only kind of nonpayment money transfers capitalist Anglo-American culture accepts as legitimate are familial – a parent may give money to his child without rationalizing it in terms of trade or merit.[20]

In this sense *Great Expectations* demonstrates how a professional home like Wemmick's Castle can officiate the business of transferring money along lines that are not officially recognized as legitimate. The job of a professional home seems to be negotiating the home–office distinction. Pip must therefore visit Wemmick in his private and personal capacity and remind him that the Castle is not his "trading place" in order to hire this legal clerk as his agent in such an illegitimate and unofficial business. Not only does the Castle space enable Wemmick to advise and facilitate Pip's ostensibly selfless deed, but it provides channels for interpersonal exchanges without requiring any justification for such exchanges. No justification, that is, beyond invoking the name of the Pleasant Home. Due to its *sub rosa* web of agents – specifically a fiancée and her brother – the Pleasant Home allows money to strengthen bonds between unrelated members of a community, such as Herbert and Pip and Wemmick and Skiffins *et al.*, instead of limiting all non-familial relations to the workplace. In other words money, once processed through the workings of the Home, functions to expand the possibilities of nonfamilial human interaction – and hence nonpersonal sociability – beyond the workplace.[21] Only through the Castle can such unearned, uninherited payments be processed into a noble and selfless "work." Thus Pip explains that it is due to Wemmick's work – work done while at home – that Pip's own Work is accomplished: "the whole business [of helping Herbert secure a position in a firm] was so cleverly managed that Herbert had not the least suspicion of my hand being in it" (317).

HOLY HOUSE WORK

That Pip's work here, the business of giving money to a biological and vocational stranger, should require such circuitous navigations divulges the usual Victorian ambivalence about money and work. Ascribing the dilemma on one level to a tradition that forbade a gentleman from working for a living, Alexander Welsh goes on to stress that the Victorian doctrine of work was also a "muffled echo" of the Calvinist paradox whereby works stand as signs of salvation but have nothing to do with achieving salvation. According to Welsh, "For Calvin's logical denial of the final efficacy of work [the Victorian doctrine of work] merely substitutes a polite agnosticism. The preachment of work is intensified, but its end is obscure" (*City of Dickens* 85).

The paradox Welsh designates as central to the Victorian doctrine of work derives from Weber's Protestant Ethic. As Weber has outlined it, the conceptualization of worldly engagement as the highest form of moral activity that an individual can assume is problematized by the doctrine of predestination, according to which work is a sign of grace but never a path to it. Only a "rationalized" method for supervising one's personal state of grace can assuage the religious anxiety of knowing one cannot earn election, only perhaps display it. Asceticism invades the everyday life of Europe because Calvinism demands, not single good works that can buy salvation, but "a life of good works combined into a unified system" (Weber *Protestant Ethic* 117) by which one shows evidence of having already been saved. What is salient here to my discussion of Wemmick's Home is precisely Weber's notion that the most spiritual form of human life is located in a rationalized method for engaging in worldly materials, which functions nonteleologically, that is, for its own sake, without a deliberate end. Leonore Davidoff has recently stressed the growing enthusiasm in the nineteenth century for the rationalizing of housework. For Davidoff, the rationalization of an economically nonrational unit, the familial household, produces contradictions – contradictions which, I would argue, reproduce themselves in the fictional spaces of Dickensian domesticity.[22]

Most critics accept Weber's version of a Protestant – and generally Dissenting – legacy as an explanation for why so many scenes of work in Dickens are blandly and hesitatingly drawn: although Welsh notes that nearly everyone in a Dickens novel has a job, he cites Orwell's complaint that "work is nowhere depicted as a concrete experience . . . 'Home life is always enough'" (*City of Dickens* 78–9). In order to be respectable, Dickensian characters will have jobs, but the specifics of work do not receive much attention. By saying, however, in this context that "home life is always enough," Orwell insinuates that whereas the details of work are neglected, it is no coincidence that the details of home life are not.

Unfortunately neither Orwell nor Welsh goes on to engage the connection between this ambivalence toward work scenes and an uncritical embrace of home sites even though they imply that one rises as an antidote to the other. Perhaps this is because they are too literal in their definition of work: for even if it is true that work does not appear in Dickens' novels in all its material details, housework certainly does, as Wemmick brushing away the cobwebs suggests and as this newlywed scene from *Our Mutual Friend* confirms:

But, John gone to business and Bella returned home, the dress would be laid aside, trim little wrappers and aprons would be substituted, and Bella, putting back her hair with both hands, as if she were making the most business-like arrangements for going dramatically distracted, would enter on the household affairs of the day. *Such weighing and mixing and chopping and grating, such dusting and washing and polishing, such snipping and weeding and trowelling and other small gardening, such making and mending and folding and airing, such diverse arrangements, and above all such severe study!* For Mrs. J.R . . . was under the constant necessity of referring for advice and support to a sage volume entitled *The Complete British Family Housewife* which she would sit consulting, with her elbows on the table and her temples on her hands . . . with all her dimples screwed into an expression of profound research. (749) (my emphasis)

In their phonemic repetitions and rhythms, the gerunds of the scene's central housekeeping sentence effect a symmetry among the various activities whereby the significance of an individual instance such as dusting is less important than the concept of the whole: housework. Exhausting in its exhaustive catalogue of household management, the scene's technical construction reveals the operation of an ethos, a spirit according to which the performance of household tasks means something more than just sweeping the floor or cleaning the dishes. Although there is no doubt that Bella is actively engaged, the passage's passive voice and subjunctive phrasing collaborate to muffle the sense in which her work might be purposeful. So while the cropped cadences and anaphoric phrasing set a quickened, anticipatory tempo, the gerunds, in their omission of direct and indirect objects, go on to convey a sense of energized movement divorced from any idea of progress, as if to suggest that home work is meaningful without being teleologically directed –

that is, meaningful in a more hidden way than goal-oriented action. In this sense, the formal technicalities presuppose a kind of organic unity, a single spirit which animates and gives meaning to such "diverse arrangements." A spirit in fact that we might call Protestant in a Weberian sense. For the effect of the passage's technical orchestration is to make home work appear as inspired and holy, but not efficacious; in the same way that there is no object pronoun for each verb, no syntactical aim for each activity and therefore literally no end to housework, there is no literal objective in the Protestant notion of work, since works cannot buy salvation.

I want to suggest that, by divorcing movement from context, the gerunds, coupled with the passage's static present-tense verbs, function very much like cinematic close-ups of incomplete and ongoing activity. In this way, the technique that constructs and conveys housework as something like a single spiritual concept might be labeled narrative montage. Montage is, in its original sense, the juxtaposition of disparate elements, but in its cinematic sense, "the production of a rapid succession of images in a motion picture to illustrate an association of ideas" (*Webster's*). According to Sergei Eisenstein, in an essay arguing that D. W. Griffith acquired his cinematic skills from reading Dickens, Griffith invents montage when he learns from the failure of "representational" montage pieces in *Intolerance* that trope in cinema can never be located in an isolated image; a static picture that "represents" an idea in literally symbolic terms cannot fully convey a sense of that idea.[23] This is why the image of Lillian Gish rocking a baby's cradle does not successfully depict the idea of eternally reborn epochs. Cinematic trope is, however, located in montage juxtaposition, that is, in the effect that the relations between a series of images produces. As Eisenstein explains it, the problem for Griffith was how to go beyond the narrowly representational and perform supra-representational, "conveying" tasks. He discovers that it is only through pictorial juxtapositions, through montage, that film can go beyond the limits of a situation, such as a stage or a set, and convey its ideological conception. As a result, montage also entails an abstraction of the lifelike representation, for, as Eisenstein points out, "Only by abstracting 'hot' from a thermometer reading may one speak of a 'sense of heat'" ("Dickens, Griffith, and the Film Today" 243). Although Eisenstein leaves unclear the relationship between montage juxtaposition and images like the close-up that work as abstractions of lifelike representations, I take him to mean that montage is most effective when the pictorials it collates consist of such abstractions – of such cuts.

As one might abstract a sense of heat by viewing in juxtaposition a thermometer reading, a bright sun and a sweaty brow, so might one read the conveying properties of the housekeeping passage; and what we abstract from the juxtaposition of housework close-up pictorials, is a sense of busy-ness – of being busy and therefore maybe even a conception of this housewife's "most business-like arrangements" as constituting a kind of business. What is happening therefore in the housekeeping passage not only conveys the impression of housekeeping as an ideological conception – as an idea lying beyond the representational limits of the material details belonging to the scene itself – but also a sense of housekeeping as business. The busyness and business of worldly engagement.

In theory, it would make sense that housekeeping might rise in nineteenth-century England as a representation of work capable of alleviating some of the religious anxieties belonging to the kind of Protestant culture Weber describes. As busyness, housework can figure as a methodical, systematized engagement with the materials of the world. Since it is continuous (though one task may be completed, the work of maintaining a house is never done) and unpaid (the housewife of this passage is no maid), it can serve as proof of a condition, such as a state of grace, rather than an attempt to win an end; whereas it would be absurd to think that dusting the table might buy a place in heaven, the condition of keeping the house might represent the work in a calling necessary as a sign of election. It is not surprising that the *OED* confirms the nineteenth-century sense of "business" as referring not only to trade, commercial transactions and engagements in general, but more frequently to "that about which one is busy," not as a quality proper to a single person, nor as a momentary state, but as something that is more distinct and discrete from the subject. Something perhaps like a methodology.

Historically, there is evidence to suggest that housekeeping attracts in the period a new kind of attention. For example, a fashionable new ornament popular among bourgeois ladies in the second half of the century was called a chatelaine. Worn at the waist, a chatelaine consisted of a collection of charms that represent in miniature various household implements, such as a bunch of keys, a pen knife, a thimble case, a pincushion, a pair of scissors, a button hook, maybe even a pencil and a note pad. Etymologically, "chatelain[e]" derives from the medieval word for a castellan, or a keeper of the castle or chateau who wore at his or her waist the keys to the castle's various rooms. The fact that chatelaines occur as couture at the height of the nineteenth century and not either previously or subsequently suggests that housekeeping functioned for a time as an available semiotic field. The fad suggests that the fact of housekeeping had turned into an idea of housekeeping. Miniaturized into representative forms, household implements surface in bourgeois fashion as something like icons whose original significance has been refined into ornamentation; collated into fashions like the chatelaine, representative housekeeperly items assume the Eisensteinian conveying task of representing the idea of housework.

Moreover, housekeeping appears in the Census of 1851 not only as an identifiable occupation, but as a position differentiated from that of a housekeeper on the domestic staff of a large estate. Thus housewifery rises as a category that designates what someone "does" – what their vocationally derived position is – but also as a category whose identification is somehow necessary to the larger process of articulating domestic ideology in terms of the spatial divisions that I have been discussing:

By mid-century the middle-class ideal of bread-winning husband and domesticated wife and children had become so widespread that the registrar general was able not only to introduce the new category of "housewife" to the census but also to state in his introduction to the report on 1851: "The possession of an entire house is strongly desired by every Englishman; for it throws a sharp well-defined circle round his family and hearth – the shrine of his sorrows, joys and meditations." (Hall, "The Sweet Delights of Home," 74)

Although there is no logical connection between the introduction of the word "housewife" in the census and the remark that the ultimate English cultural fantasy is a happy home (certainly there were housewives and housekeeping duties long before the family craze sweeps England), the presentation here suggests that the housewife would play the heroine in the nineteenth-century home-oriented fantasy. Obviously, housewifery is not an invention of the nineteenth century. But if its identification as a position, and perhaps even as a heroic vocation or calling in the Weberian sense, indicates a historical change in awareness, then we can say that Victorian domesticity functions as a representation of holy work. Surely it is no coincidence that in the depiction of the Satis House adoption fantasy cited earlier Pip portrays himself as a knight – a knight engaged in housework.

Nor is it a coincidence that the housekeeping idioms Lucy Snowe employs should serve to mark her as the narrative's unwilling heroine.

Lucy declares early on that she would "deliberately have taken a housemaid's place, bought a strong pair of gloves, swept bedrooms and staircases, and cleaned stoves, and locks" (*Villette* 382), rather than earn her living as a governess or paid companion. That she should prefer what is essentially manual labor (and we should remember that Brontë writes before William Morris boutiquerizes handicraft and commodities made "by hand") to the less manual and perhaps more intellectual services involved in being a governess is not immediately evident. It is not explicable, that is, until Lucy visits a childhood friend who, now a married and wealthy mother, makes Lucy ashamed of her spinsterhood. Rather than expanding the experience in a psychological idiom that would render Lucy's subjectivity more legible, Lucy the narrator checks the story by explaining that the purpose of the anecdote is to account for how she came to have a story to tell at all: for it is in her married friend's home that she learns through a network of housekeepers that there are job opportunities abroad. "I stored up this piece of casual information," she rationalizes, "as careful housewives store seemingly worthless shreds and fragments for which their prescient minds anticipate a possible use someday" (105). Good housekeeping as a quality of mind provides Lucy with a vocation, with literally a job, at the same time that it marks her as the narrator. Thus she insists that she mentions the incident, not because she thinks her emotional life is an appropriate topic of representation, but only to explain how she came to get a job abroad, and hence how she came to write the story; and thus how she came to be its heroine; and thus, of course, how her psychic life might after all be worthy of describing to others. By capitalizing on her constitutional and fortuitous association with housekeeping, Lucy proves a heroism she claims not to seek. She finds, in other words, a predestined novelistic election. That it requires sailing to a foreign (French) land refers us to *Persuasion*'s domesticated navy.

In returning to *Great Expectations*, it would therefore follow that if we have only cropped glimpses of what reviewing the account books or visiting the Newgate clients entails, the novel does present an elaborate pastiche of Wemmick's home work:

It was no nominal meal that we were going to make, but a vigorous reality. The Aged prepared such a haystack of buttered toast, that I could scarcely see him over it as it simmered on an iron stand hooked on the top bar; while Miss Skiffins brewed such a jorum of tea . . . The flag had been struck, and the gun had been fired at the right moment of time, and I felt as snugly cut off from the rest of Walworth as if the moat were thirty feet wide and as many deep. Nothing disturbed the tranquillity of the Castle . . . We ate the whole of the toast, and drank the tea in proportion, and it was delightful to see how warm and greasy we got after it. (315)

Again we can see the same collage-like technique that characterizes montage. Although the cuts are not as sharp nor the effect as condensed as the passage from *Our Mutual Friend*, the haystack of toast, the jorum of tea, the struck flag and the fired gun nevertheless convey the same sense of busyness that characterizes Wemmick's Pleasant Home and perhaps its novelistic desirability.

Yet even if we say that housekeeping makes the home a place of holy work, there is still another factor operating in these passages that needs to be taken into account: for what is common to most happy home scenes throughout Victorian literature is the abundance of material details. Although there is an apparent historical explanation for the sheer number of objects described in so far as the supposed increase of possessions in nineteenth-century homes would naturally register in the period's increasingly "realistic" fiction (Altick, *The Presence of the Present*), I would reject Altick's suggestion that the objects filling these kinds of scene are the material details of Barthesian "reality effects." On the contrary, such collections of knick-knacks ironically play an important role in representing the home as a place of spiritual work. For if, as Weber argues, Luther calls monastic life "devoid of value as a means of justification before God" and attributes such a "renunciation of the duties of this world" to selfishness (*Protestant Ethic* 81), a vocationally spiritual home would have to maintain the signs of worldliness in order to fulfill the strictures of selfless work. And certainly so many household furnishings would serve as signs of the worldly. But Calvinism also, Weber tells us, warns against any "relaxation in possession" that would distract from "the pursuit of a righteous life" (157). Any representation of the home as a place of righteous work would therefore have to develop presentational techniques that might process a bunch of objects into something more meaningful. Home must look worldly without looking like possession. In this sense Wemmick's Pleasant Home not only contains a collection of signs derived from the office but appears as a collection itself; a "crazy little box of a cottage," the Castle stands as a collection of curious details resembling something out of Disney World:

a little wooden cottage in the midst of plots of garden, and the top of it was cut out and painted like a battery mounted with guns . . . the smallest house I ever saw . . . the queerest gothic windows (by far the greater part of them sham), and a gothic door, almost too small to get in at . . . The bridge was a plank, and it crossed a chasm of about four feet wide and two deep . . . Our punch was cooling in an ornamental lake . . . This piece of water (with an island in the middle which might have been the salad for supper) was of a circular form, and he had constructed a fountain in it, which, when you set a little mill going and took a cork out of a pipe, played to powerful extent that it made the back of your hand quite wet. (229–30)

With its miniaturized toy-chest features, the passage communicates a playful sense of artifice not unlike the effect of wearing a chatelaine. Its diminutive representative features – sham gothic windows, a pretend moat, a *tromp d'œil* battery – suggest that the Pleasant Home is *faux* – deliberately but nonetheless seriously ersatz. Valued in fact precisely for the showiness of its fakery, the Castle seems not far from what Susan Sontag in another context has called "camp": a particular kind of sensibility, camp consists of a degree of stylization, a spirit of extravagance and artifice that is never ironic despite its self-consciousness;[24] but most importantly, camp is "alive to a double sense in which some things can be taken" (106–12). Let us put this alongside *Webster's* three-tine definition of "camp": camp as a temporary shelter, camp as a group's ideological position and camp as something so outrageously artificial as to be considered amusing. Such a spirit animates the Pleasant Home: though *faux*, the Castle is not pitched to sound phony or deceptive; though pretend, it takes itself very seriously. In this way, it is the curiousness of the passage's campy objects that produces a double sense of their participation in a greater enterprise.

Such an accumulation of details presents therefore the whole of the Castle as a collection – not only as work but as A Work – in order to suggest that, as method, its value lies in how it engages with material forms and not in the material forms themselves. After all, a collection provides the means of going about the business of possession without being distracted by the accumulation of wealth it might otherwise represent: not only is the exact monetary value of the collection often irrelevant to the collector, but a collection is an on-going task – one is always working on it. The campiness of the Pleasant Home's furnishings and its representation as a collection make it a place where worldly goods are signs of more spiritual, even if not specifically religious, values. In this sense, the Castle and the scenes presenting it appear constructed according to the demands of a calling; they are spiritually, albeit playfully, motivated.[25]

EXPECTATIONS

The Pleasant Home, as a housewifely collection, reformulates the self-interestedness of the portable property principle in terms of process and method – a kind of work that is valuable not as deed, but as condition. By divorcing the drive from the literal acquisition – the process of getting from that which is gotten – the Pleasant Home borrows from the Protestant tradition in order to legitimize the circulation of money and hence economic relations in general, regardless of the particular relationship occasioning it.[26] The result of stressing the work as a whole rather than the specifics of payment, that is, the consequence of making the work its own payment, is twofold: structurally speaking, it places means over ends, the process of doing over what is done; socio-ethically speaking, it establishes the Pleasant Home not only as a place of good or holy works but as a place where money can represent a broader, more communitarian, conception of social transactions than one predicated on the self-interest of the workplace.[27] Sociability itself emerges as an absolute good.

The complexity of this new order evinces itself in the peculiarly Protestant way in which Pip's experience with Wemmick's Pleasant Home and his initiation into the office–home antithesis changes the significance of having expectations. Pip's first view of the home–office distinction teaches him what kinds of expectations he can harbor for different kinds of interactions (that he can expect Wemmick to respond in a certain way at the Castle, that he cannot expect Mr. Jaggers to interact with him informally). When the dry Wemmick with the mailbox mouth resurfaces as they approach London, Pip knows that Wemmick will no longer function in his "private and personal capacity," that he will interact with Pip as a clerk acts with a client, not as a man with a friend. What is relevant here is that although Pip's "expectations" begin as a reference to a sum of money and to the changes in social status that having such money entails, they now mean something else. In the context of Mr. Jagger's boundaryless all-office life, expectations must refer to the money that designates income. In the context of a life that maintains this home–office boundary, however, expectations do not involve Capital, as Herbert Pocket puts it, or career or personal destiny in the conventional amorous or financial sense, but are linked specifically to bearing and conduct. This would seem fairly simple. But it is important to realize that in connection to conduct, "expectations" direct the way in which one engages in the activities of the world – how one behaves, what one does; in a way then having expectations determines one's deeds and measures their fitness. But because such expectations are part of a system – codified norms for whole categories of behavior – they evaluate the value of a single gesture only in terms of its consistency with the system. Expectations therefore make possible the legibility of "good" deeds – or works – because expectations presume the existence of a rationalized system that provides the standards for determining what counts as good. In other words, the evolving significance of "expectations" in the novel suggests that the home–office distinction ultimately represents, not the rights or wrongs of a polarity, but the ultimate rightness of a rationalized system that is valuable in and of itself, as itself good.

While this sense of "expectations" as money transforms into a sense of "expectations" as guide to worldly engagement, Pip, as the narrating voice, shifts his focus from the psychologized self of the Satis House family romance adoption fantasies to what I can only call his condition: instead of being preoccupied with his desires, Pip must focus on the conditions of his worldly life – on a state of being that must by definition be personal while still being selfless. Although *Great Expectations* begins with Pip's desire for Miss Havisham to adopt him – to call him her legitimate heir, to legitimize him with her money – that story-line ends with his desire for her to take on the business of financing Herbert – for her to legitimize his work rather than legitimize his self. In this sense, the novel uses the notion of expectations to subordinate its initial psychological concerns to the social but no less personal ones proper to the Protestant conception of a spiritual status that is reliant on worldly condition. Thus Satis House itself, once symbol of self-awareness, is by the end of the novel liquidated, turned, that is, into naked cash as if to suggest that the system of social relations represented by money has vanquished and supplanted the novel's psychologized grammar of personal desire.

This movement from a psychological understanding of the personal to a spiritually social one relies on the way in which the Pleasant Home functions in the novel to construct a notion of business that is simultaneously personal and social. To backtrack momentarily, the busyness of the Pleasant Home registers in terms of the novel's action as what the Castle effects: the business of an illegitimate fiduciary transfer – illegitimate because it seems to be the selfless gift of a biological and vocational stranger. Interestingly, the etymology of "business" includes a selfish use alongside a selfless one. According to the *OED*, "business" can carry a communitarian sense in referring to dealings or intercourse with others, as in "a man who thinks he has no business with others"; but increasingly in the nineteenth century, the term carries a more personal sense – a concern to which one is constitutionally devoted (as in, "your business is with children"), or a matter in which one has or has not certain rights (as in, "that is no business of ours" and "just worry about your own business"). When, for example, Pip announces to Mr. Jaggers and Wemmick that he did not accept Miss Havisham's money, the personal sense of business and its worldly sense seem at odds: whereas Mr. Jaggers answers that, "'every man ought to know his own business best,'" Wemmick reproaches, "'Every man's business is portable property'" (421).

But it is important to remember here that Pip's interest in the worldly business of financing Herbert is ultimately what saves him, and saves him in several important personal ways. By referring to it as "the only good thing I had done and the only completed thing I had done since I was first apprised of my great expectations" (427), Pip presents the business of financing Herbert's career as a conventionally Christian good deed. From the more cynical perspective of plot, doing a selfless deed does not preclude self-interest: for if it weren't for this "good" work, Pip himself would have ended up without any work at all (as it is Herbert who hires him as a clerk at Clarrikers). But in terms of a Protestant ethic, this middling position at Clarrikers fulfills the vocational precept characteristic of salvation: "We were not in a grand way of business, but we had a good name and worked for our profits and did very well" (489). In this sense, the "whole business" of helping Herbert, culminating as it does in the communal first person-plural-pronoun "we," straddles both the *OED*'s extroverted and introverted senses: it starts out as a nonpersonal affair to be managed and expands into a more demanding project involving the services of many other characters, but culminates in a question of Pip's individual's career and his personal state of grace. What starts out as worldly becomes deeply personal – personal, though, in a quasi-religious, not a psychological, way.

What needs, however, to be pointed out here is that at the time that Pip first arranges the business of financing Herbert, he believes he has been adopted by Miss Havisham and that his fortune derives from her, Herbert Pocket's very legitimate relation. In so far as it amounts to Pip giving money he receives from the beneficiary he presumes is Miss Havisham to Herbert, Pip's good work starts out as a gesture toward restoring the legitimate House of Havisham, realigning its inheritance lines according to its blood lines, though writing himself in as agent of the restoration. By asking Miss Havisham to take over the responsibility (once he discovers the fortune is not from her) he is only asking her to actualize a situation he had believed already to exist had his initial fantasy concerning the condition of his expectations been its reality. In other words, there is something about Pip's initial fantasy that was destined – predestined perchance – to become truth once the psychologized grammar of wish-fulfillment had been exchanged for a Protestant grammar of works proving election.

In this sense, Pip surrenders the family romance fantasy according to which the good is represented through psychological valuations (what Pip does and does not want) in order to process the psychologized inheritance tale into a Weberized career story according to which the good is represented through vocational valuations (what does and does not fit into the rationalized system marking a state of grace) – vocational valuations that are set up by the novel's domestic discourse. In other words, the domestic line of valuation that initially identified true homes from false ones based on how well they maintained the home–work boundary emerges fully developed in the Pleasant Home as a vocational standard of spiritual purport. What is crucial in Pip's ironic election-after-all[28] is that the restoration of the Havisham House rightful heir to his rightful inheritance occurs through a vocabulary of Pip's personal condition while still maintaining its status as desirable, good and rightful in an absolute sense; rightful restoration only happens as part of a predestined scheme made material in Pip's individual life.

In this way, the novel gestures at a catharsis for a hero who loses the girl but gets the job[29] only by virtue of the amateurly professional home that enables Pip to take care of business – in all its senses. Consequently, it is only having been filtered through the Pleasant Home's works that the moral or aesthetic (depending on how one interprets "catharsis") structure of the novel's plot emerges as reliant on exchanging the estate house for a Pleasant Home. It would appear then that the novel can only preserve its concern with rightful property transmissions and the conservative socio-political order embedded there by abandoning its psychological idiom so as to take up the quasi-religious ethical agenda emblematized in the Pleasant Home and its holy works.

CHAPTER 4

Dickens II: Little Dorrit *in a home: institutionalization and form*

Persuasion, Villette and *Great Expectations* allow us to see domesticity as a narrative discourse that uses a professionally charged vocabulary that, in referring, for example, to the British navy or to the Protestant ministry, conveys a sense of institutional affiliation. Domesticity's professionally charged vocabulary makes the nonpersonal sociability characteristic of home life look like work that is meaningful because it is done in service to some collective body, a household of often biologically unrelated others. In conveying a sense of institutionality, these novels generate what I would call "home effects," formal devices that take shape in a passage's stylistics or in a relationship between plotted episodes.

Certainly, the communal imperative represented in this fiction often correlated to the realities many Victorian women faced: whether they married and constructed a career around a labor-intensive household, or stayed single and, with greater difficulty, chiseled a career with the tools provided by a burgeoning number of single-sex institutions, Victorian women seem to have invariably relied more consciously on a collective body in the shaping of a personally fulfilling career. This is why Martha Vicinus, in a history concerned with recreating what constituted a middle-class Victorian woman's relationship to work, focuses on a host of developing residential institutions designed for women: Anglican and Nonconformist sisterhoods and deaconesses societies, hospitals and nursing schools, boarding-schools and women's colleges (especially Oxford's Royal Holloway College and Cambridge's Westfield College) and settlement houses. She explains her choice of vehicle:

A woman-controlled space became an experiment in the operation of what today would be described as a woman's culture. Since even women who lived outside an institution frequently worked with and through one in order to participate in the benefits of a women's community, I believe that examining work-based institutions is essential to understanding the Victorian single woman. Formal institutions were alternatives to the nuclear family.[1]

It is true that the same communal reliance can perhaps be said for many Victorian men, especially those without property or capital or, until 1867, suffrage. But surely it is reasonable to say that reliance on a small community was different for women in being different in degree.

We know this about Victorian culture, but what about the Victorian novel, which is after all a complex of ideological and aesthetic matter? If the "home epic" features a line of development that has as its bourne the nonpersonal sociability of communal life, how does that line encourage or inhibit other ones? So far I have argued that nonpersonal sociability as a narrative component opposes psychological character development and shrinks psychoanalytic interpretive space. In other words, there seems to be an opposition between a novel's preoccupation with the life of institutions and the psychological roundness of its characters. And this is perhaps why Harville's apartments, Dr. Home's home and Wemmick's castle are relegated to subplots where psychological development is less of a priority. Rarely are idealized domestic spaces integrated into the main story-line. This recurrent structural phenomenon suggests that domesticity raises aesthetic problems for novel formation. Nowhere is this more true than in Dickens' *Little Dorrit.*

We have seen that *Great Expectations*, a more inwardly turned novel than Dickens' other works, is ultimately too absorbed in the priorities of character development to fully abandon a psychological line of valuation in favor of a domestic one by which the category of what is personal would achieve a purely social definition. Consequently, *Great Expectations* is a type of domestic novel that identifies its ideal home as a subplot household.

But model homes, such as Wemmick's Pleasant Home and the Brettons' La Terrasse, do have an effect on more psychologically bound central plots when they are insinuated through a syntax of nostalgia. In this context, narrative nostalgia can be thought of as a confection that compounds the memory of a psychologically delineated subject and the geographic mobility of a particular socio-historical moment. Nostalgia allows Pip to recognize the Forge of his childhood as the Hearth he now seeks, but adds an element of enervation to the home plot that would otherwise be, and for Bella Wilfer or Wemmick is, highly charged. Whereas *Villette* does eventually accommodate the demands of nonpsychological sociability by moving the primary seat of meaningful work away from the plot's action and to the more purely formal plane of its discourse (as discussed above), even this technically sophisticated novel resorts to the *deus ex machina* of the backward gaze. Nostalgia allows Lucy Snowe repeatedly to reconstruct an auld lang syne out of materials already committed to a story of shipwreck and loss.

There seems then to be a difference between the objectiveless but energetic activity of subplot domestic work and the job that domesticity performs once insinuated into a story-line centered on a single protagonist. For this latter, there is a strong retrogressive quality that is apparently absent from the ideal homes of subplot narration. Thus we have in nineteenth-century fiction two manifestations of novel homes. Home as memory: Lucy's embroidered cushion, Marcel's madelaines – these are signs belonging to narrations invested in the idea of an autonomous individual whose psychological self provides the primary source of story. Home as activity – Tony Buddenbrook spreading marmalade and Sir Walter reading the Baronetage, Wemmick buttering toast and Rufus Lyon nursing a vagrant – these belong to narrations organized around the life of generations and local communities, families and households, towns and nations. The two types of narration seem to be mutually exclusive, but not because they replicate a false dichotomy between the individual and the community. The relationship a working-home plot bears to a remembered-home plot does suggest, however, a skepticism about a psychology that makes the autonomous individual eloquent.

In a revealing comment, Fanny calls *Little Dorrit*'s eponymous heroine a "marplot" (589)[2] – a creature that frustrates plans by meddling in them. That we will come to view the Marshalsea's "Little Mother" as an obstacle to plotted movement is borne out in her ultimate deed: burning the codicil that would have revealed to Arthur his true parentage and that, in another genre, might have signaled his spiritual or emotional rebirth. As Little Dorrit's motives are never clearly articulated, the significance of burning the codicil remains obscured. What is clear, however, is that Little Dorrit and the values she comes to represent are hostile, not so much to knowledge or progress, but to self-knowledge and psychological development.

FINDING A HOME: THE IDEA OF THE INSTITUTION

Nearly all the characters of *Little Dorrit* seem to be in want of institutionalization – that is, they either need institutionalizing or desire it.

Some like Old Dorrit need to be in debtors' prisons because they are bankrupt, some like Rigaud need to be in penitentiaries because they have committed crimes, some like Maggy need to be in hospitals because they are sick, some like Tattycoram need to be in Foundling Hospitals because they are orphans. Some, however, want to be in such places without any apparent cause at all. In this sense, it is not just that the Marshalsea casts its shadow into nearly every crevice of this vast novel, but that as the paradigmatic prison it represents the values of institutional life by showing the impossibility of instituting a self or a selfhood – as a Lucy Snowe or a Miss Wade will to do – outside a context of communal life. As the universal need of institutionalization emerges as causeless, inevitable and unlocalizable, the idea of the institution surfaces as the novel's primary unifying principle – its common denominator.

In *Asylums*, Erving Goffman defines an institution as a social establishment distinguished by spatial specificity, activity and regularity: "places such as rooms, suites of rooms, buildings, or plants in which activity of a particular kind regularly goes on."[3] To varying degrees, he continues, every institution has "encompassing tendencies" – structural features which absorb a member's time and interest thereby creating "something of a world" for him. According to Goffman, an institution's "total character" is measured by what kinds of structural barriers control contact with the outside and is symbolized by how such barriers are built into a plant's architecture in the form of locks and high walls (4). But the most distinctive feature of the total institution is its departure from the "basic social arrangement of modern society" – that is, the arrangement whereby an individual expects to "sleep, play and work in different places, with different co-participants, under different authorities" (5). The implication here is that there is something atavistic about a place that does not acknowledge any difference between work space and living space: by erasing the workplace boundaryline, the total institution is significantly divorced from life in the modern world.

The implication also is that without such spatial divisions there can be no possibility of an independent, psychologically defined self. Paid work, Goffman argues, is the precondition for the privacy that allows an individual to develop a psychological sense of his identity, because "the authority of the workplace stops with the worker's receipt of a money payment" (10). The wage, as a marker of the difference between the working world and private life, thus emerges in Goffman's analysis as a necessary ingredient in the development of psychological subjectivity. It follows that unpaid work – like that done in an institution or a home – facilitates a purely communal construction of self-identity because it has lost its "structural significance" as that which distinguishes the work-place from the world of psychological privacy. In this way, Goffman uses unpaid – and undirected – work as a sign of a premodern concep-tion of the self, a conception that emphasizes communal involvement as the only meaningful form of individual life.

However this may be (treating unpaid activities, privacy and psycho-logical self-consciousness as synonymous is not quite fair, however interesting), Goffman's linking of wageless work to an exclusively com-munal definition of the individual is borne out in how the home operates in the novels I have already discussed and how the parity between home and institution operates in *Little Dorrit*. Certainly the Marshalsea is very close to constituting a total institution. With its mock tavern, social evening club, snuggery and common kitchen, it is marked by the extent of its group activities; it is a thoroughly socializing place. It is not surprising then that the behavior that Goffman notes as characteristic of inmates in total institutions corresponds with conduct in the Marshal-sea. Similar to what Goffman identifies as a perverted work situation, many inmates of total institutions resort to a pattern of begging (11) not unlike Old Dorrit's own mendicant predilection. In what Goffman calls a stripping process, by which an inmate loses his outside identity in order to become a patient, many incessantly narrate the sad story-line of their "fall" (67), which is not unlike the narrational wonts of the Mar-shalsea's more permanent Collegians. Most relevant here, though, is the adaptational strategy that Goffman calls "colonization" by which an inmate collates data recalled from the outside world into proof of the desirability of life inside the institution (62–3) – a phenomenon which provides an appropriate analysis of Tip's "awful enjoyment of the Snuggery's resources" (85) as well as a gloss to the statement, "It was evident from the general tone of the whole party that they had come to regard insolvency as the normal state of mankind and the payment of debts as a disease that occasionally broke out" (85).

Revealingly, Goffman notes that patients who adopt this affection for institutional life are often accused of "having found a home" or suffering from "hospitalitis" (62 and note), curiously apt colloquialisms in the context of Maggy's ardor for life in the fever hospital and Arthur's extravagant attraction to the Marshalsea. What such argot reveals is that "feeling at home" occurs not so much as an independent psycho-logical condition as one might feel happy or sad, but as the symptom of a swelling (-*itis*) institution – an ever-expanding hospital; ultimately the ideational essence of home here has nothing to do with a state of mind other than in embodying the effect of institutionalization. Home appears, that is, as a collection of symptoms that inmates develop as a consequence of their institutionalization: Home emerges as a collection of institutionally derived home effects. As cause and consequence, it is self-perpetuating.

Domesticity understood as institutionitis – as an array of the symptoms or effects of communal life – provides a key for the retrograde temporality of the home-centered novel. In his discussion of "chrono-topicity" Bakhtin argues that meaning in narrative resides in the way specific "well-delineated spatial areas" make time "palpable":[4] all of a novel's ideas rely on "the special increase in density and concreteness of time markers – the time of human life, of historical time" that characterizes particular spaces – the road, the rural town, the manor house, the home. Although he does not elaborate on it, Bakhtin hints that there is something inevitably communal at the center of this process when he cites Lessing to explain that because what is static in space cannot be statically described, such objects rely on techniques that work affectively: "The beauty of Helen is less described than demonstrated in the reactions of the Trojan elders; these come to light simultaneously in the sequence comprised by the activities and deeds of the elders" (251). It follows then that the Marshalsea itself is not described as the model home; rather its status as Home – like Helen's beauty – is demonstrated through the institutionitis that infects so many of the novel's primary characters. In other words, it is a set of reactions – a collection of symptoms displayed by the novel's characters in their activities and in their deeds – that tags the Marshalsea Home.

That the task of locating this novel's home should rely on the affective dynamics of institutionitis implies that domesticity has an impact on the novel's temporal scheme specifically through Dickens' idea of character. For what *Little Dorrit* makes clear is the extent to which each character's psychological development – what might be described as that brand of emotional event which, in taking place over time, also tells a story – is devoted to the task of representing the Marshalsea: as the novel progresses, characters like Arthur and Little Dorrit consequently seem less like individuals and more like collections of symptoms in need of institutionalization. In the context of *Little Dorrit* then, Bakhtin's analysis implies that the homeward bound novel is implicated in an impossible situation: for the project of representing the Marshalsea as a paradigmatic home requires exploiting all the resources of character fixation; and once the novel's stores of psychological material are depleted, there is nothing left to make the novel's temporal scheme meaningful – no material left for weaving consciousness – no possibility of emotional maturation or epiphanic achievement. In other words, what is at issue is not that the absence of psychic texture initiates *Little Dorrit*'s recidivistic compulsions, but that the novel's preoccupation with communal life inhibits one of the narrative registers for making the passage of time meaningful: character development. Although Arthur shows some semblance of what is called subjective interiority when he first returns homeless to his mother's most unhomey house, he grows increasingly less interesting as his interest in the Marshalsea community overwhelms whatever "personality" he had initially exhibited. Arthur's story contains therefore neither the historical and legendary significance of his namesake nor the humanistic significance of a life examined. The novel does not, or cannot, make his individuation eloquent.

It is often felt that the absence of psychological depth is generally characteristic of the Dickensian *œuvre*, concerned as it so often is with the representation of the social machinery that forces itself on individual life. In *Little Dorrit,* Dickens – Homer of the Home – does not use the Marshalsea to illustrate a paradigmatic institution, but uses it to illustrate how an institution can be a home and what that parity implies. As a close replica of a total institution, the Marshalsea shows how home effects are generated and what the costs of such expenditure are for character. Obviously Little Dorrit herself offers the best example of such characterization overwrought: after all, the institution most saliently marked as the novel's Home is what serves as home to Little Dorrit – a figure whose structural centrality cannot be divorced from her stick-figure emotional constitution. Whether or not it is *Little Dorrit*'s domestic priorities that impoverish Little Dorrit's personality, or Little Dorrit's vapidness that allows *her* home to be *the* Home is almost moot; what is important is that the ethos of domestic sociability seems to inevitably coincide with depsychologized characterization.

Thus it is no accident that the Marshalsea, as Little Dorrit's birthplace, is the only living space in the novel ever called "home" (75): even though Arthur substitutes "as I take you back" because "the word home jarred upon him" (96), Little Dorrit shows no such discomfort when she declares on a different occasion, "'I had better go home!... My place is there. It is unfeeling in me to be here when I can do the least thing there ... I had far better stay at home'" (254). The Marshalsea is a home at first only in the context of Little Dorrit's life. And it is a place of return at first only through her perspective (since no one else had ever been born there). In this sense, Little Dorrit is nothing more than the mechanism that presents the communal life of the institution as not only better but also as prior to the undepictable freedom of the outside. Although the turnkey marvels at Little Dorrit's question as to whether anybody opens and shuts or locks the outdoor fields glimpsed through the Marshalsea's barred windows, the novel never does present the "free world" as free of gates and prison doors. As such a mechanism with such a job to perform, Little Dorrit designates an idea of communal life more than she adumbrates a personality.

DOMESTIC REFLECTIONS AND INSTITUTIONAL MOTHERHOOD

That the aesthetic costs of domesticity are high should not however override the novel's presentation of its virtues. The kind of "home" made material in this demi-prison institution that Rigaud sneers is nothing more than a "hospital for imbeciles" (728) is clearly of the domesticized institutional variety in vogue among the John Conolly camp of Victorian reformers (discussed above p. 55 no.16 and p. 193).[5] Although the collegians often move into the prison with their immediate biological kin, social relations in the Marshalsea are structured in imitation of a nineteenth-century household where "family" engendered a great deal of surrogate role-playing. However much the Dorrit kinship group might conjure a modern nuclear family lying at the Marshalsea's center, it is really only a composite family, its mother having died in childbirth and an uncle having joined its ranks. In this way, the Marshalsea reflects the original sense of "family" as designating not only blood relatives but all those who make up a particular household (*OED*). Moreover, it is this host of surrogate familial relations – operating both within the biologically related core of the Marshalsea as well as without it – that determines how the collegians conduct themselves. It is not just that Old Dorrit, as the core family's father, is Father of the Marshalsea with Little Dorrit as its Child, but that adoption into the Marshalsea community entails playing a variety of surrogate roles: in addition to being the Father, Old Dorrit also plays the child to his daughter's "Little Mother," a title she earns from having adopted the other "big child" Maggy in another surrogate instance.

Familial surrogation in the Marshalsea presides as the final determinant of behavior. This is important because it not only establishes the

Marshalsea as the kind of home that facilitates what I claim to be the civic sociability of household life, but it reveals that the category of the familial itself, along with its capacity to metaphorize all other kinds of interpersonal relationships, represents human relations as predicated on function rather than on sentiment. That Little Dorrit is called "Little Mother," for example, expresses her function in the community, the job she performs there, before it comes to stand for a measure of how much she is loved. Little Dorrit surfaces as the heroine of the novel not because she has a monopoly on feeling,[6] but because she does work that makes the collective living of the prison narratable, work that civilizes in that it transforms a group of strangers into a community complete with a folklorish history and locale-specific dialect.

Her epithet, Little Mother, allows Little Dorrit to be seen in the context of a strand of nineteenth-century feminism that sought an expansion of women's domestic sphere rather than a liberation from it. Unlike the strand of feminism which challenged the idea of natural sexual difference and mobilized to claim for women an equal place in the public sphere, domesticists invented what would come to be called social or civic "maternalism." Jane Lewis describes maternalism as an ingenious response to a separate-sphere doctrine that curtailed women's independence in the years immediately following the Napoleonic Wars:

> The other main strand of nineteenth-century feminism accepted the idea of women as the natural guardians of the moral order. It stressed the importance of women's domestic role and sought to expand it. The language used to make this appeal was steeped in the evangelical tradition, which in the early and mid-nineteenth-century had proved as successful as science in containing women, but which in the later part of the century was used by feminists to argue for the extension of maternal influence beyond the home.(*Women in England* 89)

This is not to say that the two strands were always mutually exclusive, or even that they may not have overlapped earlier than Lewis contends. But it does draw our attention to how slippery the separate sphere doctrine really was.

Moreover, it is striking how Lewis' description of civic maternalism recalls Harold Perkin's description of professionalism. As Perkin claims that part of the appeal of professionalism was that it could be theoretically extended to include every occupation and every worker (*Rise of Professional Society* 8), Lewis points out that "It was possible to argue for an infinite expansion of social motherhood" (95), even into Parliament, an argument that many suffragettes later deployed. Like a profession, social maternalism posited the idea that the ethic of care enjoined to define a woman was precisely what entitled her to certain privileges and rights.

It would seem, however, that social maternalism raised some difficult ironies: in real-life terms the championing of sexual difference as grounds for extending the domestic sphere into public life actually entailed its reverse: extending the public sphere into the home. This is especially true in light of the kinds of work that served to expand women's roles in public life: although philanthropic work, such as workhouse visiting and caring for the poor and infirm in local hospitals, provided the basis for women's representation on the boards of the institutions they served (as Poor Law guardians, members of school boards, organizers of local political committees) (Lewis, *Women in England* 92), most of this public service work was generally done at home. Rarely did middle-class women acquire any semblance of a separate work place. They continued to work out of their homes rather than outside them: it is at home that they assembled food baskets, sewed blankets, held meetings. Their homes continued to be where they worked even if they worked in a more public capacity.

For feminists who discarded the idea of a natural sexual difference and mobilized on behalf of woman's right to enter the public sphere as an equal to a man, there was ironically no problem in maintaining a distinction between the public and the private sphere, for the goal was only to degender it. Like John Stuart Mill, they tended to emphasize the position of unmarried women and to use "the individualistic framework of nineteenth-century liberalism and political economy" in promoting women's rights to fair competition in the fight to earn a living (89). In other words, the idea of the private sphere remained intact; what changed was who would occupy it.

For feminists who asserted these rights as predicated on a woman's natural difference, on her civic talents, the conflation of the two spheres poses a conceptual problem. Is the domestic expanded in the public, or the public contracted in the domestic; what marks the outside from the inside? The metaphor that differentiates between two types of social space – two separate spheres – becomes impossible. And indeed *Little Dorrit*'s expansion of institutional life manifests itself in an extended play on the ins and outs of a world structured like the interior of an institution.

When Mr. Meagles points to Little Dorrit as the ideal woman, it is not so much to praise her sensibility as to spotlight her performance value – her "noble service" (790). In terms of her heroism, however, the Marshalsea appears not only as an arena for Little Dorrit's "do[ing] the least thing" – which of course amounts to just about everything – but as the structure responsible for her work ethic. Given her heroism's reliance on the Marshalsea's institutional setting, it is no wonder that the only sign of her interiority is what some call an internalization of her duties to others. Even in this pop-psychological sense, Little Dorrit remains a character overwhelmed by the principle of sociability. The implication is that the expansion of institutional life, by which some women theoretically gained access to meaningful or lucrative work outside the home, entailed a notion of the individual that was so communally inflected that individual psychology could find no register.

DOMESTIC DEBT: BANKRUPTCY AND CO.

As the home of such a specimen of womanhood, the Marshalsea distinguishes itself as *Little Dorrit*'s most successful living space, even if the novel flashes glimpses of other abodes that are happier. Although the "practical" Meagles who live in the "home-limits" of a perfectly arranged suburban dwelling (186) and the Plornishes who live in Bleeding Heart Yard's "Happy Cottage" (586) provide alternatives to the tight, airless rooms that comprise Little Dorrit's home, such home-like spaces, while representing certain domestic values, ultimately fall short of representing true homes. The Meagles House, for example, is a picture of activity, its *mittbring* collection attesting to the regularity of the family's continuous, objectiveless movement. And it is a picture of non-psychological sociability as well, its architectural façade representing in material abstraction not so much the personality of each inhabitant but their relations to each other: the "hale elderly" brick portion stands for the parents, the younger "picturesque" one for the cherished daughter and the additional "conservatory sheltering itself against" the whole for the adopted orphan (185–7). But despite the family's nonpsychological, socialized bustle, its home-limits finally fail. Because its regular activity takes the form of regularly traveling, this home's continuative aspect has a stilled quality that finally keeps it empty, ever in expectation of a return that never happens – especially once Pet joins the ranks of the literally homeless expats in Rome.

And as for the Plornish's "Happy Cottage," so precipitously perched on the economic brinks of Bleeding Heart Yard, it too displays a failed home. For though the *trompe l'œil* of a thatched cottage's exterior marks the boundary between the family shop and its home (556), and foreshadows the campy artifices of Wemmick's Castle, Happy Cottage's membership in the Yard's Community of Poverty renders it too shaky to constitute a successful home, the persistent visitations of the rent collector disrupting its routines and thwarting its regularity. Although the Marshalsea too is poor, its poverty does not forbode the perilous change – the ever feared eviction – that the Yard's economic insecurities represent. The Marshalsea bodies forth as the ultimate home because it represents more a state of mind, indebtedness, than a building housing debtors. In so far as it can never be left, it is a home from which exile is impossible.

As a community premised on a condition of universal indebtedness, the Marshalsea offers a distinctly anti-capitalist social vision. The event that occasions the Dorrits' exile from the Marshalsea and from England is the recovery of their fortune. In this sense, the community constituting the Marshalsea occupies a position in the economic suprastructure framing it that reveals what is at issue in the home's relationship to money. As the Dorrit family history illustrates, economic failure literally meant a family's eviction from its place of residence: bankruptcy directly translated into the loss of home – a trauma that was not simply Dickens' own obsession[7] but common enough to have been extensively portrayed throughout Victorian art and literature.

But bankruptcy also meant finding oneself at home in the Marshalsea, a home removed from economic contingencies but not from economic relations. As the precondition for making the Marshalsea home, insolvency allows money to assume a heightened social significance. Circulated among the inmates to pay homage or to procure sundries, it moves without significantly changing how or where any one individual lives. Its presence in a place constructed on the premise of its absence lends it a more symbolic value. Thus the quality of Old Dorrit's supper relies more on his daughter's participation in procuring it for him than on any additional money that might have purchased it. In this way, money at the Marshalsea, like home work and home plotting, appears to be inefficacious even when it can be and is traded for real goods.

Bankruptcy – the immediate condition on which the Marshalsea's home status rests – and the free-floating indebtedness that emanates from it, has an effect on how the novel presents the significance of doing business. It must be remembered that the Marshalsea, as a debtor's prison, had already been dismantled by the time Dickens was writing *Little Dorrit*, an increasingly humane and reform-minded Victorian culture now finding it morally unjustifiable to imprison debtors. That the

Marshalsea which Dickens knew as a child was abandoned only a few decades later suggests that the period between *Little Dorrit*'s setting and its publication witnessed a change in the cultural status of debt, and consequently of the social significance of business practice. The change is best illustrated by the 1856 passage of the Limited Liability Act before which a shareholder in a bankrupt enterprise was liable not only for the amount of his holdings, but for the whole loss. Because a small share-holder could have the entirety of his possessions seized in order to pay creditors of whom he had perhaps never even heard, it is fair to say that doing business entailed making an extremely profound social commit-ment as the circle of liability could seem eternally widening.[8] Conse-quently, going bankrupt could be seen as a crime against the commu-nity, rather than simply a personal failing. And although this may be said of every crime, Dickens is particularly committed to saying it about capitalist speculation.

The perceived societal reach of this economic web can be attributed both to the realities of nineteenth-century business practice and to what was virtually a national experience of bankruptcy. As a consequence of wild speculation in the 1820s and then again in the 1840s, unprece-dented numbers and classes of the English population shared in devasta-ting financial failures. It is this unstable economic climate that provokes Sarah Ellis in her renowned handbook on domestic etiquette to bid the women of England to "sink gracefully" (*Women of England* 25), which entails mastering work that is done by virtue of the "feminine qualifica-tion of being able to use the hand" (20–1) and cultivating "the disinter-ested kindness" (21) that is the source of a woman's moral influence and authority. In this sense, the uncertain economic conditions of the period motivate her invention of the domestic woman. And like *Persuasion*, Ellis' book looks to the sea for a vocabulary that will represent the precondi-tions of domesticity:

it seems an ungracious task to attempt to rouse [English young ladies] from their summer dream; and were it not that wintry days will come, and the surface of life be ruffled, and the mariner, even she who steers the smallest bark, be put upon the inquiry for what port she is really bound – were it not that the cry of utter helplessness is of no avail in rescuing from the waters of affliction, and the plea of ignorance unheard upon the far-extending and deep ocean of experience, and the question of accountability perpetually sounding, like the voice of a warning spirit, above the storms and billows of this lower world – I would be the last to call the dreamer back to a consciousness of present things. (*Women of England* 17)

The urgency of this remarkable passage, discussed in more detail above (pp. 12–13), gains an immediate reference several pages later when Ellis places her guidelines in the context of current economic conditions. Her readership will be larger than her definition of the middle classes "in consequence of the great change in their pecuniary circumstances, which many families during a short period experience" (25). The domestic woman emerges as a sailor navigating her household in economic oceans.

With the press sensationalism that surrounded some of the larger financial scandals of the period and the popularity of "financial ruin" set pieces in a burgeoning mass media, it is fair to say that the experience of economic disaster, whether real or vicarious, would have been difficult for any mid-century Victorian to avoid.[9] The consequence of this collective experience was to further emphasize the social dimensions of individual life. For in the moment in which an individual businessman would realize he was bankrupt so also would materialize the host of creditors, financiers, agents and beneficiaries to whom he was tied. In this sense, bankruptcy would make it unavoidably clear that the personal career of a businessman like Mr. Merdle was interpersonally entangled in the lives of an extraordinarily complex and vast business community. In other words, what was Mr. Merdle's business was everyone else's as well.

In this way, the fact that Victorian business practices carry such significance for the collective complicates the significance of a debtor's prison. There is a sense in which, although there is something shameful in being committed to the Marshalsea, the novel is no less strangely committed to idealizing it. For what the Marshalsea consistently reveals is the extent to which business failure and sociability are paired: as the Merdles of the world generally turn out to be resourceful enough to escape penalty (whether through legal manipulation, flight or, as in this case, suicide), the only characters who end up in a debtors' prison tend to be the collaterally damaged – those who – as Arthur's case-history illustrates – are guilty by association, those who did not protect themselves from the business of their friends and relatives. Thus it is that Arthur is ruined by listening to his friend Pancks, Doyce by trusting his friend Arthur. Even Old Dorrit's career as a debtor begins with "affairs" that are "perplexed by a partnership, of which he knew no more than that he invested money in it" (57). In both of the novel's two case-studies – Old Dorrit's and Arthur's – it is entering into a "partnership" that serves as the fatal act. Seen in this light, the Marshalsea starts to look like a community of the inextricably involved – individuals too sociable to fortify themselves against the speculation fever. And this is precisely where the novel's disease metaphor links up with its financial metaphor: for once the economic tropes blossom into an interpersonally transmitted plague – and specifically into Arthur's illness – the Marshalsea becomes a place of recovery in all of its sense.

PROFESSIONAL DOMESTICITY

It is within the context of what it means to find a home in the bankrupts' institution that *homo economicus* is redefined as a social animal; for it is there where it becomes clear how money functions inefficaciously and how financial matters become public domain, and it is there where the excesses of sociability flourish. So it follows that the Marshalsea's interrogation of what constitutes a man's business – of what an individual's business means – begins early in Arthur's story when he and his mother discuss his homecoming. For Arthur has apparently come home in order to close his father's firm, finish his father's business. What that business is, however, whether it is pecuniary or personal in nature, remains murky, given the double sense of the word "House." When Arthur explains to his mother that he is abandoning the business because "our House" has so declined that "even this old house in which we speak" is no longer "a place of business and business resort," he does not anticipate that her response will be to treat the House as a home: "'Do you consider . . . that this house serves no purpose, Arthur, in sheltering your infirm and afflicted . . . mother?'" she remonstrates in a sentence that perverts Arthur's understanding of what he calls "business purposes" (44–5). What is peculiar in their exchange is that Arthur's home seems less localizable, less place-specific, than his father's business even though the literal meaning of the two words suggests the reverse: according to the *OED* there is only a vague sense in which home does not designate a specific locale, and many senses in which business does not. In this way, one of the novel's very first establishing shots depicts Arthur's homecoming as the realization that his father's business is not only not where he thought it was but not what he thought it was.

But besides showing Arthur's worldly career to be in crisis, the result of such a homecoming is that the whole notion of business, along with the figure of a businessman, assumes a malevolent hue. Despite the fact that the generous Mr. Meagles and the kind-hearted Mr. Pancks describe themselves as businessmen, the only figure the novel's omniscient voice tags a "man of business" is the stock villain Rigaud, and the only one it acknowledges as such is the infamous Mr. Merdle. More significant, however, is the fact that the novel rarely allows this villainous sense of business to occur independently of issues that might be called private; for more often than not, business coincides with engagements that characters strain to keep covert on the grounds that they are personal. Miss Wade, for example, confounds Arthur's search for information by claiming her interaction with the "man of business" was her own "business" (516); and Arthur, forced to quit his mother's home on an evening when she needs to speak privately with the suspicious "man of business" is kept from knowing the nature of what he later refers to as an "unlucky course of business," consequently validating the shadiness that Miss Wade insinuates when she remarks that "business hours on that occasion were late" (639). Moreover, Mrs. Clennam's explanation that "it will prove, no doubt, to be one more or less in the usual way of our business, which it will be both our business and our pleasure to advance" (530) conflates the sense in which business is a vocational practice by which a living is earned and the sense in which it is a personal property – a place-holder, that is, for some kind of personal boundary. By harnessing the practice of making a living to a notion of personal life, Mrs. Clennam suggests that all business is private in the extreme sense of belonging exclusively to an individual: what one does in the world of finance is as personal as what one does in one's own bedroom – precisely the place where Mrs. Clennam the perennial invalid conducts much of her financial business. In this way the novel, by dressing business in secrecy and malevolence, generates a distrust of anything that is personally private, thereby fostering an antipathy toward the no-trespass side of what might be seen as a barebones form of individualism.

When business does occur as part of a good turn, it relies on an instance of contortionist linguistics in order to redefine itself as less personal than the novel generally implies. Pancks, the busiest of all business men, for example, justifies the *sub rosa* detective work of ferreting out the Dorrit family fortune by saying, "'It may be out of the ordinary course, and yet be business. In short, it is business. I am a man of business. What business have I in this present world, except to stick to business? No business'" (267). By moving from the designation of a specific task to an ongoing job to a sense of personal identity to a reference to worldly preoccupation to an articulation of boundaries, Pancks' tautological play suggests that vocational business involves questions of quotidian activity, personal self-representation, quasi-divine duty and an ability or inability to recognize the boundaries that delimit the realm of the private. That this configuration involves so many shaded overlaps, however, makes it clear that the idea of privacy when constructed in the context of worldly business is structurally available to those in the business of such business; under the aegis of being a businessman, Pancks' statement both erects the boundaries necessary to establish an idea of what might be private in Mrs. Clennam's sense of the word, but nonetheless authorizes his mobility into such roped-off purlieus. By claiming to have no business in this world other than sticking to business, he makes the private history of the Dorrit family his business – and, for that matter, Clennam's business and the novel's as well. In other words, the novel suggests that in order for business to do good, privacy itself must be defined in nonpersonal, more communal terms. It uses the doing of a good deed as a means of reiterating that an individual's business in not exclusively his own, but imbricates that of others.

This reconstruction of business as a set of interpersonal relations occasioned but not defined by economic interactions surfaces in the expressions benevolent characters like Mr. Pancks use to rationalize their motives. When, for example, Flora wants to euphemize her previous personal relationship with Arthur, she calls her ex-suitor by his company name, "Doyce and Clennam"; and when she refers to Clennam's mother as "Clennam and Co" and describes "'a very different person, indeed . . . with no limbs and wheels instead and the grimmest of women though his mother,'" Mr. Dorrit expresses surprise that "Clennam and Co" should mean a mother, to which Flora adds, "'And an old man besides'" (604–5). Even more than illustrating the eccentric wonts of Flora's personality, her idiolect offers up the conceptualization of a business as a compound of relations rather than as an enterprise organized around procuring profit for an individual or set of individuals. Not coincidentally, the peculiar speech pattern that identifies Flora's character here is also employed in conveying this model of social relations, the novel's domestic agenda again competing with the strictures of representing personality.

Daniel Doyce defines good business as the placing of a priority on the community rather than on personal gain, whether in money or in independence. When he explains that he needs a business partner "'in deference to current opinion'" and in order to uphold "'the credit of the Works'" (184–5), he emphasizes that business credit can be seen as turning public opinion into capital.[10]

Daniel's desire for a business partner is particularly significant because Daniel is the consummate professional: not only does his vocational history consist of the lengthy and rigorous and, in Daniel's case, international training that marks professional expertise, but his "composed and unobtrusive self-sustainment" demonstrates a virtually Weberian vocational spirit. When, for example, Arthur asks him why he does not give up his struggle with the Circumlocution Office, Daniel responds in the supra-personal third person, "'He can't do it . . . It's not put into his head to be buried. It's put into his head to be made useful. You hold your life on the condition that to the last you shall struggle hard for it. Every man holds a discovery on the same terms'" (184). As a career man, Daniel combines a sense of divine order and a sense of social service: not only does he display "this adaptation" or "that combination" as if "the Divine artificer had made it, and he happened to find it" (500), but he returns to England despite an auspicious career abroad in order to "do his country whatever service he could do" (183). What is important here is that by housing his inventions, and what amounts to his decidedly professional career, in a business, Daniel seeks to bring them and himself into an English – and an historically specific English – community.

LITTLE DORRIT'S WORK: A SERVICE INDUSTRY

Daniel's vocational career is important because it provides the appropriate foil for Little Dorrit's work. Like Daniel, Little Dorrit begins her occupational training early and deliberately, teaching herself "the matter of lifting and carrying," learning to "read and keep accounts" and convincing the prison's milliner to make her into "a cunning workwoman" (68–70) – all with the objective of managing what Old Dorrit himself calls "household business" (81). But the skill most crucial to this business of home economics is Little Dorrit's ability to hide the fact that she "goes out" to work: "So, over and above other daily cares, the Child of the Marshalsea had always upon her the care of preserving the genteel fiction" (71). It would seem then that housekeeperly expertise involves circumlocuting the receipt of a wage. Like Daniel, Little Dorrit's career requires pretending to not know about what Mr. Meagles labels "practical" matters even though such practical matters are invariably philanthropic. Dedicated to the article-less concept of service – or what Mr. Meagles specifies as "noble service" (790) – rather than to the articled particulars of "a" job, Daniel's and Little Dorrit's make-believe suggests that vocational work relies on mediating an individual's relationship to cash payment, such a negotiation of wage labor again emphasizing that the true professional does not work *for* individual gain but *due to* the calling of a sociable sensibility.

But Little Dorrit's specifically domestic calling evinces one important difference from Daniel's career as a public-minded engineer. Although the need to keep up this "ceremony and pretence" seems motivated by Old Dorrit's faux-patrician sensibility, it soon becomes clear that this cloaking of outside "work" is but a complement to the equally pressing but less explicable need to hide home life: similar in a certain sense to Wemmick's commuter lifestyle, Little Dorrit, from the moment she begins working beyond the prison's walls, "found it necessary to conceal where she lived and to come and go as secretly as she could" (81). Unlike the Wemmick paradigm, however, Little Dorrit's division of space coincides with what the novel repeatedly calls her "womanly consciousness" (75). Whereas such a division of work space from domestic space in *Great Expectations* and *Our Mutual Friend* allows the home to function as a preserve of true vocational professionalism, it appears here as a hypostatization of Little Dorrit's psychological growth.

In this way, the novel presents Little Dorrit's sense of self as curiously reliant on the communal nature of her Marshalsea home and specifically on the kind of service such a home both demands and provides. Similar in this sense to *Villette*'s rhetoric of renunciation, Little Dorrit's relationship to the Marshalsea raises the question as to whether the home's collectivist principles are sacrifices or privileges. Especially relevant here is the fact that the nineteenth-century sense of "service" designates the condition of being a servant almost exclusively in terms of being a domestic servant, although sometimes also in reference to a religious or public servant in the employ of God or the state. But this "condition" of servitude is etymologically rooted in the feudal sense of service as designating the "work or duty" of servitude – specifically either a knight's pledge of fealty in money or kind to his lord, or a knight's holding. In other words, "service" can designate the property held as part of the feudal contract (*OED*). And if service can be a property, then service can be the condition necessary and sufficient to the assertion of political rights in nineteenth-century Anglo-American culture.

That the onset of Little Dorrit's "womanly consciousness" coincides with her sense of "noble service" (as the keeper of the ultimate institutional Home) suggests that in *Little Dorrit*'s vocational domesticity, gender coincides with an interpretation of property that uses community service to assert an individual's "natural" rights. In this light, natural rights derive from womanliness because womanliness entails a version of the service that originally gave feudal lords their property and their political place. A woman's gender can become the basis for her asserting her rights as an Englishman.

In this context, *Little Dorrit* uses a reductive type of developmental psychology to limn Little Dorrit's "career" as a mother who has no children. "Career," as Erving Goffman uses it in reference to the life of a mental patient in a "total institution," is a two-sided concept that involves interior matters such as self-image or identity and publicly available matters such as official position and style of living. "The concept of career," he explains, "allows one to move back and forth between the personal and the public, between the self and its significant society, without having to over-rely on the data collected from what the person says he thinks he imagines himself to be" (*Asylums* 27). But in an institution, Goffman claims, even felt identity becomes socially reliant, for, despite the accepted psychological definition of mental illness, an individual enters and quits an asylum only through a set of social contingencies – through some kind of social malfunctioning that precipitates moving in or moving out. The hierarchy and management of the hospital – how the patient is treated, where he is assigned to live, what kinds of allowances he is given – work as markers for an individual's level of social functioning: "Built right into the social arrangements of an organization, then, is a thoroughly embracing conception of the member – and not merely a conception of him *qua* member, but behind this conception of him *qua* human being" (180). Like the careers of Goffman's institutionalized denizens, Little Dorrit's career at home in the Marshalsea wholly institutionalizes her identity. But once we recognize the sense in which the novel wholly institutionalizes everyone's identity, we can see how the idea of "membership" in an institution can be expanded into a universal "membership" in the human race.

It is in this sense that the novel delineates Little Dorrit's "womanly life" exclusively in terms of her vocational ascension, her adult consciousness beginning with the onset of her domestic career as housewife to the Marshalsea:

It was enough that she was inspired to be something which was not what the rest were, and to be that something, different and laborious, for the sake of the rest. Inspired? Yes. Shall we speak of the inspiration of the poet or the priest, and not of the heart impelled by love and self-devotion to the lowliest work in the lowliest way of life! (689).

In all its sermonesque biblical echoes and rhetorical pacing, the recitative here voices Little Dorrit's domestic career as spiritually inspired, exposing housework as the bodying forth of exalted calling. That she is called to be a "something," however, divulges the price domesticity extracts: for in all its lofty representation of Little Dorrit's housekeeperly career, the passage's rhetoric slips into a chain of reductions which, in trying to convey the abstract sense – the conceptual beauty – of noble deed, cannot sustain the presence of what is human. The fatality hidden in domesticity's collectivist imperative crystallizes: it is the priority of idea that dehumanizes.

"I WILL GIVE THEE THY WAGES"

This is borne out in the immediate sequence of events leading up to Little Dorrit's final repression of the codicil, which brings the Meagles subplot into focus. The information contained in the codicil would disclose the identity of Arthur's biological mother and the wealth that Little Dorrit wants to renounce. We can recall that Arthur's father had wished that something be given to Arthur's mother after he was taken away from her. The uncle responsible provides the money too late, and so it goes to her dancing-master, who happens to be Little Dorrit's uncle. Money is given to Arthur's mother because she is his mother, but not *for* her being his mother. Little Dorrit's desire to renounce her wealth takes the shape of her repressing how money was ineffectually circuited through maternity. Arthur's sense of unlocalizable debt, which comes to a head when he is imprisoned in the Marshalsea, remains intact.

There are many reasons why money should play such a mystifying role in *Little Dorrit*, one of which emerges in the Meagles subplot. Indeed, money's role in the novel is especially interesting in light of Davidoff's observation that money is "the demystifying instrument par excellence." According to Davidoff, although the rationalization of the household advocated in domestic manuals prescribed increased use of and reference to money, the application of calculation to the family, and hence to women, met with a great deal of resistance (*Worlds Between* 83). Certainly, the centrality of indebtedness in *Little Dorrit's* institutional home draws attention to one of the problems of using the metaphor, civic motherhood, as a means of asserting a degree of financial independence for women. Motherhood is generally not a paid position, and economic independence – especially for married women, and hence for married mothers – was of very serious concern even for women and men who would not have described themselves as feminist.

The potential for the idea of payment to threaten the efficacy of a metaphor that depicted public women as surrogate mothers emerges in the controversy surrounding the seal of corporation for the Coram Foundling Hospital (now the Thomas Coram Foundation for Children), which was painted by Hogarth and entitled *Moses Brought Before the Pharaoh's Daughter*.[11] The painting depicts the biblical scene in which the Pharaoh's daughter, having adopted Moses, hires his biological mother to nurse and care for him with the phrase, "Take this child away, and nurse it for me, and I will give thee thy wages" (Exodus 2:9). As the seal of the Coram Foundling Hospital the painting implied that the Hospital, like Pharaoh's daughter, was a kind of surrogate mother who could enable women by employing them as "foster" mothers to their own biological children. The controversy occurred when the Hospital's patrons noticed that Hogarth had included a certain detail: Moses' mother wore a triumphant smile as she received a shining pile of gold in exchange for – well, ostensibly in exchange for her services, but in the context of the Hospital's role as a foster-home, perhaps in exchange for her child. To appease the patrons who were, after all, giving him his own pile of gold, Hogarth changed the painting, obfuscating the payment by blurring that portion depicting it.

The episode and the history of the Coram Foundling Hospital bring civic maternalism and the London artistic community into an interesting relationship. Founded by a sea captain in the eighteenth century, the Coram Hospital was supposed to provide a foster-home for London's vagrant children.[12] By the nineteenth century, overwhelmed with the numbers of potential wards, the hospital had regrouped along a set of new principles. Operating like a giant surrogate family it was organized around raising children rather than relocating them in adopted homes: a bevy of nurse mothers and administrative fathers were responsible for teaching the little girls about household management and for arranging craft apprenticeships for the little boys (Nichols and Wray, *The History of the Foundling Hospital*). As a philanthropic home, its primary responsibility was perceived as providing the training that would give these illegitimate children skills enough for a respectable job.

The Coram Foundling Hospital was famous for its "moral standards": it accepted a child only after the mother had proved she had expected to marry the father and that she had been coerced into the sexual encounter that produced the child (Barret-Ducrocq, *Love in the Time of Victoria*; Nichols and Wray, *History of the Foundling Hospital*). But it was also famous for its art: a monument to private philanthropy, the Hospital was a *cause célèbre* among members of the London artistic community, especially with Dickens. Its beautiful church featured an organ donated by Handel and an annual high-priced performance of *The Messiah*; its reception hall became a well-trafficked art gallery that included works by Gainsborough, Ramsay and Reynolds. The Coram Foundling Hospital turned into a space where familial philanthropy and cosmopolitan art intersected as an institution.

Although it is true that the scene from Exodus depicts compassion, the chain of surrogations highlighted in Hogarth's rendering entails an uncomfortable payment. But the inclusion of the payment itself calls attention to the fact that this particular scene is a strange choice for the Hospital's seal. In Exodus, the occasion that requires an adoption is the tyranny of a pharaoh who demanded the murder of all the Israelite first-born males. The suggestion that nineteenth-century London posed a parallel social situation implies that a world in which a single mother cannot keep her child is a world in which she is enslaved. In the biblical story, the wage is important because the Israelites *were* slaves: they were not paid for their labor. That a slave woman can be paid as a surrogate mother to her own child suggests that mothering can be paid work as long as some vested body, like the Pharaoh's daughter, intervenes. If we read the Coram Foundling Hospital as an institutionalization of civic maternalism, then we can understand the hospital as an institution that pays a mother for her motherlike work but not for her being literally a mother. That the wage of Exodus is depicted at all, when the Found-lings' biological mothers were not at all paid, further reproduces some of the ironies attendant on civic maternalism.

In the Meagles subplot, the tension between character development and domesticity recurs in the episodes involving Tattycoram. Tatty-coram, as the adopted daughter who rebels by pursuing Miss Wade's promise of a more self-gratifying life of independence, brings the Meagles household into a revealing relationship with the Coram Foundling Hospital. In recounting how Tattycoram came to get her name, Mr. Meagles explains that he and his wife and his daughter went to church one Sunday at the Coram Foundling Hospital and saw all the children and thought to bring one home. "Harriet Beadle," Tattycoram's original "arbitrary" (18) name, turns into "Tattycoram" in an Irigaryish play on the phonemes of "Hatty" (from "Harriet") and the child's institutional affiliation to the "Coram" Foundling Hospital. In a sense, the Meagles name her after her corporate parent, after a place rather than after a person. And in keeping with the principles of the Foundling Hospital, the Meagles do not adopt Tattycoram as their daughter, but as a maid to their daughter: "Let us take one of those same little children to be a little maid to Pet" (18). In a sense, they hire her, but never mention what kind of wage they pay her. The Foundling Hospital as an artistic center enables Hatty to employment, but the familial setting of that employment, like Hogarth's painting, obfuscates what kind of payment she might or might not receive.

Mr. Meagles goes on to explain that they never expected Tatty to be an ideal child:

If we should find her temper a little defective, or any of her ways a little wide of ours, we shall know what we have to take into account. We shall know what an immense deduction must be made from all the influences and experiences that have formed us – no parents, no child-brother or sister, no individuality of home, no Glass Slipper, or Fairy Godmother. And that's the way we came by Tattycoram. (18)

Although Mr. Meagles avers here that a hospital is not a home, Tattycoram, the name and the woman, is invented in his household, through his family's associations to the institution that raised her. That she comes to be their better daughter and, after Pet's unhappy marriage, their only daughter, suggests that the absence of fairy tales in institutional life produces more virtuous homebodies. Although Tattycoram enters the Meagles family as a maid, she becomes their true daughter. Her ascension is marked by her agency in the novel's denouement. For it is Tattycoram who returns the iron box containing the repressed codicil. She reunites with "Father and Mother Meagles" (789) by enabling Little Dorrit to repress those two strangely linked secrets: her wealth and the identity of Arthur's mother.

But why is it important that the novel link these two secrets in the first place? The novel presents Arthur and Little Dorrit's marriage as contingent on her maintaining a fiction of her dependence. In order to do so, she has to hide that she was made independent by an imperfect relationship between money and maternity. Maintaining this fiction results in an imbalance of knowledge between her and Arthur that serves to prevent his psychological awakening.

So it is as a "something different and laborious for the sake of the rest" – as a depersonalized embodiment of communal commitment – that Little Dorrit takes the helm of her Marshalsea home:

She took off her old bonnet, hung it in the old place, and noiselessly began, with Maggy's help, to despatch somebody else to fill the basket again; which soon came back replenished with new stores, from which a present provision of cooling drink and jelly, and a prospective supply of roast chicken and wine and water, were the first extracts. These various arrangements completed, she took out her old needlecase to make him a curtain . . . [Arthur] found himself composed in his chair, with Little Dorrit working at his side. (736)

The elongated syntax and the abundance of intermediary details underplay agency while underscoring authority. As Little Dorrit's work occurs in the durative mood, the basket seems to replenish itself, the condiments extract themselves, the arrangements complete themselves and finally Arthur is composed. That Arthur "finds himself" – returns from fevered delirium to consciousness – only as he is "composed" amidst the quiet hum of Little Dorrit's ongoing work again accentuates the way in which the domestic system of this novel assimilates consciousness; though Arthur reawakens, the terms of his recovery cannot support psychological realism. That the idea of a human community can overpower so much of what is human in nineteenth-century English individualism is the ironic, if not tragic, tale that *Little Dorrit*'s domesticity unfolds.

CHAPTER 5

Professing renunciation: domesticity in
The Cloister and the Hearth *and* Felix Holt

THE CLOISTER AND THE HEARTH

It is especially in connection to George Eliot's work that a brief look at Charles Reade's popular 1861 novel, *The Cloister and the Hearth*, yields a crucial paradigm for Victorian novelistic domesticity.[1] Based on a section of Erasmus' *Compendium* in which the late medieval scholar narrates the history of his parents' courtship and quasi-legitimate marriage, *The Cloister and the Hearth* places the idea of the Home formally in a tale of vocational choice and historically at the heart of the Protestant Reformation.[2] Set in fifteenth-century Holland, Charles Reade's widely acclaimed novel[3] opens when Gerard Eliassoen surrenders his plan of "going into the Church" (*The Cloister and the Hearth* 5) so that he might marry instead; a decision his family vehemently opposes since Gerard's ecclesiastical career would have provided them with a primary source of income. Betrothed but not yet married to the beloved Margaret, Gerard must quit his Dutch homeland and hearth for Rome. The novel's laborious, quasi-episodic yarn is thus initiated by Gerard's search for the Roman education that would turn his monk-taught skills in penmanship and manuscript illumination into an artistic career by which he might support his now pregnant wife, her father and a variety of other "friends" who have found their way into his household.

After a series of tedious travel anecdotes and picaresque complications Gerard reaches Rome, where he is tricked into believing that Margaret has died. Near despair, he attempts suicide, is saved, enters one of the ubiquitous monasteries that the novel sprinkles along each of its European highways, and finally becomes a Dominican priest sporting a new name, Clement. To benefit from Clement's oratory talents, the Roman monastery sends him to England, a nation humorously renowned on the novel's continent for its stiff-necked congregations. Before crossing the Channel, however, Clement encounters Margaret in Rotterdam, realizes that he had fallen victim to a plot, abandons the journey and confines himself to the Hermit of Gouda's cave, there assuming the hermit's cloistered career of solitude.

Margaret, having spent the intervening years supporting a "family" (which, due to her irresistible charm, now includes Gerard's once-disapproving blood kin) by freelance laundering and adjunct sewing, coaxes the "satanophobic" Clement out of his hermitage by invoking a remarkably Protestant argument: "She showed him," the narrator marvels, "in her own good straightforward Dutch, that his present life was only a higher kind of selfishness, spiritual egotism" (649). Returning him to the community domiciled in his mother's house, Margaret forces him to "eat a good nourishing meal" and rest in "a snowy bed" so that he soon awakes "as from a hideous dream, friar and hermit no more, Clement no more, but Gerard Eliassoen, parson of Gouda" (653), his literal and spiritual homecoming, almost like Lucy Snowe's Auld Lang Syne awakening, is marked by the falling away of his Roman Catholic delusions as he accepts the connotatively Protestant title of "parson."

Here the novel dilates a peculiar kind of happy ending that lasts for nearly a quarter of the whole story:

> History itself, though a far more daring story-teller than romance, presents few things so strange as the footing on which Gerard and Margaret now lived for many years. United by present affection, past familiarity, and a marriage irregular but legal; separated by Holy Church and by their own consciences, which sided unreservedly with Holy Church; separated by the Church, but united by a living pledge of affection, lawful in every sense at its date. (660)

History and romance having converged in the "footing" that constitutes Gerard and Margaret's final condition, the couple is depicted at work on negotiating a "marriage" – what one of Reade's historicizing foot-notes calls the "legal betrothal" of an engagement. Their marital home requires such work because, though recognized as legitimate, it must nonetheless be integrated into an ecclesiastical career that is by defini-tion built on its renunciation. Through paired participial phrases linked by a coordinating conjunction, Gerard and Margaret's "footing" seems to require a difficult balancing act. Composed in this way of matched predicates pivoting on a "but" axle, each semicolon-bracketed sentence fragment conveys the sense in which oppositional tension effects a balance that preserves stasis through a series of concessions, or compro-mised positions: together but separated, apart from the Church but a part of it, Gerard and Margaret are married but not married. In this way, the passage's syntactical patterning suggests that the novel's domesticity can only be represented through the negotiations of opposites.

This frustrating state of irresolution is important in two ways. From a reader's perspective, such an unlucky twist of events, though based on a historical chronicle, feels embarrassingly cumbersome, the protracted final situation narratively unhinged and aesthetically overwrought: it is nearly impossible to avoid hoping that Reade might stage the Reformation at an earlier date, as Luther is most clearly the novel's awaited *deus ex machina*. And in this sense the Dutch home that so boldly hoards the novel's sympathies, the home whose difficulties would be solved by such a historical imposition, reveals a clearly Protestant disposition. Secondly and more interestingly, however, the novel's relentless artificiality seems generated primarily by a central motivating principle: a need to illustrate the experience of renunciation. Wheresoever Gerard turns, he cannot escape renouncing, whether it is the hearth for which he took a marital oath or the priesthood that extracted as powerful a vow.

The novel's diluted Protestantism and heightened degree of artifice are related. The connection can be seen in how critics describe the popular reception of *The Cloister and the Hearth* among nineteenth-century Englishmen. That Victorians saw in Reade's novel a spiritualization of human life according to a Protestant tradition surfaces in the commonly evoked analogy between the Victorian novel and Dutch and Flemish art. In analyzing Reade's nineteenth-century appeal, for example, Elton Smith ends up explaining the Victorians' taste for Dutch interiors:

> Reade felt quite free to embellish the "musty chronicle" of Erasmus' *Compendium* with fresh motivation, with historical or semi-historical characters, and with complications of plot. In a way, the plot reveals the incredible clutter of his notebooks; but this Victorian failing significantly compares with the Flemish school of painting, which also exulted in exotic possessions such as maps, rugs, pitchers, and flamboyant textures of material . . . A contemporary journal pointed out the relationship between a Nativity painting by Hans Memling (one of the historical figures introduced for a moment in the burgeoning cast) and the narrative art of Charles Reade. (Smith, *Charles Reade* 143)

Smith implies that Protestant art forms like Reade's novel humanize the divine, so Gerard's reconstructed spiritual family is thus a humanized representation of Christian archetypal figures. But when one examines the excerpt Smith cites, it turns out that what the *Blackwood's* reviewer liked so much was how the divinity of Mother and Child is conveyed by a proliferation of background material (Smith, *Charles Reade* 143–4) – "superfluous" visual details in the painting and "extraneous" plot lines in the narrative: that is, clutter. It would appear from the context in which such clutter is treasured that the appeal of Dutch and Flemish interiors to Victorians derived not so much from any celebration of material ownership, but to the humanizing of holy ideas to which such material details can be seen to contribute, a subtle but important distinction. Moreover, what is peculiarly interesting is that the Victorian reviewer here does not see the numerous "things" of an interior scene as corresponding simply to the realistic details of the novel's descriptions, but rather to its multitudinous narrative conventions and structures: Reade's "infinite variety of scenes," his "paths innumerable" (144). Whereas the evocations and allusions that so many Victorian domestic novels, particularly George Eliot's, make to Dutch painting is usually ascribed to the commodified nature of the two cultures, the more essential source of attraction appears in the review to be the dispersion of energy each form (genre painting and novel alike) enacts. Rather than focusing on the single figure or groups of figures, Dutch interior painting effects a humanization of religious themes through a deflected lens whereby significance can radiate from a variety of sources. The English novel can be said to develop a comparable structure: as Dorothea Brooke's energies follow a network of rivulets instead of single current, so do many English novels shy away from a concentrated single plot in favor of various melodramatic coincidental story-lines. The question should be asked to what extent such dispersion, as a formal characteristic, can be traced to Protestant conceptual paradigms.

Significantly, it is out of Gerard and Margaret's irregular marital condition that the home emerges, through a particularly resonant metonymy, as a figure for sociable and societal work: for when Gerard persuades his "wife" to "warmeth [her]self at the fire that warmeth [him]" by joining him in public service, his metaphor deposits the novel's hearth squarely in Margaret's new job of managing the small district of "twenty housen" (668), a situation in which the connubial pair are featured as "two saints which meet in secret to plot charity to the poor" and the final home as "a large Xenodochium to receive the victims of flood or fire" (669). In this sense, the renunciative condition that constitutes Gerard and Margaret's happy-home ending evinces the same values that Brontë and Dickens show as proper to domesticity: nonpersonal sociability and spiritually animated work. This is especially evident in Gerard and Margaret's concluding collaboration on the "Xenodochium," a term which, obsolete by the early part of the twentieth century, appears surprisingly common in Victorian historical and archaeological chronicles as designating "a house of reception for strangers and pilgrims" and, as some of the citations indicate, for paupers and needy travelers (*OED*). Although the term's nineteenth-century popularity can be ascribed to any number of cultural developments – increased travel, increased interest in ancient history and archaeological exploration, increased use of Greek derived vocabulary – it is interesting to note in the context of my argument an increased awareness of the Xenodochium as a kind of institution – an asylum or home – whose traces Victorian historiographers claimed to find in the remains of Greek settlements and medieval monasteries. Thus the *OED*'s citations record attempts to locate Xenodochia of the past ("Many have supposed the Xenodochium . . . was placed in this division of the mansion"), to outline the Xenodochium's social function ("Within the precincts of the monastery stood an edifice, distinguished by the Greek name of Xenodochium, in which a certain number of paupers received their daily support, and which was gratuitously opened to every traveler who solicited relief"), and to establish it as part of the English contemporary religious inheritance ("Long before the era of persecution had closed, the hospital and the Xenodochium, or refuge for strangers, was known among Christians").

It would seem, then, from the finale's evocation of a prototypical public housing project and from the metaphorical warmth that such social service fires exude that the novel means to move toward a synthesis between the career and the home. The title's dyad, for instance, and its varied repetition in the novel's three types of chapter titles, "The Cloister," "The Hearth" and "The Cloister and the Hearth" suggest both an antonymic and synonymic relationship for the career represented in the cloister and the home figured in the hearth. Is the hearth an alternative to the cloister or is the spatial referent both a cloister and a hearth – a meeting of ways, one professional and one domestic, at a kind of crossroad of social work? After all, in the reader's anachronistic wait for such an incisive intrusion of history as the Protestant Reformation, patience for the story's overly contrived personal dilemma wanes. Thus the urge to immerse the self in depersonalized enterprises like social service becomes an increasingly pressing readerly matter.

In this sense, the contortions the plot must perform in order to effect and preserve Gerard and Margaret's renunciatory condition – forged letters, servant foul-ups, evil-brother machinations, tavern antics, religious epiphanies, competitive perversities of renunciation – the idea of the selfless life is thrown into high relief. Faulty as it is, *The Cloister and the*

Hearth is therefore interesting in terms of how its depiction of Gerard and Margaret's concluding home, their state of renouncement, departs from the tradition of tragic genres in which renunciation involves a choice between two incompatible ideals or desires. Exposing the narrative's willingness to go to any lengths to preserve the renunciative condition, Reade's encrusted plot and a Byzantine array of narrative devices evidence a structural desire for the selfless state; such awkward pyrotechnics can ultimately be seen as working to mystify any notion of self-sacrifice by focusing on its desirability as a purportedly but perhaps impossibly nonpersonal objective.

FELIX HOLT AND THE SELFLESS CAREER

Keeping in mind the peculiar array of conceptual touchstones that *The Cloister and the Hearth*'s failings divulge, *Felix Holt* can be seen as similarly linking what Felix himself labels his "inward vocation" (468)[4] to an idea of renunciation: in devoting his "life" – as he calls his chosen career path – to the hardly concrete objective of reforming "public opinion" (401), Felix enters the novel as a self-appointed emblem of vocational devotion. Indeed, Esther idealizes Felix as the apogee of all "nobleness of character" exclusively in terms of his willingness to "renounce all small selfish motives for the sake of a great and unselfish one" (537). It is therefore no accident that the substitutive symmetry in Esther's pronouncement here, in equating "motives" with "one," avoids specifying that which is "great and unselfish" in the shape of any concrete ideal, work or project, as if the value of vocational devotion stems more from the fact of devotion than from either its contents or its products. The logic of Esther's syntax suggests, moreover, that what Felix actually acquires through his unspecified acts of renunciation is not a deed done, but a "motive"; her grammar intimates that renunciation not only precedes motive, but somehow confers it, motive thus rising as a sign of ennoblement but renunciation featured as its agent.

It would seem then that "renunciation" does not describe what Felix does so much as it surfaces in the novel as a presence – and a presence valued precisely as a generator of value. Valuable and valuating, its status is curiously complex. For as the slippery idiom "for the sake of" indicates, the activity of renouncing not only presides over the exchange of small motives *for* the great unselfish one (whatever that may be), but acts *on behalf of* the great unselfish motive – is, in this sense, a substitute for it. Because the "for the sake of" formula yields a notion of renouncing that encompasses the sense of a verb as well as of a noun, renunciation appears to operate as both agency and property, means as well as ends. By foregrounding the priority of renunciation in the novel's representation of vocational election, Esther's encomium positions renunciation as the key term in a Victorian vocabulary that fixes on work as a conceptual activity where the meaningfulness of individual life is made manifest.[5] It is therefore not enough to say that work offers a window onto Victorian literary culture without stressing that there is, at least in George Eliot's novels, an implicit notion of renunciation that invariably qualifies it.

As the *OED* documents, renunciation nearly always entails varying degrees of self-sacrifice. But the list of senses that the *OED* includes provides a repertory for the various permutations that sacrificing a self might take. "Renounce" can designate a material divestment as in the formal surrender of the world or of worldly interest "in order to live a spiritual life"; or it can mean, as in law, the resignation of a right or trust, especially of one's position as heir (and here two of the four citations are taken from George Eliot). But "renounce" can convey an idea of self-sacrifice through an embrace of the worldly as well. In this sense, self-sacrifice can take the shape of abandoning a practice, thought or belief "in open profession" to the world – to the community – or as the disclaiming of a "personal" relationship, usually in the nineteenth century, of a blood kinship.

It follows then that what counts as selfless activity, particularly in the context of how an individual comes to devote him or her self to a life, emerges as a central complication in the novel's exploration of career and heroism – or what might be called, in George Eliot's works, of plot and character. And what her novels structurally and discursively indicate is that it is specifically home life that plays more than simply a participatory role in the battle of conceptual interests whereby individualistic concerns are pitted against socially sanctioned goods. Indeed, it is an idea of home that determines how an individual character finds a lifeplot, because it is home life that proffers a narrative occasion and evaluative rhetoric for articulating that seemingly paradoxical ideal: the desired selfless career.

A QUESTION OF CHARACTER:
MR. LYON'S VOCATIONAL CRISIS

The first few chapters of *Felix Holt* make this configuration clear in their presentation of Rufus Lyon; for the conventional personal history that serves as background to Lyon's character serves also as a compact paradigm for how domesticity renovates the meaning of vocational selflessness. The central experience of this Dissenting minister's life tells the story of how the "marks of a true ministerial vocation" – marks that for Lyon had not only been self-defining, but had provided him with a prestigious job – were overshadowed by another calling – his desire to set up house with a French Catholic woman and her daughter by another man. The difficulty in locating self-sacrifice, and more signifi-cantly in conceptualizing personal desire as possibly submerged in the rhetoric of the selfless career rather than in a vocabulary antithetical to it, surfaces when Rufus Lyon resigns his ecclesiastical position in order to take up the domestic mantle by giving Annette and Esther a home:

> Those three years were to Mr. Lyon a period of such self-suppression and life in another as few men know. Strange! that the passion for this woman which he felt to have drawn him aside from the right as much as if he had broken the most solemn vows . . . the passion for a being who had no glimpse of his thoughts induced a more thorough renunciation than he had ever known in the time of his complete devotion to his ministerial career. He had no flattery now . . . The only satisfaction he had was the satisfaction of his tenderness – which meant untiring work, untiring patience, untiring wakefulness. (173–4)

That the logistics of Mr. Lyon's narrated life posit this home in contest with his profession not only invites an equation – however contraposi-tional – between home and job as both constituting potential occupa-tions or careers, but situates the domestic within a specifically Protestant idea of vocation. That is, Lyon's biographical history represents the apparent opposition between home and profession as more importantly a question of vocational alternative; by stressing that the conflict be-tween home and profession is less an oppositionary relationship than a situation of choice, the Lyon plotline's implied distinction between opposition and alternative allows home life to share the vocabulary not only of professional life but of a spiritually inspired brand of professional life, the Protestant ministry. So it is that Lyon comes to homekeeping "as some men have their special genius revealed to them by a tardy concurrence of conditions" (168). So it is that Lyon receives the news of his now Protestant adopted daughter's inheritance as a sign of divine sanction for "the cause of congregational Dissent" (506–7). So it is that what Lyon finds by building a surrogate household for these virtual strangers is not only that the higher calling is marked by an unexpected coinciding of passion and self-sacrifice – a compound perhaps more superficially recognizable in an ecclesiastical venue – but that there is a sense in which it is the work of homekeeping that offers a more thorough fulfillment of such precepts.

By requiring more self-suppression – more renunciation than even his previously "complete" ministerial devotion – Lyon's domestic work in this passage reframes romantic passion and self-gratification as both extracting the price and conferring the privilege of the ultimate sacrifice of self. The gratification home work offers Lyon is more piercing in being less self-centered at the same time that it is more personal: for it is precisely as a consequence of the structural selflessness on which his homekeeping rests that Lyon must keep "the satisfaction of his tenderness" to himself, the very category of the personal thereby possible only according to the terms of self-sacrifice. In this way, the passage defines personal satisfaction itself – an experience that would reasonably figure as an objective or result of the domestic work Lyon does – as the work itself: "untiring work, untiring patience, untiring wakefulness . . . " Through anaphorically dilated compounds that yield a sense of active stasis, ongoingness divorced from any idea of progress, and a gerund-accented vision of effort that turns work into a revisitable state of mind or condition of soul, the phrase limns vocational domesticity as what I shall provisionally call a profession – that is, a profession of renunciation.

"LOVE OF THE CREATURE"

The difficulties involved in domestic renunciation emerge at the end of *Adam Bede* when Dinah Moore, having "made great advances in household cleverness" (534)[6] surfaces as the novel's heroine when she trades in her work as a Methodist preacher for the housework of being a wife. When she explains to her aunt why she must return to her solitary ecclesiastical career, she articulates what is at stake in homekeeping:

Your wish for me to stay is not a call of duty which I refuse to hearken to because it is against my own desires; it is a temptation that I must resist lest the love of the creature should become like a mist in my soul shutting out the heavenly light. (520)

What Dinah's plot will eventually reveal is that the higher sacrifice lies in giving in to her own desires, giving in to that "love of the creature," a strange phrase indeed, that, in an almost gruesome way, comes to stand for a life devoted to homecare.

The phrase echoes Romans 1:25 when Paul condemns the gentiles because they "exchanged the truth of God for a lie, and worshipped and served the creature more than the Creator." In requiring her to accept "love of the creature" as the higher calling, Dinah's spiritual crisis demonstrates a repudiation both of Pauline doctrine and of an asceticism that is villainized throughout English domestic novels for being Roman Catholic.

But we can only read Dinah's spiritual renunciation of spiritual life as a vocational awakening in light of the historical fact that women preachers were prohibited from public speaking by the Wesleyan Methodists after 1803. The epiphanic moment in which Dinah accepts her domestic mission directs our attention towards a surrogate for public work. When Adam's mother becomes too tired to keep up "her dilettante scouring and polishing" (534), Dinah stands in with a vocational version:

She laid by the brush and took up the duster; and if you have ever lived in Mrs. Poyser's household, you would know how the duster behaved in Dinah's hand – how it went into every small corner, and on every ledge in and out of sight – how it went again and again round every bar of the chairs, and every leg, and under and over everything that lay on the table, till it came to Adam's papers and rulers, and the open desk near them. Dinah dusted up to the very edge of these, and then hesitated, looking at them with a longing but timid eye. It was painful to see how much dust there was among them . . . It was as if Dinah had put her hands unawares on a vibrating chord; she was shaken with an intense thrill. (535)

Dinah's relationship to Methodism and public preaching makes her domesticity into a career whereby loving the creature entails an unparalleled sacrifice: the sacrifice of a religious self. And it is there where Eliot places both homekeeping and the writing of prose. Indeed, as Stephen Gill points out, Elliot articulates her own goals as a novelist precisely in the terms that Dinah uses to describe her ministry (Notes to *Adam Bede* 594).[7] They are both conceived in professional terms.

DOMESTIC PROFESSIONALISM

I do not mean to say that homekeeping in Victorian England was a profession no different from that of being a surgeon, lawyer or military officer. But within a historical context, home work does, however, look strikingly similar to the kinds of occupation Victorians were beginning to call "professions." In fact, the ways in which novels like *Felix Holt* depict homekeeping suggest that it can be clearly seen as participating in what Burton Bledstein has identified as a nineteenth-century Anglo-American "culture of professionalism" – a concept which provides the terms for recognizing professionalism as an essential property of domesticity.[8] According to Bledstein the characteristics associated with the highly developed capitalist environment of Victorian England and America, such as increased divisions and specifications of time and space (e.g. breakfast-time, weekends, department stores, public parks, private bedrooms) applied also to the occupations according to which a man or woman might make his or her living: not only were leisure activities such as playing ball organized into "professional sports" whereby a "player" received wages to exercise his talents, but divisions within livelihoods such as medicine or education entailed a heightened degree of specialization whereby doctors or surgeons became, for example, orthopedists or cardiologists or podiatrists. Whereas a "professional gambler" might refer to the amateur card-player who showed a marked degree of expertise, the term came to include as well the individual who made playing cards a primary source of income (*OED*); and whereas an "amateur" once designated someone who acted out of love, the word now came to carry a disparaging connotation in the context of professionalism's new scale of value.[9] So it is in this climate of professionalism that the merchants of Treby-Magna criticize Felix's authority to debunk his father's apothecary business on the grounds that such a pronouncement comes from "one who is not a "'professor'" (*Felix Holt* 241). Although at this relatively early stage in professionalism's development, it is not specifically a degree or certificate that the townspeople want to see as proof of Felix's apothecariacal knowledge, their objection exemplifies the loose way in which the nineteenth century's vocabulary of professionalism animated so many evaluative statements.

A profession, as Bledstein outlines it, is a full-time occupation that provides a permanent source of income; it requires a lengthy process of education in an "esoteric but useful body of systematic knowledge" by which an individual turns mere talents into trained expertise and at the end of which he receives documentation as proof of his skills (*Culture of Professionalism* 86–7). Most significantly, a professional, particularly in England where those who counted themselves as members of the professional orders were more eager than their American counterparts to distinguish themselves from tradesmen, is marked by his or her devotion to "an ethic of service" – an ethic that underscores the professional's interest in a good other than material personal gain or financial profit.[10]

It is important to note, however, that there are two sides to Bledstein's historicized definition of a profession: descriptive and prescriptive. For in wielding the term "profession" both as a description of certain already recognized nineteenth-century careers (like, for example, the law or the military) and as a prescription according to which certain occupations (such as designing a building or teaching a child or commenting on a musical production) attained professional status, Bledstein plies an image of Victorian professionalism as a process – a process not unlike institutionalization. Implicit here, however, is the suggestion that professionalism, in its potential application to each and every human endeavor, functioned not only as a practical means of distinguishing various pursuits, but operated as well as a kind of judicious spectrometer by which a scale of human activities might be glimpsed: art, religion, craft and service industries alike were subject to its reach, each measured and/or shaped in terms of the degree to which each met "professional" standards. Although such standards grow more concrete as the century progresses, the values they initially measured appear strangely vague, the professional's ascension seemingly predicated on a social function that was curiously divorced from social effect. Consequently, mid-century professionalism can be historicized as something like a fad rather than as, for example, a material means of improvement. Certainly, it can be argued that the increase in professional training and standardization improved the way in which specific jobs were performed. And certainly the rise of professions played a significant socio-historical role in allowing members of the lower-middle classes to become "gentlemen" while enabling the younger sons of the aristocracy to remain so despite their need to work for a living. But the purely spiritual dimension of the professional standard, the ethos of professionalism, nevertheless appears to have an almost independent history. Depicting professionalization as a kind of Dickensian fever, for example, Bledstein attributes to it an inflated self-perpetuating quality: indiscriminately applied to each and every category of human life, the professional eye exposes "abnormality," irrationality and immorality everywhere, thereby making the job of the specialist that much more crucial to the communal welfare (*Culture of Professionalism* 102).

The reverence surrounding professionalism derived not only from this potentially universal applicability of its standards, but also from the perceived certainty of its methods: because the professional "excavated nature for its principles," professional expertise was no less than the virtually faultless means of grasping "the concept behind a functional activity" (88). Importantly, however, it is only in the context of the professional's selflessness, as evidenced by his or her remove from moneyed interests, that the surety of methodology evolves into transcendent work:

The professional did not vend a commodity, or exclusively pursue a self-interest. He did not sell a service by a contract which called for specific results in a specific time or restitution for errors. Rather, through a special understanding of a segment of the universe, the professional person released nature's potential and rearranged reality on grounds which are neither artificial, arbitrary, faddish, convenient, nor at the mercy of popular whim. Such was the august basis for the authority of the professional. (890)

In its analysis of the professional's social function, the passage makes it clear that the general societal good relies on a compound of specificity and self-sacrifice: for it is only the professional's knowledge of a particular space – a "segment of the universe" – and his or her selfless commitment to that space that ensures the community's well-being. A watered-down kind of positivist emphasis on observed particulars combined with some sign of self-sacrifice, most readily attained through a material surrender, infused professional work with its spiritual purport.

But on what basis Victorian professional standards determined the incorporation and elevation of some practices and some practitioners while barring others remains hazy. At its simplest, the professional tag can be said to amount to a question of training. Casaubon will fail in a career as a philosopher because he has not been educated in German language and literature; Gwendolyn Harleth cannot turn her drawing-room talents into an acting career because her voice has not been trained; Dinah's gift for preaching does not translate into a religious career because she has not received a clerical education. But another salient feature of professionalism, the ethic of service, poses a way in which the professional ethos distinguished activities for which training was actually irrelevant. In its deemphasis on income, English professionalism's ethic of service elevated certain religious, artistic and political callings as that much more professional, despite the absence of training required for their pursuit. With this in mind, it is possible to identify two strains of Victorian professionalism: a spiritual form, resembling what Max Weber will generally call a "vocation," developing alongside a more practical form, marked by a quasi-scientific emphasis on specialization. Although these strains are by no means mutually exclusive, it seems possible to trace a predominance of one or the other in a given historical period or culture.

In discussing what he calls George Eliot's novel of vocation, Alan Mintz identifies "the rise of the professions" in the nineteenth century as a socio-historical medium that "made it possible for the impulse toward self-aggrandizing ambition and the impulse toward selfless contribution to society to be united in a single life" (*George Eliot and the Novel of Vocation* 2). Although he does not directly address renunciation as a crucial ingredient, Mintz follows Weber's lead in tracing Eliot's use of the professions as a spiritualization of work that, in following a secularized Puritan model, combined self-realization and social participation (6). But because characters with ambitious vocations tragically cannot overcome the domestic imperatives of romance and household life, "vocation," according to the argument "is viewed as a desire that by definition cannot be fulfilled" (7). Setting up domestic ensnarement as a kind of minotaur to whom the best girls and boys are sacrificed (*Middlemarch* 253),[11] Mintz thus locates the heroism of characters like Dorothea and Lydgate in the tragic surrender of their vocational visions. Ultimately, the "talk of model farms, model hospitals, colonies of workers' cottages, and scientific farming" (*Felix Holt* 3) remains undone as each hero is as well undone by homely realities.

Although Mintz is absolutely right in emphasizing the vocational contest, the question remains why it should always be home life that inevitably wins the battle, what is it about the domestic line of development that makes its conquest such a convenient vehicle for representing tragic heroism. After all, it is certainly possible to imagine other *force majeure* realities – national events, physical or emotional diseases, wars, environmental catastrophes – that would serve to extract that same surrender of the vocational fantasy. The answer I think lies in a reevaluation of the domestic plotline precisely within, and not outside, the Protestant vocabulary Mintz uses. For it is in this sense that imagining homekeeping as a kind of profession changes the significance of the battle: it is not that the vocational path is abandoned, it is simply relocated. As Mintz says, vocation is certainly desire, but I would add that it is not facilely unfulfillable "by definition;" it is simply a particularly subtle kind of desire, the kind that demands nonpersonal gratification. And this is why I would argue that marriage, rather than disrupting the novel of vocation, cannot but be incorporated into it, precisely because the home emerges as the strongest preserve of what is so crucial to authentic vocational choice, renunciation.

If homekeeping is like a profession but nevertheless not quite the same as a profession – not quite as close to the superlative pole on the profession continuum as a career like law – the question must be asked, why draw attention to the similarity, why place it in the professional bailiwick at all? The answer is that it is only by situating domesticity in this Victorian vocabulary of professionalism, with all its spiritual and self-sacrificial specters still alive, and along the evaluative scale such a vocabulary impresses, that certain truths about what is called domestic ideology can surface. To be clear, I have argued so far that domesticity in novels like *Felix Holt*, regardless of the historical facts concerning domestic ideological imperatives and the false consciousness that the ideological label insinuates, can be described as a depiction of a specific category of activity, the work involved in devoting a life to building and maintaining a home – work that is continuous, nonteleological and self-sacrificial and that therefore constitutes a higher calling in the Protestant tradition. It is important to note that at the same time that such representations of homemaking as a spiritually inspired vocation abound in Victorian culture, there develops as well a spiritually inflected vocabulary of professionalism. In the context of *this* vocabulary, domesticity is not a leisure pursuit, not an antithesis to industrial production; the home not an antidote to the capitalist workplace or a place of material consumption or bourgeois sport. Rather it is, in nineteenth-century terms, a vocational profession.

THE HIGHER CALLING

Returning for a moment to Mr. Lyon, what his foray into homekeeping tells us is that at the heart of an individual's career choice lies this question of self-sacrifice. By placing such a premium on the renunciation of self-interest in the context of choosing a life, the novel questions what kind of relationship links this notion of vocation to what starts to look like a recurrent professing or profession of self-sacrifice; as Esther's comment on Felix's nobility indicates, it is not simply that commitment to an ennobling calling entails renunciation, but that renunciation becomes the condition that is necessary, and perhaps even sufficient, for having a calling in the first place. From this perspective, it appears that the content of Felix's character – and any action that might demonstrate it – is less important than the fact that he can be said to have it. After all, what precisely Felix does for a living, how he intends to fulfill his calling, remains perversely vague: occupied in either random "watch and clock-cleaning, and teaching one or two little chaps" (144) or in arbitrary tavern visits to "pick up conversation," with local workmen, Felix never explains with what tools or in what sense he will accomplish his purpose: reforming "the ruling belief in society about what is right and what is wrong, what is honourable and what is shameful" (401). Never does he articulate a realizable social vision or plan of action, preferring instead simple statements of moral distaste for the selfishness that drives political or socio-economic ambition and for the self-absorption that allows people to be "ground by wrong and misery, and tainted with pollution" (211). "I go for educating the non-electors," he tells Esther, "so I put myself in the way of my pupils – my academy is the beer-house" (155). Despite his propaedeutic claim, his colloquial idiom and academic metaphor ensure that how and what he will teach remain inchoate.

But as the Lyon backgrounding episode imparts, the difficulty in recognizing activities like Felix's politicking or Lyon's homekeeping as the professions and higher callings they are derives from the complexities inherent in the rhetoric of self-sacrifice – a rhetoric with which Felix is particularly enamored. In explaining to Esther, for example, why he has forsworn marriage and thereby taken a virtual vow of celibacy, he professes, "The old Catholics are right, with their higher rule and their lower. Some are called to subject themselves to a harder discipline, and renounce things voluntarily . . . It is the old word – 'necessity is laid upon me'" (363). What Felix means by these "things" is clear from the novel's onset: the inconvenience of having to financially support a wife and children, burdens he is certain would force him to "lie and simper a little, else they'll starve!" (156). Evincing a great deal of self-satisfaction in his self-sacrifice, Felix brandishes the vocabulary of the domestic life he eschews – marriage, family and livelihood – as metaphors which – as long as they remain figurative – can turn what he has renounced into what he has kept: because he has chosen to devote himself to "a family with more chances in it" rather than a family of fortune (367), Felix assures himself that no matter what the outcome of his trial, "they can't rob me of my vocation. With poverty for my bride, and preaching and pedagogy for my business, I am sure of a handsome establishment" (468). In this sense, the rhetoric of self-sacrifice converts a loss–gain dichotomy into something more complex when the loss so invariably resounds as a gain: Felix cannot be robbed because his state of self-sacrifice has already changed the idea of being without into an idea of possession. Surely it is not accidental that the tropes Felix finds most apt to convey this retributive rendering of renunciation and self-sacrifice are connubial, household commonplaces.

In the context of such a renunciation-mathematics, it is not surprising that, according to the *OED*'s final listing, "renounce" was often used in popular nineteenth-century cardgames to refer to playing a card of a different suit from that which has been led, implying either the possession or want of a proper card. In other words, Victorian parlour-game sociability accommodates the sense in which renunciation entailed unexpected reverses in loss–gain ratios. It is not until another instance of parlour sociability, a love scene with Esther, that it becomes obvious how the "things" renounced and the role of self in the renunciation economy might have lost their purported clarity:

"I want you to tell me – once – that you know it would be easier to me to give myself up in loving and being loved, as other men do, when they can, than to – "

This breaking-off in speech was something quite new in Felix. For the first time he had lost his self-possession, and turned his eyes away. He was at variance with himself . . .

"This thing can never come to me twice over. It is my knighthood. That was always a business of great cost" . . .

Felix reproached himself. He felt that they must not marry – that they would ruin each other's lives. But he had longed for her to know fully that his will to be always apart from her was renunciation, not an easy preference. (418–19)

In prose divided between thought-report and dialogue, aurally fractured by aposiopesistic speech and visually broken by dash-designated qualifiers and hyphenated compounds, the object of Felix's renunciation materializes simultaneously with the object of his desire: fancying his newly realized passion for Esther to constitute a test of his heroism – of his knighthood – he loses "possession" of himself, is "at variance with himself," requires another to confirm what had until now been an independent inward conviction. Felix breaks off because the economics of renunciation have gotten too complicated, the formula that charts what is lost, gained or traded has in fact reversed its terms: whereas it is clear in Felix's idiolect that taking Esther as his wife would require him to "give up [him]self" – or what until this point has amounted to himself, his vocation – it becomes clear in the passage's structure that Felix has sudden doubts as to what falls on which side of the renunciation equation. It would be easier to give himself up than to do what? Than to give up himself? In other words, it is easier to forswear a home with Esther than to acknowledge that the conditions securing his supposedly self-abnegating "vocation" are in actuality self-affirming and thus in some sense evidence that his celibate vocation is a sham, is nothing more than a product of false consciousness no matter how well intentioned. The repressed phrase that Felix wants Esther to voice – that she recognizes his sacrifice as *self*-sacrifice – is never confirmed as being the case; it remains at the end of their dialogue as Felix's un-uttered desire for Esther to think that his "will" to renounce her is different from his desire to have her – and for her to believe that his passion for his work is not desire. For clearly the question has become which is the more difficult job? Which requires the most work? The most sacrifice? Would it really be easier for Felix to give himself up or is that precisely the cost of this knighthood business – precisely the price vocational commitment extracts – precisely the ironically sought-after renunciation: giving up the self-sacrificial career in an ironically self-sacrificial gesture. By the end of their exchange, renunciation itself thus surfaces as the prize: it is no longer quite something done, but a property that Felix wants to hear that he has. In this sense, it is the alternative life Esther offers – presumably a home – and thus the eruption of a marriage plot into Felix's career path – that throws into question what possessing selflessness might mean.

THE WORK MADE MANIFEST

For all the priority it places on the spirit of the moral work for which Felix is willing to sacrifice so much, the novel never fully discredits the value of that work's substance; but it does rely on a domestic story-line of romance, marriage and home to reveal that Felix's occupation is more than a botched attempt to halt a riot. The sign that Felix is in fact engaged in something more than ambling around the countryside exuding righteousness emerges in the effect he has on Esther, the deeds and choices that compose her own lifeplot thus serving as the only available proof of Felix's work.[12] So it is that by claiming not to have been able to "see the meaning of anything fine" until "hearing what Felix Holt said, and seeing that his life was like his words" (537), Esther legitimizes Felix's vocation not only literally by defending him at his trial but, more importantly, in the language of her own psychological character development. But it is ironically this rhetoric of self-denial that animates Esther's epiphany in two important ways: for what it is about Felix that effects the change in Esther and how the novel makes her personal realization manifest pivot on a valuation of nonpersonal categories and the degree to which self-sacrifice as a quality of mind might stand as their expression. After all, what makes an impression on Esther has more to do with Felix's purportedly selfless life than with any compassion for the suffering poor or the unenfranchised laborers he wants to reform: for not only do nearly all of Felix's conversations with Esther either highlight his electing "hardship" and "privation" as a "better lot" (537) or showcase his proud conviction that "the universe has not been arranged for the gratification of his feelings" (556), but Esther never indicates that she has caught his averred concern for social principles. Indeed, her heroism relies strictly on the particular moment of her "final choice" (590): whether to marry Harold Transome and assume her rights to the Transome estate or to renounce her claims and hope for a life alongside the selfless and hence morally superior Felix. How it is that the novel situates the right choice in a home with Felix depends precisely on the rhetoric that makes self-sacrifice a vocational property – a good in and of itself. From a practical point of view, had social welfare really been Esther's objective, surely her position as mistress of the Transome estate and heiress to its family's wealth would have afforded her a practical means of doing great good: the possibility of a career in philanthropy, a choice that so many wealthy Victorian men and women actually did make.[13]

The rightness of Esther's choice, however, relies – like Felix's – not so much on performing specific good acts, but on her willingness to surrender something (in her case, the estate) and what such an act of surrendering represents. On the one hand, there is in Esther's choice an embrace of renunciation by virtue of the material sacrifices it would entail: marrying Felix, she muses, would mean accepting "the dim life of the back street, the contact with sordid vulgarity, the lack of refinement for the sense, the summons to a daily task" (591). Such article-headed nominal clauses, however, offer up a pastiche of abstract static states that makes her future life looks less like an impoverished lifestyle than a collection of spiritual properties: despite the bald qualifying phrases represented in the "back street," the "vulgarity" and the "daily task," the sentence convenes "life," "contact," and "summons" in a quickened visionary triptych that adds a hallowed aura to this vision of Esther's future. In this sense, Esther's marriage choice is not a vote for Felix. It is not simply Felix the beloved who figures as the "gain that was to make that life of privation something on which she dreaded to turn her back," but the idea of renunciation that contact with him has made manifest. Although it is unclear whether Felix will ever really have an effect on any workers, the narrated phrases of Esther's imagination apotheosize him precisely as that force which will check "her self-satisfied pettiness with the suggestion of a wider life" (468). It is here in the workings of a narrated mind that Felix's work evinces itself as a higher calling.

In this sense, the novel uses Esther's psychology as a kind of showcase for an idealized selflessness. And certainly what she gives up by surrendering the "imaginary mansion" of her childhood fantasies (500) is the psychologically self-centered Freudian family romance fantasy of noble-birth-after-all, thereby embracing a very different kind of personal past: the childhood household of her adopted father's home. Significantly, the novel adumbrates her final rejection of Transome Court with the oblique statement that she began to understand "what it would be to abandon her own past" (496). The question immediately registers, which past does she mean? The childhood experience of Mr. Lyon's home or the childhood fantasy of an aristocratic estate that an older past of blood relations might now legitimize? Through a syntactical ordering that places the future before the past and a subjunctive phrasing that allows biographical time to make the Transome home and the parish home interchangeable, Esther's statement suggests that the choice of home is a choice of what kind of past will serve as "her own past" – the one of selfish fantasy and familial blood ties or the one of household routines and adopted relations. Her final choice suggests that the right home is the task-filled cottage belonging to a biological stranger, a place gained only if a psychologically delineated personal past of fantasy is renounced.

The personal past of fantasy that the rhetoric of renunciation renders undesirable is linked in an unexpected way to an idea of change. For although the most striking feature of Transome Court is its stillness, such motionless desuetude always conveys a sense that it had not always been so: its "darkened" windows, uncut grass, unswept fallen fir needles and absence of gardeners or servants thus conspire to impress the Transome estate's representation of the past with the signs of change – change which can figure only as devolution. But whereas this renounced home divulges an alliance between stillness and change, motion is found in the changeless activities of "the old-fashioned, grazing, brewing, wool-packing, cheese-loading life of Treby-Magna" (124). Embedded in this montage of cropped, collaterally arranged and anaphorically united scenes, the Dissenting pastor's home is metonymically associated with the gerund-wrought continuity of small-town workings. The homey virtues of the right home materialize in the hometown details of a past marked by an almost oxymoronic active changelessness. And this is where the recidivistic leanings characteristic of so many domestic novels appear in *Felix Holt* to result from the way in which literary montage can depersonalize the past. That is, the active changelessness limned in Treby-Magna's hometown-iness is the effect of a technical device: the literary collage. As the right past, this Treby-Magna home comes to supplant Esther's own personal, imagined past. But because this right past cannot be separated from the montage technique that presents it as such and because this technique also presents such a past as actively changeless, the recidivism of domestically committed plots is more complicated than simply a yearning for the way things used to be, the world of the past or the past of personal origins. The Bretton residence in England, Joe Gargery's Forge, the Marshalsea, do not become idealized homes simply because they represent a lost past, but because they embody a spirit of ongoing activity that precludes differentiating any notion of the past in the first place.

Meanwhile, change in this novel, when not typified as devolution, seems either to disappear or to be channeled into a notion of character that can develop only along domestic lines. Although Esther's choice of the right home's bustling changelessness results from the fact that she herself has changed, this personality conversion crystallizes only through domestic gestures that carry a heightened sense of significance. When, for example, Esther demonstrates affection for her adopted father by making his tea, the minister muses "with wonder of the treasures still left in our fallen nature" (214); and when she carries his things upstairs and makes him porridge the narrative comments, "Very slight words and deeds may have a sacramental efficacy, if we can cast our self-love behind us" (546). It is not simply that contact with a domestic implement confers nobility or designates election, but that in the context of a plotline that presents home life as a career and profession reserved for the spiritually elect, such domesticities appear charged with meaning. The novel illustrates the difference when, upon her return from Transome Court, Esther immediately combs her father's hair and straightens up his study, inveighing now against Lyddy's false religious enthusiasms because they keep her from "brushing [Mr. Lyon's] clothes and putting out [his] clean cravat." Although Esther had always criticized Lyddy in a vocabulary of household words, complaining that Lyddy's crying over the soup made it too salty, the censure now carries the stamp of a critique, of a loftier, perhaps even more expert, judgment: for it is the selfless concern for another that makes the details of housework more than matters of convenience or comfort. In this way, Esther establishes her own housekeeperly authority when she pronounces upon Lyddy by turning evangelical expressions into domestic metaphors: "[Lyddy] is always saying her righteousness is filthy rags, and really I don't think that is a very strong expression for it. I'm sure its dusty clothes and furniture" (504). Good housekeeping emerges as the ascendant mode of ethical valuation.

And this is precisely when the structural status of the Lyon vocational crisis episode, once repressed as parenthetical external analepsis meant to gloss Mr. Lyon's character and his relationship with Esther, returns as central to the novel's primary plotline. For the most tangible effect of Felix's exemplary career, besides the domestication of Esther's personality that marks her as the heroine he is destined to marry, is how his influence ultimately breathes life into the surrogate father–daughter relationship lying at the heart of Esther's domestic awakening. In this sense, the "retribution" that Felix teasingly calls his future marriage to Esther (603) occurs structurally when the satellite background material of Lyon's foray into homekeeping is recovered on a higher narrative level as a kernel function essential to the meaning of the story as a whole.[14] A reconstruction of the plot will then yield the following scenario. The novel marks Esther's character development by showing her engaged in activities and committed to choices that legitimize a surrogate familial relationship; this surrogate father–daughter relationship, resulting as it does from Mr. Lyon's domestic episode, represents in condensed form a valorization of Lyon's experience of homekeeping as a vocation; a legitimization of her adopted father's domestic professions, Esther's household conduct also happens to provide the sign of Felix's hitherto invisible work. Her domestic activity shows Felix's vocation itself to be, after all, literally home-making.

FELIX THE HOMEKEEPER

How Felix "The Radical," whose tremendous physical stature and roughly-hewn carriage generally code him as virile, finally reveals himself as homekeeper *par excellence*, can be seen in how the novel surreptitiously mines his vocabulary for a pattern of terms that lead to home via a gender-neutral vocational corridor. In articulating his inward calling, for example, Felix asserts that he cannot expect to see the results of his "particular work" (556) because "'Where great things can't happen, I care for very small things, such as will never be known beyond a few garrets and workshops'" (557). In thus exhibiting what can be called an ethos of particularization, Felix speaks in a Protestant ideolect whereby the summons to worldly engagement can take the shape of involvement in the minutia of daily life. In so far as these Protestant values have been secularized, it follows that Felix should speak Professionalism as well: like the specialist described by Bledstein, Felix concentrates in his worldly work only on that small "segment of the universe." Hence Felix's Protestant-esque professionalism is established by the way the attention he pays to the small and the narrow play into the novel's spiritually resonant accentuation of the particular.

Showing Felix to have adopted this Protestant elevation of small worldly works, the novel goes on in a different instance to equate worldliness as a quality of mind with domestic expertise: the oddness of Mr. Lyon's manners and social behavior thus due to his "unworldliness . . . in small matters" (163). Noteworthy here is that the novel, in its depiction of Mr. Lyon's character, does not cite his sex as the cause of his domestic illiteracy, but stresses instead his absentmindedness, a trait that makes him a comical (however lovable) figure to the townspeople, not to mention a minor minister in a less than prestigious pastorate. Unworldly as he is in the small matters that preoccupy his neighbors, Mr. Lyon is consequently caught off-guard when the otherwise histori-cally resonant year of 1812 turns out to be significant primarily as the date on which "romance did befall him" (163). In the metaphorical vanquishing of Mr. Lyon's "fall" before romance and in his consequent lackluster ministerial career, there is a shadowy sense that had Mr. Lyon been more domestic, been perhaps as methodical as Felix, he would also have been more of a man.

This is not to say that gender plays no role in novelistic plots centered on domestic story-lines; it is only to call attention to how *Felix Holt*, in its severe focus on the Protestant spirit and the formal structures that spin out of it, makes such topics less relevant than they may have been in the "real" life of its readers. When sexual difference is addressed, as in fact it often is, the novel pointedly uses its ethos of particularization to dismiss it as precisely that veil which hides the higher calling. For example, when Esther and Felix discuss the difference between men and women, Felix presumes that women never choose hardship like his "unless they are Saint Theresas or Elizabeth Frys," to which Esther counters that a woman cannot but choose "hardship as a better lot" because only "meaner things are within her reach" (367). Although superficially commenting on the different socially prescribed destinies that divide the sexes, Esther rhetorically checkmates Felix by translating his idea of hardship into her "meaner things," thereby resituating his apparent Protestant sensibility in a grammar of genderless professional particularization. As a life of these meaner things is presumably what both Esther and Felix seek, it follows that the spirit of specialization that infuses such quotidities with higher meaning also desexualizes the whole process of vocational election. In other words, the banter here is less concerned with sexual difference – whether real or perceived – than with locating the pivotal characteristic of vocational election in the domestic plottings of hearthside meaner things.

What kind of homekeeper Felix represents, however, shows the homewardly developed Victorian novel in a social role different from that which can be seen in either Brontë or Dickens. True, the end of Felix Holt pictures Felix and Esther bound for a spiritually lofty, never-never-land home ostensibly devoted to an abstracted idea of social work and communal imperatives. But the ethos of particularization that professionalizes both Esther and Felix, the spiritually infused methodology that makes them into domestic specialists, shows them not quite as housekeepers at work in preserving arenas of nonpersonal sociability, but as professional keepers of a specific set of communitarian-like ethics. It is through the training Esther receives in Felix's presence that she acquires a certain kind of moral appreciation – what might be called a kind of ethical taste that makes selfish actions not simply wrong, but unpalatable. The aesthetic component mixed into her ethical epiphany surfaces in the metaphors the novel conjures in describing Esther's moment of romantic choice. Prefacing her final decision, this aesthetic-ethic hybridization first appears when Harold assures himself that "Esther was too clever and tasteful a woman to make a ballad heroine of herself, by bestowing her beauty and her lands on this lowly lover" (536). Relying on a correspondence between aesthetic valuations and class structure, Harold's rhetoric uses the kitschiness of a ballad to invoke an idea of taste as a final arbiter in questions of social correctness.

But Esther overturns his judgment by revealing herself to possess too tasteful a sensibility and too professional a taste to fall for such middle-brow reasoning as that which would define the valuable as no more than economic standing. Demonstrating precisely the refinement Bledstein ascribes to the professionalized intellect, Esther reasons with precision, plumbs what Bledstein calls the "esoteric, but useful body of systematic knowledge" (*Culture of Professionalism* 86–7) that here one might call ethics, in order to identify those "principles" (88) by which the valuable might be glimpsed: half-wishing to be saved "from the effort to find a clue of principle amid the labyrinthine confusions of right and possession," Esther deliberates on how difficult it was "by any theory of providence, or consideration of results, to see a course which she could call duty" (*Felix Holt* 524). Having received the education of witnessing Felix's exemplary vocational renunciations, Esther finally arrives at a scale of valuation that counters Harold's overly literal idea of worth:

> this life at Transome . . . gave an air of moral mediocrity to all her prospects . . . All life seemed cheapened; as it might seem to a young student who, having believed that to gain a certain degree he must write a thesis in which he would bring his powers to bear with memorable effect, suddenly ascertained that no thesis was expected, but the sum (in English money) of twenty-seven pounds ten shillings and sixpence. (524)

By demonstrating her good judgment, Esther's choice of the right home suggests the extent to which her judgment is depicted as professional. Here there is a loose parallel between what Freedman discusses as "aestheticist professionalism" and George Eliot's brand of vocational domesticity, the rise of the professional aesthete as a keeper of "culture" thus comparable in a certain sense to the rise of the domestic professional as a keeper of "ethics" – a kind of ethicete. According to Freedman's argument, English aestheticism participated in English professionalist culture by mirroring and generating that "discreet form of professionalism" which I have called professionalism's spiritual strain: emphatically divorcing themselves from "the acquisitive, work-oriented ethos of the bourgeois economy" (*Professions of Taste* 53), late nineteenth-century aesthetes constituted "a new caste of professionals who designated themselves as experts in cultural knowledge, and who defined their own role as that of instructing others in the lineaments of that knowledge" (55). Indeed, Esther evinces in her metaphor's decided rejection of the moneyed path to scholarly expertise a reliance on a spirit of specialization that changes the terms according to which the valuable is determined: value is not an easily locatable object indiscriminately accessible to any seeker willing to pay a literal fee, but a whole life of "prospects" available only to those spiritually correct professionals chosen and trained to fossick for it. With this in mind, it is peculiarly interesting that *Felix Holt* closes with Esther reminding us that she is a teacher: "'I mean,'" she tells Felix in describing what their future home will be like, "'to go on teaching a great many things'" (602). Although the prospective Holt home is not the literal schoolroom that closes the pages of *Villette* – even if Felix does tease Esther that her plans must include improving his French accent – there is at the novel's close a clear propaedeutic imperative, albeit articulated obliquely.

CHAPTER 6

A prejudice for milk: professionalism, nationalism and domesticism in Daniel Deronda

Emerging from *Felix Holt* is a vision of the homecrafter as a civics specialist. She, or he, qualifies as a kind of civics professor not only by doing selfless work for a collective good but by virtue of the exemplary value residing in a career composed of such deeds. In this the home-crafter resembles the professional Weber describes in a different context as following an ethic of ultimate ends.[1] Whereas the professional who follows an ethic of responsibility might, like Will Ladislaw, choose a political career whereby he could vote for laws requiring factory-owners to pay their workers a minimum subsistence wage, the professional who follows an ethic of ultimate ends might, like *Shirley*'s Caroline Helstone in her self-flagellating relationship with the factory-owning Robert Moore, believe that playing cards or reading Shakespeare in the company of a specific factory-owner can eventually instill in him a sense of responsibility for his workers' welfare.[2] For Weber, both careerists are professional politicians, but each perceives the primary sphere of moral action in different places.

In this light, the homecraft typical of Victorian mid-century domestic plots can be understood as a type of ethical profession and the home-bound novel seen as a version of the novel of vocation rather than an alternative to it. As professional culture develops during the last part of the nineteenth century, however, domesticity becomes one among several other competing lines of professional plot development.

DOMESTICITY AND PROFESSIONAL CULTURE

Although domestic heroes and heroines like Anne Elliot, Lucy Snowe, Wemmick and Pip, Little Dorrit, Rufus Lyon and Esther (as well as Carolyn Helstone and her mother, Dinah Morris, Dorothea Brooke and Mary Garth) illustrate domesticity as a spiritually elevated vocation, they maintain an amateurish air that qualifies their professionalism and

151

distinguishes it by virtue of silent self-sacrifice: good deeds anonymous and unacknowledged. Deeds hidden, that is, until they are publicized by a novel. In other words, the domestic worker's amateurism, her or his working for love rather than for a living, preserves some notion of self-sacrifice in so far as it requires work to be wageless unrewarded in the most literal sense. In the amateur professionalism of homecraft, the absence of a wage serves as a kind of objective correlative for the selflessness associated to spiritual election. Alternatively, the specter of the wage calls attention to another issue; for it stresses the extent to which an exploration of the symbiotic relationship between Victorian domesticity and professionalism inevitably touches on the role of the "middle class" and its "domestic ideology."

Can the Victorian domestic plot be discussed independently of class? Yes and no. "Class," in the strict economic sense of a group's connection to the means of production, is seen among some historians as a relatively insignificant category in English nineteenth-century history. David Cannadine, for example, writes:

The Industrial Revolution has been reinterpreted as a gradual process, which produced neither a self-conscious working class nor a homogeneous bourgeoisie . . . Throughout the mid-Victorian period, the middle class remained weak and divided, and there was no such thing as a labor aristocracy. Even in the closing decades of the nineteenth century, the bourgeoisie failed to achieve economic or cultural preeminence, while the working class was predominantly conservative and quiescent, often divided internally against itself. Instead of being a society torn apart by class antagonisms, nineteenth-century Britain was a country characterized by a high degree of consensus . . . where national loyalties outweighed sectional interests.[3]

But, as Cannadine goes on to point out , "class," in the sense of "those finely graded distinctions of prestige ranking to which sociologists give the name status," is unquestionably central to the Victorian frame of mind: "Yet, despite the best efforts of many of today's historians to take class out of the nineteenth century, the fact remains that the Victorians were obsessed with it – or, at least something like it" (57). It would seem that though Victorians might have belonged to a specific class, rarely did they exhibit a consciousness of that class. They did nevertheless speak incessantly of class as a general category, as if its terms were open to interpretation. Sarah Ellis, for example, begins her domestic conduct book by addressing the middle classes as those who have "one to four domestics – who on the one hand, enjoy the advantages of a liberal education, and on the other hand have no pretension to family rank"

(*Women of England* 24–5). But that definition soon gives way when she states that these parameters should not restrict her audience because, given the period's economic uncertainties, members of one class are always in danger of slipping down into the next. If the upper classes were slipping into the middle, while the middle were slipping into the working, Ellis implies, it is probably best that everyone expect to be both middle class and not middle class – that is, middle class or "something like it."

Describing that category – that "something like class" – is the difficulty confronting theorists of the novel, an aesthetic form that has been connected to the rise of the middle class since Watt and Lukács[4] wrote their pioneering studies. The history of the novel, like the history of domesticity, presumes the centrality of a capitalist middle class. This assumption causes problems, however, when it becomes the backdrop for reading certain types of scenes. In a paradigmatic domestic segment at Wemmick's castle, for example, Dickens emphasizes that Miss Skiffins "washed-up the tea things, in a trifling lady-like amateur manner that compromised none of us" (*Great Expectations* 315). Some question of class is clearly there, but fraught by various apparent ironies. That Miss Skiffins washed the dishes *herself* is as important to the scene as the air of leisure she assumes. The dynamics of the scene and its precious self-consciousness appeal to a relationship between two ostensibly antagonistic elements: work and leisure. Surely if the need were simply to distinguish Miss Skiffins from the manual-labor working class, it would not be necessary to show her routinely putting her hands to work every Sunday afternoon. She might have been depicted only as a middle-class lady generally is: as an administrator, the head and not the hands of the household.[5] As I have argued before, Protestant cultural residues complicate the scene's work ethic. But even an English sociology of religion loses its coherence when it incorporates nineteenth-century class distinctions: the socio-economic composition of Dissenters, for example, when compared to say, Low Anglicans, is so overdetermined by a set of plastic dichotomies (urban versus rural, manufacturing versus agricultural, Oxbridge versus locally educated) that calling one middle class and one lower class loses its usefulness.[6]

This is only to point out that the subtleties and ironies of Miss Skiffins, "trifling, lady-like amateur" work are unrepresentable in the terms provided by those historical accounts of domesticity and those histories of the novel that do not acknowledge the presence of a professional class and a professional ideology in Victorian literary and intellectual culture. The explanation for this missing piece of the jigsaw is not necessarily that Marxist history or Marxist criticism overemphasizes the endemic and often cooptive presence of capitalist ideology; for professionalism itself can be legitimately seen as a sophisticated extension of that capitalism. I do not mean to suggest that these writers wrongly represent Victorian reality, only to suggest that Victorian literature may not have represented that reality accurately. While this possibility is hardly an insightful proposition, it helps to explain why a particular set of truisms that literary critics have borrowed from historians sometimes distorts the significance of middle-class ideology in the Victorian imagination.

OFFENDENE AND IMAGINED DOMESTICITY

Nowhere is the presence of professionalism and the erosion of conventional conceptions of class more evident than in the cosmopolitan world of *Daniel Deronda*. The first home presented in the novel raises important questions about the relationship of the home both to class and to nationhood. Humiliated at the gambling tables of the continent, Gwendolen Harleth returns to her English homeland and to Offendene. "Just large enough to be called a mansion," Offendene is difficult to rent because it has no landed property attached to it and so is "rather too anxiously ornamented with stone" (51),[7] an adverbial mismodifier that inscribes English architecture with the signs that all is not well in the state of England. Gentility, however, is still self-evident:

> But inside and outside it was what no beholder could suppose to be inhabited by retired tradespeople: a certainty which was worth many conveniences to tenants who not only had the taste that shrinks from new finery, but also were in the border-territory of rank where annexation is a burning topic. (51)

Socio-economic anxiety, the possibility of falling into a lower class, is assuaged here by the "certainty" of having "taste." But the sentence nevertheless culminates in a striking metonymic figure: the English upper classes are depicted as a "border-territory" vulnerable to "annexation." Despite the certainty of taste, the Englishmen of the passage face a double-edged threat in an annexation of which they may be either objects or agents.

Collapsing anxiety and ambition in this way, hypothetical annexation presumes a plot of social positioning perfectly in keeping with the conventions of the Continental drawing-room comedy of manners. What is interesting here, however, is that the domestic discourse of the manor house is taken over by territorial tropes. Interrupting the description of the Offendene home, a new catachrestic figure emerges: the geopolitical rhetoric that seizes on a border-territory's vulnerability to annexation in order to represent socio-economic uncertainty presumes that it is possible to match the idea of a home to the idea of a national territory.

In this sense the domestic figure that dominates Gwendolen's home-coming not only conveys a sense of nationalistic anxiety, but locates that anxiety in an often neglected social class. As Bourdieu has maintained, this class is not defined, as Marx would have it, by its economic relationship to the means of production, but by a complicated notion of prestige – a prestige whose reactionary anti-materialist modesty relies nevertheless on a tacit elitism. So it is that the shabby "sombre furniture and faded upholstery" (51) of Offendene, Gwendolen's subjunctive home, is morally preferable to the wealthy and onomastically tainted Diplow and Ryelands. Removed both from secure land and from capitalist enterprise, the border-territory that functions as Gwendolen's adopted home tells the story of the way in which class identity can be somehow implicated in an unsettled sense of national consciousness. The passage thus indicates that the English novel of 1876 is not about class, but about nation.

Given these variables, it is no wonder that the domestic lines of development of *Daniel Deronda* will ultimately turn away from the home and towards a more abstracted community: the homeland. Although the domestic community of a household can be abstracted, in theory, in the minds of those who have left it, it can also be experienced first hand. The domestic community of a nation, however, can only be imagined. As Benedict Anderson has argued, the nation "is *imagined* because the members of even the smallest nation will never know most of their fellow-members, meet them, or even hear of them, yet in the minds of each lives the image of their communion" (5–6).[8] Abstracted, imagined, the community of the nation poses a set of new difficulties for the narrating of domesticity.

Offendene is Gwendolyn's subjunctive home in the sense that Eliot uses this house that is not home as an occasion for ruminating on the origins of that "wider life" – that broader vision whose conspicuous absence is of such pressing concern to the narrator:

Pity that Offendene was not the home of Miss Harleth's childhood, or endeared to her by family memories! A human life, I think, should be well rooted in some spot of native land, where it may get the love of tender kinship for the face of the earth, for the labours men go forth to, for the sounds and accents that haunt it, for whatever will give that early home a familiar unmistakable difference amidst the future widening of knowledge: a spot where the definiteness of early memories may be inwrought with affection, and kindly acquaintance with all neighbours, even to the dogs and donkeys, may spread not by sentimental effort and reflection, but as a sweet habit of the blood. (50)

A human life, she intones, should have a native home base because that is where a series of desirable desires are shaped. The operative phrase of the second sentence's complicated syntax is "love of tender kinship for." A home cultivates "love of tender kinship for" a host of objects: for earth, for labor, for sounds and accents, for whatever will preserve the home in memory. The home emerges here as an intellectual ability, a way of thinking "amidst the future widening of knowledge." It is a way of thinking that looks very much like what Harry Frankfurt calls a "second order desire," by which he designates a desire for a desire: "Besides wanting and choosing and being moved *to do* this or that, men may also want to have (or not to have) certain desires and motives."[9] For Frankfurt, desire of a second order differentiates humans from animals; it is the sign taken as a precondition for civilization, which is precisely what Eliot is interested in when she talks about the good of "some spot of native land." Such a spot of native land produces that higher state of civilization known to intellectuals as universalism; for Eliot's virtually Germanic compound subject, "love of kinship for mankind" designates, not a love of mankind, but a love of loving mankind, that is, a type of second-order desire. As both sign of and precondition for, second-order desires can be both cause and consequence of civilization. And so Eliot's phrase, "a love of kinship for" invokes a desire of a desire as an object impossibly connected to civilization, to "the labours men go forth to," but her protracted syntax circumlocuates how native soil produces love of kinship for humanity. For at the same time that native land produces love of kinship for "the face of the earth" (humanity), for the work men do and the languages they speak, the ultimate direct object is "for whatever will give that early home a familiar, unmistakable difference," which is to say, this love of kinship for universal mankind returns us tautologically to loving our original spot of native land.

Although Henry James, in reviewing *Daniel Deronda* for *The Nation*,[10] praised the novel for its sense of the universal, the famous Offendene passage discloses a central ambiguity in how Eliot constructs events that transform, as another reviewer put it, Daniel's "capacities into acquisitions, by leading him home to his own race."[11] Eliot wants to convince her readers not only that this figure of racial homecoming signals the materiality of interiority, the making of a capacity into an acquisition, inner quality into outer property (exactly the opposite of what Jeff Nunokawa has rightly claimed she does in earlier novels),[12] but that racial homecoming can also signal a higher state of civilization, universality. The question emerges as to why the narrative should strain so to use the home as a representation of universality. For how can an object marked by its "unmistakable difference" function as a producer of universal kinship, that is, of sameness?

James' comment is based on Klesmer's denunciation of a Bellini aria as an expression of "a puerile state of culture – no sense of the universal." And his conclusion remains valid as long as Eliot confines herself to the international world of professional art. But when Eliot attempts to locate that sense of the universal in a habit of the blood, the narrative falters. The idea that domesticity, imagined here as habits of the *blood*, can produce a higher state of civilization, one based on a second-order desire like universality, gets lost in the muddle of the passage's protracted syntax, as if to suggest that in the metaphoric expansion of the home into the nation, the distinction between fantasy and reality, novel and experience, is unsuccessfully camouflaged. This is important to the history of literary domesticity in so far as Eliot's failure to make the home the nation calls into question the usefulness of metaphorical domesticity in the legitimization of extradomestic activities at all. Whereas Oliphant, for example, like many other conservative Victorian feminists, could envision an expansion of the female private sphere by collapsing public politics into drawing-room sociability, Eliot's narration discloses the speciousness of publicizing the private. As this discussion will hopefully demonstrate, the novel's home fails to expand, cannot fill the cultural universalism that forms its outside space, because Eliot makes it clear that the act of making the home public by making it professional is an artistic act. By making the artistry of professionalizing the home overt, Eliot's domesticity must unmask the essential oxymoron at the heart of the professional home. This disclosure takes shape in the terms of an intellectual's vocational crisis and his remedial turn to nationalism for a succor that will reinscribe the amateur–professional dialectic in novelistic discourse.

CITIZEN OF THE WORLD: IMAGINED DOMESTICITY AND IMPARTIALITY

Let us return to the Offendene passage and further explore how Eliot traces love of kinship for universal mankind to territorial instincts. In a muffled echo of Edmund Burke's conception of the nation's origins, Eliot uses domesticity to discuss the origins of civilization.[13] As if to explain the apparent circularity of an argument that begins and ends with "habits of the blood," she enjoins another set of metaphors:

At five years old, mortals are not prepared to be citizens of the world, to be stimulated by abstract nouns, to soar above preference into impartiality; and that prejudice in favor of milk with which we blindly begin, is a type of the way body and soul must get nourished at least for a time. The best introduction to astronomy is to think of the nightly heavens as a little lot of stars belonging to one's own homestead. (50)

Although Eliot ranks "preference" below "impartiality," preference – or prejudice – is still the only road to those higher impartial ways. But "impartiality" raises a set of difficult issues for the novel, particularly in the context of the grammar according to which Daniel's heroism is inscribed. Rather than beginning with a preference that will take him to impartiality, Daniel begins at the end, already occupying that impartial state.

Daniel's impartiality initially emerges as a tragic flaw in a scene that seems to satirize what is now called professional culture at the same time as it devalues domestic surrogacy. When the receipt of a letter from a Cambridge Don gives Daniel's surrogate uncle Sir Hugo an "air at once business-like and leisurely" (215), Daniel sees an unexpected opportunity. The "air," metonymically transferred through the letter to the London home from Oxbridge, positions Sir Hugo as a familiar intermediary who will secure for his promising young "nephew" placement in a profession by taking advantage of any number of family networks, a common means to successful professional establishment in the days before the 1870s and 1880s civil service and educational reforms (Davidoff and Hall, *Family Fortunes* 263; Cannadine, *The Decline and Fall* 238; Perkin, *The Rise of Professional Society* 119). The reference to Sir Hugo's proximity to Cambridge Dondom, however, does not incite Daniel to pursue information about the expected family connection (the Oxbridge contact), but rather spurs him on to inquire into another family connection, the very literal question of his mysterious heritage and feared illegitimate birth. Professional protocol yields narrative space to a story fraught with potential psychological resonance.

Only a paragraph earlier, the novel makes it clear that Daniel is haunted by his imagined illegitimacy: Daniel begins his novel with "his mind turned to a cabinet of estate maps in the library, where he had once seen an illuminated parchment hanging out, that Sir Hugo said was the family tree" (210). Familial lineage is Daniel's apparent concern. But Sir Hugo understands the "lineage" of kinship in terms of institutional affiliation, that is, in terms of careerism. The misunderstanding is suggestive of the key languages informing the novel's discourse. For although Sir Hugo's air of leisurely business is not the invitation to intimacy Daniel seeks, leisure business appears here as a precondition for asking such psychologically resonant questions as "who is my father?" and "who am I?" This air of mock business, of business-likeness or *playing* at business, straddles the central opposition of domestic ideology – that between work and leisure – at the same time that it conditions the representation of Daniel's psychological interiority.

So it is that when Daniel asks his euphemistic uncle, "What do you intend me to be, Sir?" (215), the idiom most immediately available, "to be something," marks a peculiarly pregnant moment: for in the metaphorical tealeaves of being something Daniel seeks to trace out his past through some vision of his future, thereby endowing vocational identity with a timeless stability that, with Evangelical undertones, only waits to be revealed. But the virtual epic catalogue of professions that comprises Sir Hugo's answer baffles:

Whatever your inclination leads you to, my boy. I thought it right to give you the option of the army . . . The university has a good wide opening into the forum. There are prizes to be won, and a bit of good fortune often gives the turn to a man's taste . . . You might make yourself a barrister – be a writer – take up politics . . . I am glad you have done some good reading outside your classics, and have got a grip of French and German. The truth is, unless a man can get the prestige and income of a Don and write donnish books, it's hardly worth while for him to make a Greek and Latin machine of himself . . . That's all very fine, but in practical life nobody does give you the cue for pages of Greek . . . But talking of Dons, I have seen Dons make a capital figure in society; and occasionally he can shoot you down a cartload of learning in the right place, which will tell in politics . . . we want a little disinterested culture to make head against cotton and capital, especially in the house . . . (215–17)

Accoutered in learned sound-bite equivalents, Sir Hugo's hypothetical intellectual is commercialized in anti-industrial terms: rather than make himself into a "machine," he invests his capital in the appeal of "disinterested culture," and sees its return in the shape of political clout. But Daniel is determined to reject "politics as a profession" (434) and refuses to see himself and psychologically "find himself" in Sir Hugo's list of professions not only because he shrinks from such implicit social climbing, but because what he really wants to hear is who his mother is. In this sense, Daniel's quest for personal identity becomes inseparable from his thirst for an inspiration he can only conceive as a career, but this desire for a career is presented as a surrogate for knowing his mother's identity, for a childhood experience. For Daniel, a career not only signifies a desire for what object-relations theorists call mothering, but conditions the interiority that conventionally marks the humanist subject. The dialogue climaxes in a moment of excruciating emotional pain for Daniel. With "feelings clogg[ing] his tongue," he remains isolated, his chosen ergologics unable to convey appropriately his emotional life: "A moment was passing by in which a question about his birth was throbbing within him, and yet it seemed more impossible than ever that the question should find vent . . . " (216)

<h2 style="text-align:center">MATERNALISM AS PROFESSIONALISM</h2>

The novel's plot is launched by this invocation of the traditional professions (Cannadine, *The Decline and Fall* 237; Mintz, *George Eliot and the Novel of Vocation* 14; Davidoff and Hall, *Family Fortunes* 260; Perkin, *Rise of Profession Society* 16) during a period in which, according to many historians, the professions themselves were becoming more efficient at transforming services into income-yielding property (Perkin, *Rise of Professional Society* 7) thereby posing a structural challenge to a class-stratified society: by borrowing the doctrine of work from the Evangelical working and lower middle classes and the ideal of a gentleman from the landowning aristocrats and wealthy bourgeoisie, members of the professional classes are represented as engaged in promoting a social ideal that was avowedly national, cultural and anti-capitalist (Perkin, *Rise of Professional Society* 120–1). In other words, professionals, without evincing any group consciousness themselves, strove to cut across class distinctions in the name of national and cultural good. If literature of this period is, as Alan Mintz has argued, engaged in substituting a consideration of man's relation to the world for a consideration of man's relation to woman, moving that is from romance to work in a reorientation by which the novelist appropriates for writing "the central experiences of the age: work, vocation, and the passion to improve the world" (Mintz, *George Eliot and the Novel of Vocation* 55–6), we need to ask here why Sir Hugo's litany is represented as an intrusion – as inadequate to Daniel's maternal desire – whether we understand that maternal desire as a need to know about his mother or a need to act like a mother.

Indeed *Daniel Deronda* asks us to situate middle-class career professionalism in the context of a gendered and nationalistic conflation of discourses and measure what kind of formal force it thus poses for novel formation.

As discussed before, historians and critics have characterized nineteenth-century professional society as organized according to three criteria: (1) expertise or specialization, often in an esoteric or abstract form of knowledge; (2) associations and institutions that "gate keep" by conferring and/or recognizing the training and education necessary to such specialization; and (3) an ethic of social good attendant on the performance of professional work (although not necessarily its efficacious performance) by which society is persuaded of a professional's right to resources and rewards. Although American historians tend to see professionalism as an outgrowth of late capitalism whereby services and know-how – and human capital generally – are commodified like commercial products (Bledstein, *Culture of Professionalism* 34), English historians see Victorian professionalism as a precursor of the twentieth-century welfare state in so far as its emphasis on institution-centric rewards for social work and cultural expertise foreshadow nationally scaled state-sponsored welfare programs (Perkin, *Rise of Professional Society* 129–30). Indeed historians on both sides of the Atlantic seem to see professionalism as negotiating a nineteenth-century dialectic between capitalist enterprise and labor activism in so far as the organizing principles of professional society are potentially applicable to every job, every member of the nation. Hence the nineteenth-century burgeoning of institutions associated to various kinds of "employment" – whether that employment is a paid service like administering medical advice or an unpaid occupation like distributing Bibles to the working classes – is read as the same structural phenomenon: the expansion of professional society. In this sense, professionalism cuts across economic class difference without doing away with an idea of privilege and prestige.

This is not to say, however, that professionalization can be defended as definitively more egalitarian than laissez-faire capitalism. As Mary Poovey's work demonstrates, successful professionalization entailed marginalizing various groups, particularly women whose "natural" identity was constructed in correspondence to the amateur, or the nonprofessional (*Uneven Developments* 9; 25). But if we accept Davidoff and Hall's definition of the professions as entailing "the sale of services, particularly those involving the manipulation of words, visual forms and abstract ideas" (*Family Fortunes* 269), then we can see how Perkin's

Victorian intelligentsia, many of whom were indeed women, gained increasing social clout, as well as economic and political power, without becoming overt capitalists or pretend men. It is in light of this incipient professional culture that Sharon Marcus explains Charlotte Brontë's access to a novel-writing career as relying on her capacity to abstract and thereby advertise a gender-neutral writerly personna.[14]

Placing women novel-writers in the context of the theoretically endless applicability of Perkin's professionalism – its expansiveness – has broad implications both for the way in which women's novel-writing strove to achieve a semblance of professionalization and for the way in which the representation of domesticity, the female sphere and women's vocation influence and are influenced by the values current in professionalism. That professionalism is potentially applicable to every activity from doctoring to decorating and from science to sports, but actually applied only to some suggests that the resemblance between professional work and both domestic management in Victorian culture and the realities of female novel-writing in the nineteenth-century literary marketplace is a matter of representation: the imagining of an ethical expertise that was at once learned and innate, Utilitarian and Romantic, professional and not. Thus one 1877 reviewer writes that Eliot's "conception" of her "specimen" derived from a power of perception that was "as relentless as that of a naturalist who has a jelly-fish under his microscope, and as tenderly considerate as that of a mother who holds her new-born babe in her arms."[15] In the context of novel-writing, a woman's work is comparable to that of a scientist, the ethical good of maternal love akin to the professional expertise of the trained scientist. It is no wonder then that Eliot's career-long endeavor to define and validate Authorship by insisting that the job of a writer is to produce "moral taste"[16] echoes Sarah Ellis' plea for the "science of good household management" by which all the "highest and best feelings are called into [the] exercise" of moral influence (*Women of England* 31–2). The question emerges as to whether the promotional strategy that depicts the novelist as a producer of social knowledge can be read as a sign of the professionalization of the domestic woman's claim to an ethical monopoly.

If we allow that the kind of novelistic realism Eliot practiced purportedly provided a means of producing social knowledge and that, as Sharon Marcus has argued, successful authorship required the marketing skills understood as pivotal in the commercialization of an increasingly professionalized economy ("The Profession of the Author" 207), then the "realignment of social forces precipitated by the specialization of function" that Mintz sees as residing in the emerging dominance of the professions (*George Eliot and the Novel of Vocation* 14) allows us to read *Daniel Deronda* as a representation of professional ideology. In other words, it allows us to read *Daniel Deronda* as what Bruce Robbins calls an "allegory of vocation" by which professionalism's romance is exposed in its normative set of polarities: "female experience and male expertise, private ends and public means, politics and professionalism" (*Secular Vocations* 55). The advertising techniques of Marcus' literary market-place, the work ethic central to Mintz's novel of vocation and the allegories that Robbins' institution-based intellectuals reenact demon-strate the way in which the concept of a professional culture provides a means of accounting for the intricacies and apparent ironies imagined in Victorian domestic fiction.

Although by professionalism Robbins really refers to a contemporary idea of the professional critic, particularly the "professor" housed in the modern and generally American university where institutional affili-ation is somewhat different than that governing other more conven-tional professions, his discussion is pertinent here, since Sir Hugo finally settles on intellectual life as the profession that will "tell in politics" by virtue of its claims to "disinterested culture" – a puzzling line of reasoning since presumably what has weight in politics, what is politi-cally committed, is presumably not disinterested. Sir Hugo's solecism is of course nothing new in so far as modern secular intellectuals, in their commitment to disinterestedness, have traditionally borne a tortured relationship to political and social practice. What is interesting here, though, is that the intellectual's age-old moral conundrum occurs as Sir Hugo's professional discourse makes Daniel's maternal desire legible. In the shape of Daniel's emotional constitution, the novel's psychological line of development disrupts Sir Hugo's professional expectations by invoking some inchoate type of maternalism, as if to suggest that the novel's reproduction of male professional culture produces a great deal of anxiety about female identity and the appropriateness of emotional and psychological concerns to professionalized art forms.

For the novel, professionalism makes legible what Daniel does not have, whether that missing piece is a career or, what Robbins sees as its opposite, an experience (in this case, a maternal experience). As Eliot goes about the work of conveying social knowledge – that is, the work of fictionalizing Daniel – the question emerges whether the relation be-tween profession and experience is really one of antithesis or of comple-mentarity.

This absence of a professional story alongside the absence of a maternal history initiates a crucial narrative line when the allegedly illegitimate birth that haunts Daniel's silence before a set of Oxbridge professional choices returns in the shape of a particular emotional asset: citing Daniel's unknown birth as the single influence that makes his birthright a question of character, Eliot explains that Daniel's sympathy for others derives from his "sense of entailed disadvantage." The property of an entailed estate conventionally associated to English novelistic discourse thus returns here as an intellectual property that still retains its hereditary connotations.

In a sly proleptic wink at the novel's conclusive Zionism, Eliot explains that this possession of dispossession is by no means a sufficient condition for sympathy, for such a sense in an introverted personality would produce only an "Ishmaelite." But in the "rarer sort" like Daniel, "the inexorable sorrow takes the form of fellowship" (215). Potential (and importantly not actual) illegitimacy provides Daniel with a great deal of emotional and ethical capital: a sense of fellowship that appears disinterested, similar indeed to what Sarah Ellis cites as the definitive characteristic of an English domestic woman: the "disinterested sympathy of a generous heart" (*Women of England* 21). But the free-floating nature of Daniel's sympathy allows his imagined dispossession to endanger the efficacy of his sense of fellowship. Daniel's initial flaw, Eliot intones, is a "plenteous flexible sympathy" – a sympathy that is too indiscriminate, overly disinterested. Many Victorians would have associated this sympathy to intellectual life: Daniel's vocational crisis, as one reviewer writes, stems from "the comprehensiveness of intelligence and of sympathy" (Whipple, *North American Review* 49). Not only has Daniel's " sensibility to the half-known facts of his parentage made him an excuse for lingering longer than others in a state of social neutrality" (*Daniel Deronda* 220), but a "too reflective and diffusive sympathy was in danger of paralyzing in him that indignation against wrong and that selectness of fellowship which are the conditions of moral force" (413). And so an analysis of Daniel's character yields an ethical critique of Arnoldian disinterestedness and one of the novel's potential psychological subjects ossifies into a new type of anti-hero: the intellectual citizen of the world.

In a doctrinaire diagnosis of Daniel's ineffectual moral constitution Eliot flashes a vision of the great antidote by collapsing the temporal and spatial dimensions of Daniel's biography, a move that has led Deirdre

David to see the collapse of the novel "from social realism into pseudo-epic":[17]

> But how and whence was the needed event to come? – the influence that would justify partiality, and making him what he longed to be yet was unable to make himself – an organic part of social life, instead of roaming in it like a yearning disembodied spirit, stirred with a vague social passion, but without fixed local habitation to render fellowship real? (*Daniel Deronda* 413)

Implicit in Daniel's need to "justify partiality" is a desire to reject an impartiality that has kept him isolated from the biases of a group as well as a desire to distance himself from a disinterestedness whereby his freedom from selfish motive would keep his social passions "vague." He laments that his freedom from selfishness and bias, in a sense his intellectualism, have prevented his Gramscian "organic" social growth.

But let us return to the question of "soar[ing] above preference into impartiality" (50) and how that is connected to a "love of tender kinship for" a spot of native land. When Eliot tells us that preference is the road to impartiality, we cannot help but ask why she would then use Daniel's diffusive sympathy to blur the distinction between disinterestedness and impartiality. Defined here as the state of being "stimulated by abstract nouns," impartiality is the intellectual state of the citizen of the world. It is the Saidian nation of the homeless intellectual and the Robbinsian university of the professional critic as much as it is Arnoldian disinterestedness. In this sense, home, a site for acquaintanceship and affection, becomes the nest of impartiality, but it is a strange impartiality indeed, no less so than in the context of Daniel's plenteous sympathy. In other words, the passage begs the question how an impartiality that involves being stimulated by abstract nouns pertains to Daniel's plenteous sympathy, his social neutrality and his moral paralysis. Is the love of kinship that culminates in impartiality nothing more than an indiscriminate sympathy born of dispossession? Is the state of being stimulated by abstract nouns nothing more than entailed disadvantage? If Catherine Gallagher is right that the professional critic is illegible as a political signifier,[18] then Daniel's dilemma, and perhaps even Edward Said's, can be seen as falsely resolved in a peculiar form of twentieth-century nationalism, one that emerges in the novel as a remedy to the necessary absence of political commitment, the disdain of interestedness, characterizing professional life. Certainly Eliotian professions of worldliness risk falling prey to a nationalism that, despite its ideal merging of local commitment and communal universalism,[19] contradicts the key terms of both intellectualism and professionalism: disinterestedness.

But I have neglected the figure that heralds Eliot's nation-state of impartiality: the "homestead" and "the little lot of stars" belonging to it. A homestead implies a communal enterprise organized around some kind of production. If a homestead is literally associated to agricultural production, here as a metaphor it produces the impartiality necessary to the citizen of the world; it manufactures intellectualism. This image of the home as a workshop for intellectual properties crystallizes in the gendered shape of the Meyrick household, whose "vision" beckons Daniel (235) to seek it as a heaven for Mirah, the Jewish "poor wanderer" (241). Not unlike the *Pensionne des Desmoiselles* of *Villette* (which also serves as safe harbor for a tempest-tossed woman), the Meyrick home is an all-female cloister so enclosed (between a river and a garden) that, despite its location in the middle of a city, it is sealed off from urban noise and blight. Half workplace, half reading room, it recalls the fairytale subplot of *Middlemarch* in which Mary Garth, having become mistress of the Stone Court where once she served as maid, produces with her co-author husband a handbook on farming as well as a storybook version of Plutarch.

Indeed, looking at the Meyrick home is like looking at a pastiche of advertisements for reading, the details all collated to focus attention on an ethics of literary consumption: not only is its sequestered front parlor quiet enough for Mrs. Meyrick to read aloud to her children with the window open, but its hospitality is predicated on Daniel's conviction that the "motherly figure of quakerish neatness" and her three daughters "hardly knew of any evil closer to them than what lay in history books and dramas, and would at once associate a lovely Jewess with Rebecca in 'Ivanhoe'" (235). Eliot is hardly subtle in her suggestion that the Meyrick women come to know how to do the right thing due to their readerly imaginations. That the moral lesson in this case derives from Walter Scott's novel about the forging of an English national consciousness suggests that to take in a Jew is to participate in a particularly nationalistic English literary tradition. Indeed, Michael Ragussis has convincingly situated *Daniel Deronda* as a whole in a revisionist tradition of the novel whereby the representation of Jewish conversion furnishes a vocabulary for debating the historical meaning of Englishness.[20]

The Meyrick home reproduces the business of busyness that can said to be characteristic of a domestic vignette. Rooted in the durative of historical present tense, the first description of the home shows it as a workplace. Drawing, sewing, reading – the manual mixes with the intellectual and the scene's chiaroscuro lighting casts a penumbra around the alliance: "The candles were on a table apart for Kate, who was drawing illustrations for a publisher; the lamp was not only for the reader but for Amy and Mab, who were embroidering satin cushions for 'the great world'" (237). Although their work may be amateur in that the only training they received would have been at their mother's hand, it is clear that they are not only paid for their productions, but the household, including the sole and absent male, is economically dependent on such payment, compensation that is neither the laborer's wage nor the professional's fee, but typical of an artisanal economy. In this sense, the scene replicates an ongoing irony about novelistic domesticity; it highlights, indeed sometimes glamorizes, a type of manual work that never takes the form of alienated labor.

But handicrafts are not the scene's only products. For featured at the scene's center is Mirah in the middle of entertaining her coworkers by reading to them while sitting on a camp stool, thereby serving as model "for a title-page vignette, symbolizing a fair public absorbed in the successive volumes of the Family Tea-table" (538). Sitting, reading, entertaining, Mirah, by modeling for a publisher's advertisement, portrays domestic work as implicated in the marketing of a popular magazine. In a kind of *Las Meninas* self-disclosure, Eliot's domestic scene here illustrates its own manufacture as ideological commerce: it overtly claims an ironic commercial appeal as an organic extension of its domesticity. In other words, part of the scene's very appeal derives from its ironic disclosure of its own artifice, a disclosure that invokes the same kind of campiness characteristic of Dickensian domesticity. In this, it resembles a nineteenth-century version of what Mark Miller identifies in television advertisements of today as a preemptive irony that co-opts all skeptical postures;[21] the element of self-mockery implicit in either twentieth-century television or in this domestic scene's self-reference prevents perceiving it as ideological fare or propaganda.[22]

Certainly these diminutive women nested in their tiny rooms, who, "if they had been wax-work, might have been packed easily in a fashionable lady's travelling trunk" (238) recall the playland miniature moat with bridge and garden estate of the campy Castle Dickens gives Wemmick. But the telling sign that this home differs from any Dickens would have built is the conspicuous presence of something entirely new: what is called "culture.'

it is pleasant to know that many such grim-walled slices of space in our foggy London have been, and still are the homes of a culture the more spotlessly free from vulgarity, because poverty has rendered everything like display an impersonal question, and all grand shows of the world simply a spectacle which rouses no petty rivalry or vain effort after possession. (237)

If we take Eliot at her word, it would seem that in domestic culture poverty curbs investing material objects with psychoanalytic properties. The tables and chairs of the parlour may anthropomorphically materialize like "old friends preferred to new" (237), but they do not reflect anyone's personality, psychological history, preference or taste. Display for this culture can never be personal; it is "free" from efforts after possession, free from the desire to own. The implication of Eliot's idyll is extravagant, if not patronizingly reactionary: poverty precludes egoism?

Indeed the ethos is avowedly anti-materialist and intellectually elitist in so far as it appears to champion an idea of cultural appreciation very much in keeping with the Oxbridge-centered attack on property that Perkin describes as central in a professionalism from above (*Rise of Professional Society* 123–41)[23] and that Freedman describes as characteristic of the anti-establishment ambivalence of intellectual aesthetes towards capitalist commodification (*Professions of Taste* 53). The diminutive *parole* constraining the home and its inhabitants appears as nothing more than a showcase for cultural breadth, a version of the perspectival leitmotif played incessantly throughout the novel as a whole: "But in these two little parlours with no furniture that a broker would have cared to cheapen except the prints and piano, there was space and apparatus for a wide-glancing, nicely select life, open to the highest things in music, painting, and poetry" (237). It is no wonder that they are willing to house Mirah, a figure whom the novel similarly metaphorizes as an *objet d'art*: "image of unhappy girlhood"; a version of other "girl tragedies" (228); "an impersonation of misery" (227). Mirah fits in very well with the only other objects in the house that actually do have literal market value: the prints and the piano. In other words, Eliot connects nonpersonal sociability – that lack of interest in the personal – that makes the Meyrick household such an authentic home to a cultural appreciation that is by no means independent of economic concerns. We find ourselves in another border-territory where just enough money affords a piano without the too much money associated to an "effort after possession," that shameful desire to own. In this sense, Eliot's social critique acknowledges the financial quiddities that her cultural program elides.

This is borne out in the William Morris-esque way in which the Meyrick homecraftsmanship links cultural appreciation to a collectivist spirit. As a kind of advertising agency for that combination of the intellectual and the aesthetic known as culture, Eliot's home defines the very bond joining the mother to her daughters as a rather strange amalgam of biological and professional virtues: "family love; admiration for the finest work, the best action; and habitual industry" (238). That family love coincides with habitual industry is typical of domestic discourse from Sarah Ellis onward. That the paired superlative sandwiched between them associates an aesthetic appreciation (the finest work) with an ethical admiration (the best action) suggests that the home produces both kinds of specialists; it links art and morality under the aegis of domestic connoisseurship.

The significance of connoisseurship to the novel's domesticity surfaces in the fact that it is through Mirah, the wandering homeless amateur professional, that the Meyrick household is registered as the happy home: structurally, it is through a metonymic line of development beginning with her that the narrative arrives at the Meyrick's when Daniel brings her there and it is there, amid all the accouterments of English taste, that she is recognized by Herr Klesmer as a professional. In the first of the novel's various recognition scenes, Mirah's professionalism serves as her Odysseus scar. In this sense, the novel's initial movement from the Gwendolen plot line to the Mirah one, and from an English woman without a home to a homeless woman without a surrogate one, takes place in a professional idiom, for the recognition that Klesmer accords Mirah is precisely that which he withholds from Gwendolyn. Mirah's fitness for the role of heroine in the novel is expressed as her fitness for the drawing-room career in which Klesmer launches her.

Indeed Klesmer represents professional authority. He stresses the importance of training by telling Gwendolen that loving art is not enough: "'genius at first is little more than a great capacity to receive discipline'" (300). He celebrates a Protestant sense of election in vocations requiring inefficacious "self-denial" – self denial from which no issue can ever be expected (300): "'you wish to try a life of arduous, unceasing work, and uncertain praise . . . you could do nothing better – neither man nor woman could do anything better'" (297–8). He even employs professional jargon when explaining to Mirah what she would need to do to hone her skills: he spoke "in noises which sounded like words bitten in two and swallowed before they were half out" (542). And he emphasizes the disinterestedness of service in a professional community:

I will ask leave to shake hands with you on the strength of our freemasonry, where we are all vowed to the service of Art, and to serve her by helping every fellow-servant . . . Where there is duty of service there must be the duty of accepting it. The question is not one of personal obligation. (304)

Despite these signs, however, Klesmer encodes a professional ethos that is peculiarly domesticated in being peculiarly gender-blind for, as I have argued before, homecraft as imagined in domestic novels is theoretically open to all. Invoking "freemasonry" as his professional model, Klesmer seems to refer to those fourteenth-century itinerant stoneworkers who signaled their expertise by means of a secret system of signs and passwords. By the middle of the nineteenth-century, however, freemasonry commanded a host of other associations, as the freemasons themselves had regrouped in 1717 and revised the society's objective from that of serving as a kind of qualifying association to that of "mutual help and the promotion of brotherly feeling" (*OED*). In other words, eighteenth-century ethical culture substitutes for medieval craftsmanship as the society's organizing principle. The irony emerges in the nineteenth century when, despite their origins in guild-based skilled labor, the freemasons become "one of the most influential and wide-ranging of the masculine associations" characteristic of nineteenth-century English middle-class life (Davidoff and Hall, *Family Fortunes* 425). In this sense, the freemasons of the nineteenth century exemplify a segment of middle-class culture where para-professional structures serve to organize social life. And this evolution seems to have included an ambivalent assertion of sexual difference as well: rallying around a set of collectivist values many of which derived from eighteenth-century Dissent – solidarity, charity, trust, tolerance (426) – , the freemasons championed as masculine the same virtues that Sarah Ellis claimed for domestic women. That female domesticity and male freemasonry may be thought of as two versions of the same set of principles emerges in the freemasons' commitment to marriage and to family life:

Freemasonry helped to give location to young men who could not yet marry and set up on their own and, "as a single sex organization with a strong moral code, it served as a protection against disastrous liaison and premature marriage." Indeed it provided a hearth for those who did not have a home. (Davidoff and Hall, *Family Fortunes* 426)

By invoking freemasonry in addressing a woman, Klesmer conjures a fantasy that the artistic professions he represents could bridge what did in fact if not in theory separate the home from the masons' lodge: gender.

This romance between domesticity and artistic professionalism crystallizes when Klesmer blows into the Meyrick dollhouse. Despite Eliot's praise of the home's poverty, the Meyricks are at first embarrassed and self-conscious when the blustery composer's theatrical air makes the house look like a collection of ridiculous toys (539). The novel reassures us, however, that Klesmer appreciates the home because he is a Bohemian: "He remembered a home no larger than this on the outskirts of Bohemia; and in the figurative Bohemia too he had had a large acquaintance with the variety and romance which belong to small incomes" (539). The double sense of Klesmer's bohemianism is not fortuitous: the information that his childhood home is Bohemia and that his calling as an international musician entails his living like a bohemian, "a gypsy of society, especially an artist, literary man or actor" (*OED*) has the effect of redeeming the Meyrick house from its self-consciousness and certifying it as a home: for it is due to his bohemianism, in both senses, that Klesmer puts his imprimatur on the Meyrick rooms. In this sense, the English home's identity becomes linked to an ironic representation of national origins that derives from Klesmer's career as a professional artist. Recalling that one of the necessary conditions of professionalism is certification, we can discern here a mock certification scene, cleverly staged among performers of the novel's domesticity; at the same time that Klesmer recognizes Mirah's vocal expertise, the combination of her talent and her training, he recognizes the house as a home. The parodic nature of the scene's professionalism seems to make fun of professional values at the same time as it ironically accords just such value to the "amateur" spheres it purportedly excludes.

ARTISTS AND NATIONS

Although "Bohemia" refers to a geographical place, it also denotes the rootlessness of artistic life. This cleverly contrived way of representing Klesmer's identity, and the authority that derives from it, suggests that Eliot's concern with Klesmer's romantic home on the outskirts of a

figurative Bohemia (539) is a concern that links domesticity and professionalism to nationalism. Nationalism, in the sense of a willingness to
mobilize politically on the basis of national identification, is considered
by writers like Eric Hobsbawm and Ernest Gellner in association to
nineteenth-century political and ideological shifts.[24] Whereas they have
focused on political mobilization as the definitive quality of nationalism,
Benedict Anderson has considered the origins of that national identification itself, which he locates in the vacuum created by the disintegration
of a unified sense of religious institutional life.[25] Interestingly, both
schools of thought emphasize the role of the intelligentsia. For Anderson, print culture – the newspaper and the novel specifically – provide
the instruments for national imaginings (*Imagined Communities* 24 – 5). For
Hobsbawm, linguistic criteria are pivotal in the identification of a nation
defined by its ethnic composition rather than by its economic and
political viability. The linguistic rallying point of modern nationalism,
Hobsbawm points out, originates with "people who wrote and read, not
people who spoke" (*The Age of Empire* 147). According to this argument,
the nineteenth-century ethnic-linguistic claim for political autonomy
generally involved languages (Gaelic, Macedonian, Yiddish) that were
really no more than "local and regional dialects" (147). Hebrew, the
focus of nineteenth-century Zionism and of central concern to *Daniel
Deronda*, provides an extreme example of this "localness" in having been
limited exclusively to liturgy and ritual for centuries (146). As nationalism theoretically evolves, these languages demand compilation, standardization, modernization (147) while their associated cultures (folk-
lore, mores, customs) require written historicization and codification. In
other words, Hobsbawm and Anderson insinuate that nationalism was
not only a job and a job opportunity for specialists and experts, it
contributed significantly to the professionalization of social knowledge,
an enterprise in which Eliot herself was clearly invested.

In his discussion of late nineteenth-century nationalism, Hobsbawm
differentiates between a nationalism that rested on a territorial program
modeled after the "territorial state of the French Revolution" and an
alternative "nonterritorial nationalism" developed among Europe's historically migratory peoples (especially in the Habsburg Empire and
among Jews) according to which nationality is inherent in a person no
matter where she lives (147–8). He identifies nonterritorial nationalism
by outlining how a Diaspora people's sense of a home as "the locus of a
real community of human beings with real social relations with each
other" turns into the "imaginary community" of the nation state (148).

For Hobsbawm, the degeneration of the "real" community into an abstracted one is an unfortunate prelude to territorial aggression. For Eliot it poses a formal problematic. In detaching the home from any geographic specificity and pinning it to a vocational community of professional artists, Klesmer's bohemianism suggests that in the professionalization of art and literature the idea that a home can be a profession turns into the idea that a profession can be a home. The distinction is vocational domesticity taken to its logical extreme, renunciation turned in on itself. What is lost, however, when a profession becomes a home is a sense of generational continuity, a sense that can presumably be recovered by conjuring the historically rooted imagined community of the nation. So in its emphasis on exile – on homelessness – the novel's professionalism (writ as bohemianism) relegates domesticity to a strictly metaphorical level; the home is processed into a more abstract and more potentially nationalistic idea of community: the homeland.

It follows then that within this professional grammar, Mirah must figure as the heroine, not only by virtue of her amateur professionalism, but by virtue of her nonterritorial nationalism – that is, her Judaism. But in this sense, the nonterritorial nationalism of the novel engenders a proto-Zionism that posits territorial acquisition at the same time as it champions an international spirit of Diaspora. The purpose of Mordecai's visionary mission to the East is not to end the Diaspora but to restore the soul of the Jewish people living in it: by replacing their dried-up superstitions and superannuated rituals with a sense of "common action" (585), Mordecai's imagined "national hearth" (596) would make Jews better citizens of the world. "The life of a people grows," he preaches, " . . . it absorbs the thought of other nations into its own forms, and gives back the thought as new wealth to the world" (585). Rather than increase the world's wealth materially, Diaspora Jews would increase the world's wealth spiritually if only they could be reinspired by a territorial center – a territorial center that, as Mordecai makes clear, would resemble England. So again, Eliot's reach for universality resolves itself into loving a spot of native land. By making Jewish nationalism a replication of English nationalism, the novel – in a phrase Eliot uses to describe Lydgate's foolhardy romance with Rosamond in *Middlemarch* – gets tangled in its own metaphors.

In the context of *Daniel Deronda*, the double sense of bohemianism describes how an artist makes a profession a home only to compensate for the resulting loss of generational continuity by imagining a national identity. The novel turns toward nationalism when it becomes clear that professional art, however glamorized by Klesmer, can never be a viable alternative for any of the main characters. Professional art cannot satisfy the demands of domestic vocational longing. In so far as it is Klesmer the professional artist who chooses Mirah and her potential nationalism as the conduit whereby a meaningful life may be envisioned, it is professional art that, in its failure to sustain that meaningful life, summons nationalism. In other words, whereas professional art cannot sustain the novel's domestic plot of vocation, the imagined nation can. The home in Bohemia that allows Klesmer to recognize the Meyrick household's domesticity will ultimately depart from a set of artistic connotations in order to settle in a real place, on a real piece of land. Thus the nationalism of Mirah and the Jewish plot wins out over the marketplace popularity of Gwendolen and the English plot.[26]

How the intellectual qualities important to a bohemian artist can be linked to a nation's land emerges elsewhere in Eliot's writing in her representation of the German peasant's relationship to history. In "A Natural History of German Life," she explains how it is that the German peasant will not change his grandfather's home with any improvements, but will dismantle a medieval church so as to use its stones for his backyard fence:

Riehl well observes that the feudal system, which made the peasant the bondman of his lord, was an immense benefit in a country the greater part of which had still to be colonized, rescued the peasant from vagabondage, and laid the foundation of persistency and endurance in future generations. If a free German peasantry belongs only to modern times, it is to his ancestor who was a serf, and even, in earliest times, a slave, that the peasant owes the foundation of his independence – namely, his capability of a settled existence, – nay, his unreasoning persistency, which has its important function in the development of the race. (*Essays and Leaves from a Notebook* 204–5)

In her praise of the German peasant's independence from the past, Eliot makes similar moves to those that complicate her explanation of the citizen of the world's impartiality in the homestead passage above: independence is defined as a settled existence tied to territory in the same way that impartiality can be traced to a prejudice for milk. In order for Eliot to locate the source of independence in a history of bondage and the source of impartiality in prejudice, she needs to redefine independence itself as a quality of mind, as an intellectual property. Both analogies reveal Eliot's preoccupation with conceptualizing an intellectual independence that can be defended as rooted in the life of generations, in a historical order of things that would ironically curtail that very independence. Bohemianism seen as a professional home thus encodes an impossible dream: the legitimization of independent intellectual work in the communal terms of a historical nation. In this mythology of Klesmer's own home in Bohemia, the professionalization of *Daniel Deronda*'s domesticity turns into an intellectual romance with nationalism.

The alliance between artistic professionalism and nationalism asserts itself as a formal force in the novel during a drawing-room music party at the Arrowpoints' estate. At first blush, the scene suggests that a comedy of manners had revisited England: in an urbane and aristocratic salon an ironic exchange of witticisms matches two men against each other in competition for the presiding lady's favor. The conventional banter, however, does not rely on the usual epigrammatic subtext of essentialist sexual differences. For Eliot's vintage rendition here substitutes a remarkably compatible nationalist type-casting. The scene is, in fact, like much of this immigrant-populated London-centric novel, perversely concerned with national difference, and much of the scene's humor pivots on the effectiveness of its racist caricatures. The Jew Klesmer speaks in "odious German staccato endings" like an Irishman's resuming his brogue when upset (*Daniel Deronda* 78) and the English MP Bult, a model "party man" (283), calls a performance of coloratura offensive and Polish. The nineteenth-century conflation of race and nation informs the stereotypes Eliot uses to satirize the English themselves, with their fastidious costuming (135 – 6) "suffusive pinkness" (283) and "phlegmatic solidity" (285). The English gentleman, Eliot remarks, "objects to looking inspired" (135). In fact, Eliot's concern with national or cultural traits is most pronounced in her diagnosis of England: the problem with English culture, she repeatedly makes clear, is its constitutional resistance to idealism, its unanchored sympathies: and here disinterestedness itself is portrayed as a kind of curse visited on the English nation.

From his position as an artistic professional, Klesmer occupies center-stage at the Arrowpoints' salon. And from his position as a bohemian, he attacks the "lack of idealism in English politics, which left all mutuality between distant races to be determined simply by the need of a market" (283). Klesmer sees the English mentality as molested by the same social neutrality that hounds Daniel: in suggesting that both England and Daniel make choices, but never with that "selectness of fellowship which [is] the condition of moral force" (413), the novel likens the commercialism that informs England's international neutrality to the diffusive sympathy that informs Daniel's moral paralysis. In this light, Klesmer's critique of impartiality suggests that it is not merely a temporary political condition, but a moral deficiency – both in English culture and the individual lives that constitute it.

Dodging the charge, Mr. Bult the politician and expectant peer commends Klesmer for his command of the English language and his rhetorical sophistication: with "the general solidity and suffusive pinkness of a healthy Briton on the central table-land of life" (283), Bult confesses his astonishment at Klesmer's "ability to put a point in a way that would have told at a constituents' dinner" and speculates that Klesmer must be a refugee, "a Pole, or a Czech, or something of that fermenting sort, in a state of political refugeeism which had obliged him to make a profession of his music" (284). Bult seems to find Klesmer's bohemianism explicable only as a symptom of his exile: it is inconceivable to Bult that a man would willfully either leave his country or make an amateur pursuit like music his career. Upon asking whether Klesmer is a "Panslavist," however, the German musician retorts, while standing before a piano, that his name is Elijah, the "Wandering Jew," at which point he punctuates his *pronta riposta* with a crashing *glissando* that dramatically wins him the match.

Bult's evasion of the charge that the English lack political idealism can be seen as the novel's response to it: in emphasizing Klesmer's command of English, the novel immediately directs our attention to the presence and idea of this flamboyant professional musician who, a cosmopolitan no less at home in his professional calling as a native would be in his homeland, erupts out of the scene like a deus-ex-machina antidote to England's lack of political idealism. That Klesmer speaks English like a statesman and impresses audiences by virtue of his professional flair forces nationalism and professionalism into a contrapuntal relationship, whereby the English can cure their lack of political idealism by conceptualizing England as a nation of professionals – expert managers who provide the world with crucial cultural services. But Klesmer's condemnation of the English for their willingness to leave "all mutuality between the races" – that is, all reciprocal exchange, all communication and intercommunication among peoples – to "the market" suggests some ambiguity as to whether the market is an emblem of self-interestedness or an emblem of disinterestedness. The diagnosis of English national identity reenacts the doubts that molest the professional who gains materially from her presumably disinterested vocation.

An analogy emerges then between the professional and the Englishman in so far as both identities are based on an implicit contradiction between the soul that is disinterested and the soul that is profit-seeking. That Eliot arrives at this illustration of Englishness through a racist typecasting that begins with her representation of the Jews suggests that the nonterritorial nationalism associated to Jewishness might pertain not only to the Diaspora peoples Hobsbawm mentions, but to a Britain in which Englishness was not always a question of geography. Indeed the English mentality that leaves all mutuality between the races to the market is for Eliot no different from the Jewish mercantilism she decries in "The Modern Hep, Hep, Hep." There Eliot criticizes the Jewish Diaspora for producing in the Jewish character a "cosmopolitan indifference"[27] that takes the form of an intellectual faculty for abstracting "all national interest" into what Catherine Gallagher describes as an inhumane "calculus of lendings and borrowings."[28] Invoking an alchemy of difference and sameness in her opening remark, "To discern likeness amidst diversity, it is well known, does not require so fine a mental edge as the discerning of diversity amidst general sameness" (*Impressions* 259), Eliot asks how an Englishman is to judge among the many calls for national self-determination: recounting the parable of the husband who, when told by a physician that his wife cannot eat salad, asks if she might eat lettuce or radishes, Eliot concludes that the "physician had too rashly believed in the comprehensiveness of the word 'salad,' just as we, if not enlightened by experience, might believe in the all-embracing breadth of 'sympathy with the injured and oppressed'" (287). While supposedly arguing in favor of the specificity of difference, Eliot likens sympathy to a salad in an instance of professional artistry whereby metaphor-making exonerates finding likeness amidst diversity just as her polemics condemn it.

What allows for discriminating among the ingredients of a salad as well as among peoples with whom to sympathize is "experience." In the case of nations, Eliot refers Englishmen to their own sense of national consciousness, which derives from a history of generations. In this sense of historical national consciousness, the English would find sympathy for the Jews: "There is more likeness than contrast between the way we English got our island and the way the Israelites got Canaan" (207). In the same way that the consciousness of "having a native country, the birthplace of common memories and habits of mind, existing like a prenatal hearth quitted but beloved," saves "migratory Englishmen from the worst consequences of their voluntary dispersion," so would a "renovated national dignity for the Jews" inhibit the "cosmopolitan indifference" that international assimilation threatens (278). So when Eliot says that in this modern context the "idea of Nationalities" has value (285), it is not clear whether she means to protect the English at home or abroad: it is not simply Zionism at issue when she endorses Mordecai's vision of the Jews as "a nationality whose members may still stretch to the ends of the earth, even as the sons of England and Germany, whom enterprise carries afar, but who still have a national hearth" (*Daniel Deronda* 596). The antidote for salad-like sympathy amounts to a national hearth built on a single idea: separateness with communication. But this recipe for a Jewish national hearth derives directly from Eliot's explanation of English nationalism: not only does this likening of cosmopolitanism to mercantilism imply that the international intellectual's professed disinterestedness is nothing more than professional self-interest, it connects the Diaspora Jews living in England to the Englishmen living in "voluntary dispersion."

FEMINISM AND PROFESSIONALISM

According to this vision, both the Jews and the English are each separated from their respective homelands but connected to each other by virtue of their national imaginings. This model of nationalism, which posits a separate-but-connected doctrine, gives Daniel's story of development a direction in a particularly gendered way. Katherine Bailey Linehan has pointed out, in following Rosemarie Bodeheimer's notion of the "female paternalist," that *Daniel Deronda* cultivates a "romance of the male maternalist" according to which the border delineating the sexual separate spheres is invoked as necessary to the nation's proper management but transgressed by male figures who have learned to perform female "nurturing" work.[29] This reading, understood in the context of Eliot's separate-but-connected model of nationhood, suggests that the novel's psychoanalytic discourse bears less of a resemblance to Freudian theory than to that of object-relations: for the self-identity ostensibly achieved in Daniel's embrace of a national separateness with communication, an embrace that relies on the discovery of his mother's identity, prefigures the model of selfhood that twentieth-century object-relations theorists use particularly for female self-differentiation. As

Nancy Chodorow articulates it, object-relations theory sees individuation as an "oscillation between connection and separation."[30] Rather than pivoting on a disruption of a child's narcissistic relationship to reality through its recognition of the mother's otherness, child development entails a child being cognitively able to recognize the mother's subjectivity alongside her otherness. The process by which a child successfully differentiates a sense of selfhood requires developing what is called a "relational" self: a sense of separateness that relies on "a particular way of being connected to others" (107). According to Chodorow, in a society that privileges independence while disparaging community, neither the absolute individual autonomy prescribed for male children nor the absolute merging with others experienced by female children produces well-adjusted adults.

Although the operative binary of Chodorow's relational individuality, separateness and communication, has been criticized for its race and class specificity, the narrowness of its applicability and its participation in the "connection thesis" (the idea that women are "connected" – whether biologically or sociologically – that is, kinder and gentler, more compassionate etc.), its emphasis on the nurturing of a community has held a historically important place in the evolution of feminism in the broad sense. Whether female morality is seen as collectively bound due to childrearing practices, as some contemporary feminists argue, or due to divine mandate, as nineteenth-century evangelists believed, or to a scientific division of labor that ensured mankind's progress, as many secular Victorian feminists maintained, the communal ethos that is claimed by many feminists as female and as morally superior to the claims of individualism is part of a by-now conventional Anglo-American middle-class conceptualization of gender. In this light , we can see how the Victorian separate-sphere doctrine itself, an oppressive condition from many standpoints, could have been used in good will if not always to good effect as an instrument for improving the condition of middle-class women, particularly when social reform and "kinder" public policy programs came into vogue (as they do both in the 1960s and 1970s as well as in the later half of the nineteenth century). Moreover, the moral superiority encoded in the separate-sphere doctrine explains how it came to be the artistic professions that first opened to middle-class women as both groups (professionals as well as women) aspired for different reasons to mystify their class origins, one in the name of a higher god, Art, the other in the name of the entire sex, Womankind.

This brings us back to some of the definitive binaries subtending professional ideology, binaries that become problematic when "amateurs" like women, or writers, claim or achieve professional status. The struggle Robbins observes in the institutional feminism of today can be likened then to the drama played out in *Daniel Deronda*. The "feminist assault on the experts" in avenging a professionalization that violated the traditions of women's care (quoted in Robbins, *Secular Vocations* 49–50) is preface to the professionalization of particular politics much in the same way that Daniel's rejection of politics as a profession marks his embrace of a maternal legacy whose ethnic particularity ultimately demands an exceedingly partisan political program. Daniel's Palestinian destiny raises the question as to whether the professionalization of amateur occupations – female work, intellectual work, cultural work – necessarily summons an age in which the personal can be nothing other than political.

WANDERING JEWS

The implications of politicizing the professional domestic plot are dramatized by Eliot's use of the legend of *The Wandering Jew* in her representation of Klesmer, the figure who connects domesticity and artistic professionalism to nationalism in the first place. Klesmer, who finds his home in his passionate identification with the profession to which he has connected himself and the international community with which his art authorizes him to communicate, declares that he is a Wandering Jew in response to the English politician's narrow conception of cosmopolitan culture. But Klesmer's heralding himself as the Wandering Jew carries some puzzling associations and calls our attention to how the figure and its various avatars (Althusarus, The Flying Dutchman, Enoch Arden, Cain, Elijah, Don Juan) haunt so many nineteenth-century texts. *The Wandering Jew*, a story which had acquired a legendary status by the beginning of the nineteenth century,[31] especially among folklorists and antiquarians,[32] and had proliferated in art-form versions around the same time, tells of a Jew who refused to allow Jesus to rest while carrying his cross to Calvary and heckled him to walk faster. The Jew is punished by being forced to wander the world until Christ's Second Coming. Having repented, however, he eventually comes to call the world to reform, reminding them through his words and his appearance of the inevitability of Judgment Day. He stands then both cursed and blessed, a personification of exile as well as a sign of that ultimate universal homecoming, the future Kindgom Come.

What does Klesmer's applauding himself as the Wandering Jew mean in the context of Eliot's admonishment of both the Jews and the English for their diffusive sympathies (the Jews for their mercurial interests, the English for their imperial ones)? Although as a homeless Jew he would be susceptible to the charge of alienism, Eliot's term for international disinterestedness, as a professional musician Klesmer is interested. Like the Wandering Jew himself, he has an international calling that can substitute for nationality. Professional election, in a sense, redeems him. Though Klesmer does not have the homestead the absence of which also marks Daniel and Gwendolyn, his profession (his bohemianism) is home enough to make his likeness to the Wandering Jew the ironic blessing that rhetorically wins for him a position of authority. Daniel, however, is a Wandering Jew of a different sort. The comparison between Daniel and Klesmer suggests that the alternative homes – an artistic career or a national territory – present a pairing: artistic professionalism and nationalism seem to serve the same domestic literary purpose in providing alternative vocational plot-lines.

The extent to which the archetypal wanderer is given a professional purpose inflected by an English nationalist specificity surfaces in one of Eliot's favorite versions of the Wandering Jew theme, Wagner's 1843 *The Flying Dutchman*, one of the few of Wagner's operas she admired,[33] and one of the cultural phantoms haunting *Daniel Deronda*. Indeed, in Klesmer's representing a composite of Mendelssohn, Liszt (a friend of Lewes) and Wagner (an acquaintance), his remark in the scene recalls Heinrich Heine's treatment of the "Flying Dutchman, the Wandering Jew of the Ocean."[34] Having been especially moved by the element of high-relief self-sacrifice central in Heine's version, which appeared several years before he wrote his own, Wagner apparently based his Flying Dutchman on the theatrical production of the same title described in the seventh chapter of Heine's "Memoirs of Herr Von Schnabelewopski." *The Flying Dutchman* tells the story of how a sailor swears to round the Cape of Good Hope even if it takes him until Judgment Day; his audacity is punished when the devil condemns him to everlasting wandering.[35] Heine and Wagner's plot innovation is simply the caveat that the Wandering Jew of the Ocean can be redeemed by a woman who pledges her love to him. Perversely, both versions demand that the woman demonstrate her devotion in a suicide made all the more gruesome by her expressed desire to perform the most literal of self-sacrificial acts.

In Wagner's opera, we see a professional sailor seeking personal spiritual salvation through a love that is repeatedly discussed in terms of self-sacrifice and *Heimatland*. The libretto's choice of *Heimat* (the community of a collective imagination) in lieu of the colloquial *Heim* (or *Daheim*, as in a place of origin) appears especially relevant when the second act opens on to a domestic household composed, like so many nineteenth-century English novel households, of a group of female workers, the hum of their spinning wheels orchestrated to cast a phonemic penumbra around the space that, wider and more inclusive than any possible stage "ship," promises to end the cycle of the solitary professional man's wanderings. Moved by the story she has heard and retells so often, Senta expresses – not love – but such a desire to sacrifice for the Dutchman (what she calls a "longing for the sky")[36] that the home, a place of ongoing, end-less activity, shows itself as a force that can make the wanderer's plot linear and simultaneously transcendent. Structurally, then, the home appears as a reclaiming agent, however veiled its thematic attributes.

Sailors and seamstresses: the first theme sung by a crew of male sailors finds its development in a staff of female spinners. Indeed the opera reaches its crescendo when both groups sing their respective themes together in complementary juxtaposition in the third act. The sailors' rolling waves seem virtually overcome by the sewers' spinning wheels. An ageless – as old as the "young Ulysses" to whom Eliot compares Klesmer – archetypal oscillation between the home and the sea awakens a nostos that relies exclusively on Senta's desire to sacrifice herself. But what such a sacrifice would entail is elided: the Dutchman is stunned by her willingness to commit herself to such a life of wandering even though (as she knows from the start) her willingness to commit would presumably end that wandering. The specifics of what is sacrificed and the logic of its renunciation plot seem less important than the idea of Senta's final monstrous self-immolation.

The almost hysterical yearning for transcendence that the recitative dialogue between Senta and the Dutchman conveys is, however, repeatedly interrupted by a prosaic melody sung by Senta's seafaring father, Daland. Indeed, the merchant sailor can hardly contain his yippy-ai-yah anticipation of getting the Dutchman's treasure, which the forlorn captain promises him in exchange for his daughter's hand. That their deal, which (like so much of operatic plot detail) looks gratuitous at first, should precede the Dutchman and Senta's first meeting makes it important in several ways. It suggests that Senta's fantasy of self-sacrifice concurs with her father's fantasy of getting some pirate booty and thereby promotes Senta's heroic self-sacrifice by presenting her as her father's chattel. At the same time, it suggests the sense in which domestic work is implicated in making a living from the sea. The juxtaposed musical collage of the sailors returning tired and hungry alongside the seamstresses sewing and cleaning and cooking in preparation for the homecoming equates the two spheres as national workplaces. But Daland's money-grubbing interludes put a primal home–sea link into a nineteenth-century context: as members of an emerging respectable profession, sailors were often wealthy enough to make respectable middle-class husbands. And in this light, the Flying Dutchman is an idealized professional: his extraordinary wealth only a coincidental by-product of his relentless maritime wandering. No longer a journey or a voyage, the wandering presents itself as a kind of vocation: predestined to continuously spread Christ's word, the Wandering Jew is saved and his itinerant work portrayed, much like that of the Victorian traveling surgeon, estate surveyor or Imperial civil servant, as a condition of his election.

The Wandering Jew's maritime twin, though a Hollander, would carry British associations in the nineteenth century. Not only was Heine's version and Wagner's original set in Scotland, but Wagner's diary reveals that archetypal male oceanic exile has a peculiar relevance to nineteenth-century English domestic concerns. While he was thinking about the Wandering Jew as a possible subject, Wagner and his wife are caught in a storm at sea on their way to London. After being briefly sheltered in Sandwike, the Norwegian fjord where he will eventually set *The Flying Dutchman*, he and his wife finally reach London by means of a steamship from Gravesend. Wagner's description of his waterway entrance into London transforms a tempest at sea into the cosmopolitan storm of nautical London:

As we neared the capital, our astonishment steadily increased at the number of ships of all sorts that filled the river, the houses, the streets, the famous docks, and the other maritime constructions which line the banks. When at last we reached London Bridge, this incredibly crowded centre of the greatest city in the world, and set foot on land after our terrible three weeks' voyage, a pleasurable sensation of giddiness overcame us as our legs carried us staggering through the deafening roar. (Quoted in Blyth, "Wagner's *Flying Dutchman*" 7)[37]

Wagner emphasizes here the extent to which London, the heart of the late nineteenth-century English empire, was built by professions of the sea. And thus we come full circle to *Persuasion*: the English home's national significance emergent in its professional naval origins. According to Wagner's vision, at the symbolic heart of the English nation lay the structures, values and assumptions of professional seafaring. That is, at the heart of English culture lay a profession that, given its national military and economic importance – or what Jane Austen called its national importance and domestic virtues – rested uncomfortably on the paradoxical union of a putatively disinterested vocational spirit and its commercial interests. Whereas literary domesticity assuaged for a while the anxiety attendant on this union, its late nineteenth-century nationalist version makes that anxiety only more overt.

In this sense, *The Flying Dutchman* represents the domestication of *The Wandering Jew* legend in so far as it rewrites an open-ended story of worldly and circular male wandering by providing it with the romantic closure of female renunciation and sacrifice, a type of closure critics have associated with the female *Bildungsroman*. *The Wandering Jew* is domesticated both nationally in that *The Flying Dutchman* is born of Wagner's entry into nautical and imperial London, as well as literarily in that is places a wandering tale at home in the tradition of linear Western European *nostos* like the *Odyssey*. Ironically, entry into that tradition pivots on the inclusion of a plot device built on female self-sacrifice. Given the *fin-de-siècle* effeminizing of the Jew in anti-Semitic European discourse, it makes sense that the assimilation of a Jew's tale into the English literary canon should entail borrowing a plot convention that is usually associated with female narration.

In returning from this excursion to *Daniel Deronda*, it would appear that Klesmer's remark is important in a variety of ways. Klesmer, a Wandering Jew in England, evokes the domestication of *The Wandering Jew* legend not only by virtue of his loose association to the professional artists behind *The Flying Dutchman*, but quite literally in that he, a homeless Jew, is by no means a wanderer; he is a professional artist. And it is from his vantage point, from that of the professional artist, that Eliot criticizes English mercantilism. But, as her figurative language has suggested, English mercantilism is for Eliot no different than the intellectualism of universalism. And so the domestication of the Wandering Jew is conflated with the domestication of the intellectual, which, given its ethnic insinuations, can only signal the nationalization of intellectual life. As the Offendene passage first indicated, once domesticity becomes linked to intellectual disinterestedness, its only recourse is to a jingoism by which habits of the blood are given responsibility for creating positive meaning.

This is why the focal home of *Daniel Deronda* cannot remain in Chelsea. Mirah does not marry Hans, the strategically situated love interest, does not substantially integrate with the Meyricks' domestic rhythms and does not ever reveal the domestic ambitions of a conventional home-making heroine. Nor does her amateur professionalism ultimately qualify her: although the novel's professional discourse taps her as chosen, her membership of the Chosen People blocks all professional lines of development. Thus it is not "culture" that informs her future domesticity, but nation. Ethnic identity substitutes for vocational commitment. And Daniel the broad-visioned intellectual exchanges the disinterestedness of criticism for the partisan politics of a narrow strip of territory called Palestine.

Afterword

In 1871, George Eliot called the Victorian novel a "home epic" and identified the familial household as the primary "bourne" of nineteenth-century English narrative (*Middlemarch* 890). Several years later, that household is legible only by virtue of a homeless Jewish artist's appreciation, and that bourne figures as a national territory. The narrative inclusion of professional art and of international intellectualism seems to have directed literary domestic lines of development towards a collective ideal absent in the British novel since Sir Walter Scott: the national homeland.

Professional domesticity began by reconsidering a set of truisms literary critics have borrowed from social historians about nineteenth-century domesticity. It has argued that domestic tropes work to represent the home as a vocational calling and the novel form itself as a practice of ethical and social knowledge at a time when many novelists were beginning to shape their careers around an idea of intellectual property, and many feminists were using communitarian definitions of the household to expand the middle-class woman's "private" sphere. By forging spaces of nonpersonal sociability and by playing peek-a-boo with received definitions of "institution," the domestic novels under study here invite rethinking some of the binaries that have characterized the home in Anglo-American culture: leisure against work, private against public, female against male, consumption against production. Most importantly, they invite placing the idea of the home on a continuum of professionalism, which changes how we understand Victorian domestic ideology. In the course of demonstrating formal anxiety about introversion and interiority, these novels suggest a great deal of cultural ambivalence towards nineteenth-century individualism.

In her discussion of the rationalization of housework, Leonore Davidoff stresses the tension between the enthusiastic application of calculation to each and every aspect of social life and the resistance, actual and spiritual, of the familial household to the demystification promised by numbers (*Worlds Between*). Although I would not want to trace the figure of the professional home as it is imagined in the Victorian novel to the story Davidoff tells, I would want to point out that where she sees historical contradiction, the literary critic finds complex aesthetic artifacts. Thus Davidoff points out that a complete economic analysis of household labor itself, especially that performed by wageless, middle-class, emotionally invested women, is irretrievable: how much they saved the household by making jam, by caring for a sister's baby, by obviating the need for hiring an extra servant *cannot be known*, the historian says. Although household manuals proscribed the middle-class housewife from performing much manual work, Davidoff asks how many Miss Mattys simply closed the curtains (87). Again, a historian's voice confesses, Victorian domestic experience *cannot be known*. But, as Davidoff suggests, it can be imagined, was and is imagined, and so she refers us to Gaskell's novel. This intellectual honesty is exciting, but poses problems for both the historian and the literary critic alike. Davidoff brings us back to questioning the role imaginative literature may or may not play on a cultural stage where the statistical assemblage of social knowledge, indeed its very professionalization, has taken up more and more room.

That national imaginings might emerge from the ambivalent and paradoxical narrative about the rationalization and professionalization of home work should not come as any surprise to readers of these stories. For the "true" homes of these novels are located in an experience of alienation that coincides with a sense of vocation. The alienation can take various forms, but it usually involves some real or metaphorical exile from one's national and traditional culture: Anne Eliot in Bath; Lucy Snowe in Brussels; Little Dorrit in Rome; Daniel Deronda in Germany. The vocational awakening can take various forms as well, but it generally involves an ironic renunciation of the pleasures of self-sacrifice. This set of English novels does not, for example, depict home as a real place that must be renounced when a young man leaves for the city to awaken self-consciously to a world of tragic choices and lost illusions; rather, it depicts home as a metaphoric space where leave-taking and vocation merge so that personal fantasies are realized precisely because they correspond to social imperatives. That this fantastic recipe came to dominate the English mid-century novel implies that literary professional domesticity subsumes another equally powerful story about English national identity.

Notes

INTRODUCTION

1 John Ruskin, "Of Queen's Gardens," *Sesame and Lilies* (New York: Chelsea House Publishers, 1987), 85.

2 Margaret Oliphant, *The Autobiography*, ed. Elisabeth Jay (Oxford and New York: Oxford University Press, 1990), 30.

3 Margaret Oliphant, *Phoebe Junior* (New York: Virago Modern Classic– Penguin Books, 1989), 12.

4 Harold Perkin, *The Rise of Professional Society* (New York: Routledge, 1990).

5 *Blackwood's Magazine*, May 1899, 895.

6 Elisabeth Jay, *Mrs Oliphant: A Fiction to Herself* (Oxford: Oxford University Press, 1995), 280.

7 Mary Poovey, *Uneven Developments: The Ideological Work of Gender in Mid-Victorian England* (Chicago: University of Chicago Press, 1988).

8 Nancy Armstrong, *Desire and Domestic Fiction: A Political History of the Novel* (New York: Oxford University Press, 1987).

9 George Eliot, *The Mill on the Floss*, ed. Gordon S. Haight (Boston: Houghton Mifflin Company, 1961), 361.

10 Max Weber, *The Protestant Ethic and the Spirit of Capitalism* (New York: Charles Scribner's Sons, 1958), 47.

11 J. A. Sutherland, *Victorian Novelists and Publishers* (Chicago: University of Chicago Press, 1978), 5–6.

1 PERSUADING THE NAVY HOME:
AUSTEN AND PROFESSIONAL DOMESTICISM

1 Mrs. Sarah Stickney Ellis, *The Women of England: Their Social Duties and Domestic Habits* (Philadephia: E. L. Carey and A. Hart, 1839), 17.

2 Gary Kelly, *Revolutionary Feminism: The Mind and Career of Mary Wollstonecraft* (New York: Macmillan, 1992), 12–13.

3 Jane Austen, *Persuasion* (New York: Penguin Classics, 1985).

4 Marilyn Butler, *Jane Austen and the War of Ideas* (Oxford: Clarendon Press, 1987), xxiii.

5 Jane Austen, *Pride and Prejudice* (New York: Penguin Classics, 1987), 267.

6 C. Northcote Parkinson, *Britannia Rules: The Classic Age of Naval History 1793–1815* (Gloucester: Alan Sutton, 1987), 12.

7 Roger Morriss, *The Royal Dockyards during the Revolutionary and Napoleonic Wars* (Leicester University Press, 1993), vii.

8 See ibid.; Peter Padfield, *Rule Britannia: The Victorian and Edwardian Navy* (London, Boston and Henley: Routledge, 1981); and Dudley Pope, *Life in Nelson's Navy* (London: Unwin Hyman, 1989).

9 Captain E. E. Sigwart, *The Royal Fleet Auxiliary: Its Ancestry and Affiliations 1600–1968* (London: Adlard Coles Limited, 1969).

10 Martin Ridge (pers. comm.) has called my attention to the idea that what Parkinson calls a "change in professional attitude," other military historians call "total war." Ridge speculates that "total war" has less to do with men inspired to fight for the ideas of the French Revolution than it has to do with the need to prove masculinity in terms other than those previously set by an all-aristocratic fighting force.

But there is no reason that these need be mutually exclusive terms. That the ideals of the French Revolution, as represented in a newly democratized navy, might have produced a military situation requiring a new proof of masculinity is implicitly borne out in David Simpson's argument that the "construction" of the national character in Great Britain was significantly influenced by the French Revolution and took the shape of a set of corresponding binaries that posited virility and femininity, the ordinary and the fanciful, alongside the British and the French. In the British embrace of a literature of the everyday that is nevertheless fanciful, these oppositions grow in complexity. See David Simpson, *Romanticism, Nationalism and the Revolt of Theory* (Chicago: University of Chicago Press, 1994).

11 Although I rely most heavily on Harold Perkin's work on professionalism because it takes into account the specificity of English intellectual sociology and its twentieth-century ramifications, I have nevertheless distilled for the immediate purposes of this project the invariants common in work by Burton Bledstein, *The Culture of Professionalism* (Toronto: Norton, 1976); David Cannadine, *The Decline and Fall of the British Aristocracy* (New Haven and London: Yale University Press, 1990); A. J. Engel, *From Clergyman to Don: The Rise of the Academic Profession in Nineteenth-Century Oxford* (New York: Oxford University Press, 1983); Jonathan Freedman, *Professions of Taste: Henry James, British Aestheticism and Commodity Culture* (Stanford: Stanford University Press, 1990); W. J. Reader, *Professional Men: The Rise of the Professional Classes in Nineteenth-Century England* (New York: Basic Books, 1996); Bruce Robbins, *Secular Vocations: Intellectuals, Professionalism, Culture* (London: and New York: Verso, 1993); Sheldon Rothblatt, *The Revolution of the Dons: Cambridge Society in Victorian England* (New York: Basic Books, 1968); W. D. Rubinstein, *Capitalism, Culture and Decline in Britain 1750–1990* (London: Routledge, 1993).

12 The Arts and Crafts movement will later use "craft" as a buzzword whereby

a critique of consumer culture could be launched from a position historically and morally external to urban late industrial society. See Freedman,
Professions of Taste, 59–64.

13 Jane Lewis, *Women in England 1870–1950: Sexual Divisions and Social Change*
(Bloomington: Indiana University Press, 1984), 112.

14 George Eliot, *Selections from George Eliot's Letters*, ed. Gordon S. Haight (New
Haven: Yale University Press, 1985), 477.

15 Charlotte Brontë, *Jane Eyre* (New York: Penguin Books, 1981), 297.

16 Nina Auerbach, *Romantic Imprisonment: Women and Other Glorified Outcasts*
(New York: Columbia University Press, 1986), 48.

17 Denise Riley, *"Am I That Name?" Feminism and the Category of "Women" in
History* (Minneapolis: University of Minnesota Press, 1988), 48.

18 Susan Staves, *Married Women's Separate Property in England 1660–1833* (Cambridge, Mass. and London: Harvard University Press, 1990), 32, 133.

19 Richard H. Chused, "Married Women's Property Law: 1800–1850," *Georgetown Law Review Journal*, 71 (1983) 1360; Alan Roth, "He Thought He Was
Right (But Wasn't): Property Law in Anthony Trollope's *The Eustace Diamonds*" *Stanford Law Review* 44 (1992) 891.

20 Emily Eden, *The Semi-attached Couple and The Semi-detached House* (New York:
Virago Modern Classics–Penguin Books, 1979).

21 Leonore Davidoff and Catherine Hall, *Family Fortunes: Men and Women of the
English Middle Class, 1780–1850* (Chicago: University of Chicago Press, 1987),
420.

22 In discussing the "unmotivated" episode of romance narrative, McKeon
sees a "qualitative completedness":

> omission of episode and detail not on the authority of what is required by the
> empirical nature of the subject but according to an invisible principle, rhetorical or
> theological, the intuition of whose authoritative workings is necessary to render
> complete that which only appears partial.

See Michael McKeon, *The Origins of the English Novel 1600–1740* (Baltimore:
Johns Hopkins University Press 1988), 38.

2 HOMESICK:THE DOMESTIC INTERIORS OF *Villette*

1 Charlotte Brontë, *Villette* (New York, Viking Penguin, 1987), 450–1.

2 Tony Tanner, Introduction, *Villette*. By Charlotte Brontë (New York: Viking
Penguin, 1987), 15.

3 I choose a continuum as a spatial model because what the passage questions
is how to conceptualize an individual life – whether to articulate it in terms of
self-consciousness or in terms of social engagement; positioned on a continuum, such polarities suggest an oppositional relationship that is never one of
mutual exclusion, but always one of degree.

4 Mark Lilly, Notes to *Villette*, 616.

5 George Eliot, *Middlemarch* (New York: Viking Penguin, 1986), 890.

6 Richard Sennett, *The Fall of Public Man* (New York: Vintage Books, 1978).

7 The distinctions among these family types are essential for anyone claiming that intimacy, as the open and warm expression of feeling between people who are emotionally invested in each other, is the property of the family; if the family is a large, fairly heterogeneous household, the kind of exchange characterizing it might be anything but intimate. See Lawrence Stone, *The Family, Sex and Marriage in England 1500–1800* (London: Weidenfeld and Nicolson, 1977).

8 Sennett depicts eighteenth-century civic life as some kind of wondrous carnival where the average citizen daily engages in a variety of exchanges with a variety of people. Despite the fact that Parisian buildings on the Left Bank housed relatively wealthy families on the *rez-de-chaussée* and relatively less wealthy tenants on the sixth floor, it is nonetheless unlikely that anyone other than perhaps a day servant in an upper-middle-class household on his way home from work would actually experience the heterogeneity that Sennett thinks is typical. I find it hard to accept that there would be a number of laborers taking coffee at Sennett's newly "democratized" cafes, let alone "giving" an evening at the opera, despite the fact that ticket sales were no longer strictly allotted to aristocratic patrons. According to Fernand Braudel, even eighteenth-century Paris and London, despite their increasingly democratized parks, boulevards and theatres, were still composed of highly partitioned and self-sufficient neighborhoods, hardly offering the cultural odyssey Sennett envisions. Thus Braudel records how the districts of Paris were quite distinct when he quotes: 'there is as much money in a single house in the Faubourg Saint-Honoré [in about 1782] as in the whole of the Saint-Marcel district" (278). See Fernand Braudel, *Civilization and Capitalism*, trans. Sian Reynolds (3 vols., New York: Harper and Row, 1981), vol. 1

9 I choose "nonpersonal" instead of "impersonal" because I want to emphasize this kind of sociability as a neutral category, and avoid the negative connotations attached to "impersonal."

10 If, for example, I had to classify what kind of sociability a game of whist represents, why would I consider the relationship between the players to be the determining factor rather than the nature of the activity? The terms according to which the players know each other – even if they are class- or gender-based terms – need have nothing to do with the experience of the game. It seems just as possible to me for a consumer bartering in a marketplace to imagine himself working through an Oedipal struggle as for a son to eat dinner with his father without producing any material remotely psychoanalytic.

11 Peter Laslett is quite explicit in challenging the notion that the values of individualism are related to the hypothetically increasing number of nuclear family households in the eighteenth century, the aim of his *Household and Family* being to effect "the abandonment of the rise of individualism as universal explainer of family change." See Peter Laslett, *The Household and Family in Past Time* (Cambridge: Cambridge University Press, 1977), 7.

Less explicitly, other social historians still describe the nuts and bolts of life at home in ways that look blatantly nonpersonal, even while they simultaneously record the apotheosizing language of home life as a celebration of the self and of self-awareness. It is very easy to see an increase in attention paid to personal life when examining household or apartment blueprints which suddenly start to show private bedrooms, water-closets and studies; but even historians committed to documenting domesticity as an ideology concomitant with individualism include descriptions of domestic pastimes and duties hardly tailored to personal concerns. See the entries in the bibliography for Bertholet, Braudel, Briggs and Perrot.

And more recent socio-historical work also supports this notion of the home as an arena of nonpersonal sociability. In their work on the English family, for instance, Leonore Davidoff and Catherine Hall establish a "flexible concept of family" whereby extensive "networks of kin and friends" provide familial communities with population resources necessary in the event of "demographic failure, incompetence or disinclination of their own offspring to join the productive enterprise" (*Family Fortunes* 31). With a host of inns and public houses available to informal visitors, and the common practice of boarding and part-boarding with neighbors, great varieties of casual relatives and friends were constantly included in a given "family." Although Davidoff and Hall suggest that the middle classes of the later nineteenth century may have conceived of a more circumscribed definition of family predicated on allegiance to a business house, they state in no uncertain terms that there is no empirical evidence supporting such a claim.

12 Henry James, "Preface to *The Wings of the Dove*," *French Writers, European Writers, The Prefaces to the New York Edition* (New York: Library of America, 1984).

13 Witold Rybczynski, *Home: A Short History of an Idea* (New York: Viking Penguin, 1987), 39. Rybczynski's remarks about middle-class homes are similar to Lawrence Stone's recent analysis of the architectural renovations in aristocratic manor houses that took place during the next century. See Lawrence Stone, "The Public and Private in the Stately Homes of England 1500–1990," *Social Research* 58:1 (1991), 227–51.

Although I by no means want to deny that household arrangements throughout the century changed in ways that provided more personal privacy (separate water-closets, separate bedrooms, a dining room set apart from the kitchen area), I am skeptical that these changes can be adduced as part of a middle-class ideology that isolated the immediate family from the rest of its local community. On the contrary, the "division of labor" among rooms can be seen as representing a division of activity (sleeping in one place, dressing in another) that induced more sociability – now organized according to activity – as much as it may have entailed a division of classes.

14 Sigmund Freud, "The Uncanny,' in *The Standard Edition of the Complete Psychological Works*, ed. James Strachey (24 vols., London: Hogarth Press and the Institute of Psychoanalysis, 1953 – 1973), vol. XVII: 245.

15 Relevant here is Gillian Brown's discussion of female subjectivity in the context of Anglo-American Lockian humanism in "Anorexia, Humanism and Feminism," *Yale Journal of Criticism* 5:1 (1991), 192 and note.

16 Elaine Showalter documents the fact that an innovation characteristic of British psychiatry during the nineteenth century consisted of what she and others have called the "domestication of insanity." Beginning with the Lunatics Act of 1845, England and Wales underwent a virtual revolution in the caring for and curing of mental illness through asylum renovations. The lynchpin of the "moral management" and "moral architecture" that Victorian psychiatry made its *modus operandi* was a "domestication" that entailed applying a family pattern to the organization and operation of insane asylums:

> The public asylums were organized on the family model, with the resident medical superintendent and his wife (usually serving as the matron) playing the roles of father and mother, the attendants as elder brothers and sisters, and the patients as children. The most important feature of the asylum, one doctor wrote, was its "homishness." Another noted the resemblance of a lunatic asylum to "a nursery or infant school . . . "

See Elaine Showalter, *The Female Malady* (New York: Random House, 1985), 28.

17 According to Arnold Simmel, "Privacy," in David L. Sills, ed., *The International Encyclopedia of the Social Sciences*, vol. XII (New York: Macmillan, 1968), 481, the "private" increasingly refers to the rights belonging to and distinguishing the individual rather than a term that delineates and protects a particular group.

18 This perhaps explains why Lucy constantly claims that her novel is not about herself: when she includes, for example, the segment at Mrs. Barrett's (105), she explains it is not her motivation to talk about herself, only to explain how it is she came to find work abroad. The segment, you see, wasn't about her, only about what happened to her. An interesting distinction.

19 Unlike *Jane Eyre*, for example, *Villette* offers up a series of dissected moments in Lucy's life. In denying Lucy Snowe a David Copperfield-esque "I was born," and opting instead to leave the background of the picture unfinished, Brontë foregrounds Lucy with an almost unpalatable concentrate of present tense, thereby subscribing, in a certain sense, to what Svetlana Alpers has called in her examination of seventeenth-century Dutch pictorial art a "descriptive" mode of representation rather than a "narrative" one: "narrative" pictorial modes take their cues from received mythical or religious histories, whereas "descriptive" modes rely on a nonhistorical moment:

> The stilled or arrested quality of these works is a symptom of a certain tension between the narrative assumptions of the art and an attentiveness to descriptive presence. There seems to be an inverse proportion between attentive description and action: attention to the surface of the world described is achieved at the expense of the representation of narrative action. (xxi)

Although Alpers presents this shift toward descriptive models as the disappearance of narrative, I would call it a relocation, particularly when applied to narrative itself; in descriptive genres, the plot relocates to the space of reading, into the arena of sense-making, hence displaying its readerly priorities. It's not that there is no story, but that the story often focuses on the piecing together that has to take place between the artist and the audience (why is she looking out the window that way, who is the man, do they know each other, are they saying good-bye, etc.). It seems to me that an invariant property of domestic scenes, whether occurring in pictorial or narrative art, is precisely this focus on the sense-making arena. This suggests that domesticity is more a language, a collection of colloquialisms, rather than a topos. See Alpers, *The Art of Describing* (Chicago: University of Chicago Press, 1983).

20 Roland Barthes, *S/Z* (New York: Hill and Wang, 1987), 18–20.

21 In its aestheticized presentation, the Faubourg Clotilde home calls attention to the fact that domestic discourse is a nonreferential one – not about actual homes, but about utterances that are pleasurable for reasons other than their semantic content. Like poetry that luxuriates in the materiality of its phonemes rather than in the appeal of its referentiality, the Faubourg Clotilde home thus unveils itself accompanied by music: when M. Paul speaks to Lucy in the "deep pervading hush" of this aerie, his voice "mixed harmonious with the silver whisper, the gush, the musical sigh, in which light breeze, fountain, and foliage intoned their lulling vapor" (588). Even their dialogue aspires to the condition of music: "'Pretty, pretty, place!' said I,'" Lucy breathes, "M. Paul smiled to see me so pleased" (585). Symmetrically flanking a rhythmically and lexicographically central "I," alliteration and assonance conspire to add the finishing touch to this quaint scene.

22 Asa Briggs, *A Social History of England* (New York: Viking Press, 1983), 240.

3 DICKENS I: *GREAT EXPECTATIONS*
AND VOCATIONAL DOMESTICITY

1 Charles Dickens, *Great Expectations* (London: Penguin Classics, 1985).

2 D. A. Miller, *The Novel and the Police* (Berkeley, Los Angeles, and London: University of California Press, 1988).

3 Michelle Perrot, "The Family Triumphant," in *A History of Private Life, Vol. IV: From the Fires of Revolution to the Great War*, ed. Michelle Perrot; trans. Arthur Goldhammer. Gen. eds. Philippe Ariès and George Duby (Cambridge, Mass. and London: The Belknap Press of Harvard University Press, 1990), 108. See also Elaine Showalter, "Family Secrets and Domestic Subversion: Rebellion in the Novels of the 1860's," in *The Victorian Family: Structures and Stresses*, ed. Anthony S. Wohl (London: Croom Helm, 1978).

4 Catherine Hall, "The Sweet Delights of Home," in *A History of Private Life Vol.IV*, ed. Michelle Perrot, 91.

5 Walter Arnstein, *Britain Yesterday and Today: 1830 to the Present* (Lexington: D. C. Heath, 1983), 79–80.

6 Alexander Welsh, *The City of Dickens* (Cambridge, Mass. and London: Harvard University Press, 1986), 142.

7 Walter Benjamin, *Reflections*, ed. Peter Demetz (New York: Schocken Books, 1986).

8 Benjamin attributes this division between home and office to an economic and political, rather than a religious, overarching scheme – specifically to the "extension of the democratic apparatus" under Louis-Philippe whereby the new ruling class "makes history by pursuing its business interest (*ibid.*, 154). Whether authorized by irresistible historical forces or by divine ordination, the message is nonetheless the same: domesticity occurs as synonymous with a polarized notion of experience.

   Additionally, I should point out that by focusing on the political situation in France, Benjamin's analysis does not entirely take into account that the division of such spaces and the domestic idealization it evinces are, at least discursively speaking, of British origins. English words like "home" and "comfort" appear even in the generally Anglophobic society of nineteenth-century France. Although the expanded political enfranchisement traumatizing France had occurred in England as well, it did so earlier and more gradually and long before the home–office antithesis surfaces. There may be, then, something misleading about attributing domesticity to radical political changes without explaining its peculiarly English history.

9 Witold Rybczynski, *Waiting for the Weekend* (New York: Penguin Books, 1992).

10 I argue here partly in response to the two lines of valuation that Alan Mintz and Franco Moretti discuss. As I will try to demonstrate, home narratives (novels or parts of novels invested in the line of valuation that a discourse of domesticity imposes) must banish psychological priorities – what some would call subjectivity – in order to redefine and thereby reconcile the renunciation of self-interest and the choice of vocation. See Franco Moretti, *The Way of the World* (London: Verso, 1987), 216–17; Alan Mintz, *George Eliot and the Novel of Vocation* (Cambridge, Mass. and London: Harvard University Press, 1978).

11 Sigmund Freud, "Family Romance," in *The Standard Edition of the Complete Psychological Works*, ed. James Strachey, vol. IX, 263–41.

12 Because Pip actually is an orphan and because his home is already a surrogate one, his fantasy of adoption into Estelle's nonworking "family" is not as implausible as it would otherwise seem. But at the same time that the novel makes that wished-for family plausible, it makes equally plausible any variety of hidden parentages, surrogate or biological, including of course Magwitch.

13 The deserted brewery additionally marks the curious position Satis House would occupy on the Victorian social scale according to which brewers were an exception to the rule that the further an income was from the grubbiness

of hard currency, the better. Wholesalers, for example, enjoyed less social stigmatizing than retailers, who were closer to physically handling the specie in which they dealt. But, according to Richard Altick, brewers provided a unique exception: "Of all middle-class commercial aspirants to the rank of gentleman," he notes, "they had the best chance of making it" (629), an observation that Herbert Pocket corroborates – though neither Altick nor Pocket speculate as to why. One answer may have to do with the beer industry's campaign to publicize its use of domestic agricultural products: beer was one of England's few entirely home-grown and home-manufactured products.

   If proximity to the handling of money is the issue, though, then certainly the presence specifically of a brewery clarifies that the Havisham house, regardless of its social prestige, has not adequately processed the signs of its economic base. See Richard Altick, *The Presence of the Present* (Columbus: Ohio State University Press, 1991), 622–37.

14 Burton Bledstein records that in nineteenth-century America, for example, the title "Professor" was faddish argot for anyone claiming to make a living from a particular skill: barbers, dancing-masters, banjo-players, tailors, phrenologists, acrobats, boxers, music-hall piano players and public teachers all called themselves "Professor" (*The Culture of Professionalism* 21).

15 Bledstein describes professionalism as the authorization that election to a group confers, *ibid.*, 34, 86–7.

16 Charles Dickens, *Bleak House* (London: Penguin, 1982), 117.

17 I refer here to Max Weber's sense of rationalization: a rationalized life, according to Weber, is a planned, methodical, unified system whereby any one act can be judged only according to its fitness in relation to the whole (*Protestant Ethic*, 116–19).

18 It is important here to keep in mind the differences among money, capital and property within the context of the novel. Although generally capital means goods or the value of goods, when Herbert Pocket talks about accumulating enough capital to get married, he really means accumulating enough money to secure a position. Regardless as to whether a position in a firm might count as capital, his preoccupation is really with cash. Property can of course refer to money or goods or even land – and though Wemmick refers to the Castle, his rings, and the chicken as property, Magwitch's money is also property. The point is that even when the novel touches on forms of wealth that are not immediately liquidatable, its overall concern tends to be with money, with the material specie. Interestingly enough, Pocket's elision of what mediates between capital and marriage (that is, a position in a firm) is what Pip eventually gets instead of a marriage.

19 I refer here to the distinction between a mercantile drive and the "*auri sacra fames*" Weber identifies as common in most cultures but antithetical to capitalist ethos (*Protestant Ethic*, 71–2).

20 Charity is the relevant exception, although Victorians evince a great deal of ambivalence about both private philanthropy and public assistance.

21 In this way, it can be argued that Dickens uses the financial subtext of domesticity to construct a defense of charity as predicated on the virtues of nonpersonal sociability.

22 Leonore Davidoff, *Worlds Between: Historical Perspectives on Gender and Class* (New York: Routledge, 1995), 88.

23 Sergei Eisenstein, "Dickens, Griffith, and the Film Today," in *Film Forum: Essays in Film Theory*, ed. and trans. Jay Leyda (New York: Harcourt, Brace, Jovanovich, 1977), 195–255.

24 Susan Sontag, "Notes on Camp," *A Susan Sontag Reader* (New York: Vintage Books, 1983), 111.

25 In a complementary way Benjamin describes the collector as a kind of secular savior pursuing a tragically noble business: the collector, he muses, "makes the transfiguration of things his business. To him falls the Sisyphean task of obliterating the commodity-like character of things through his ownership of them" (*Reflections* 155). When, however, Benjamin declares the collector to have failed because in the end he must make do with giving his property a connoisseur value rather than restoring its intrinsic value, he does not take into account how the notion of a collection might square with a secularized Protestant ethos.

The gendered nature of collecting, as well as of kinds of aggregations (including the taxonomies organized by gentlemen scientists) is relevant in seeing the home's Protestant underpinnings. More amateur than the taxonomy, as Tim Dolin has recently pointed out, the collection is associated to a female domesticity. See Dolin, "*Cranford* and the Victorian Collection," *Victorian Studies* 36:2 (Indiana University Press, 1993) 179 –206.

26 In other words, the value of the social interaction that the transfer of money represents outweighs any wrongfulness that might be associated to financial transfers between illegitimately related individuals. Thus the concept of interaction as a universal good supersedes the principle according to which sociability is limited to a set of specific relationships. Relevant here would be the continuum I constructed earlier which maps an instance of sociability according to activity not relationship. In both *Villette* and *Great Expectations*, homes appear through their anchorage in parlour scenes (rather than bedroom or boudoir scenes) and are thus invested in interaction rather than in the cultivation of particular privileged relationships.

27 As Braudel reminds us, money is not the same thing as wealth, but only represents a means of measurement, a language that marks a type of definitively social interaction (*Civilization and Capitalism*, vol. 1, 439): "Like ocean navigation or printing, money and credit are techniques, which can be reproduced and perpetuated. They make up a single language, which every society speaks after its fashion and which every individual is obliged to learn" (477).

28 In this sense, Pip's election-after-all rewrites the paradigmatic Tom Jonesian noble-after-all plot resolution, and is fully in the tradition according to which English novelistic plot conventions make conservative moves

at the same time that they make individualistic and more politically progressive gestures.

29 Obviously I take the novel's original ending as its appropriate one.

4 DICKENS II: *LITTLE DORRIT* IN A HOME AND THE INSTITUTIONALIZATION OF FORM

1 Martha Vicinus, *Independent Women: Work and Community for Single Women, 1850–1920* (Chicago: University of Chicago Press, 1989), 7.

2 Charles Dickens, *Little Dorrit* (Ontario: Meridian Classsics, 1986).

3 Erving Goffman, *Asylums* (New York: Anchor Books, 1961), 3.

4 Mikhail Bakhtin, *The Dialogic Imagination* (Austin: University of Texas Press, 1981), 250.

5 As a biographical reference point, it should be noted that John Conolly, the first proponent of using familial models in reforming mental hospitals, was a prominent figure in the London artistic community as well as a good friend of Dickens.

6 This argument is contrary to what Edward Shorter, among others, claims about the development of "intimacy" in the nineteenth-century family, which he attributes to changes in infant mortality rates and child-rearing practices (see Edward Shorter, *The Making of the Modern Family* [New York: Basic Books, 1977]). But it stands in a more complicated relationship to what Nancy Armstrong (*Desire and Domestic Fiction*) claims about the role of women and the authority of emotion in the ideological evolution of the novel. That Little Dorrit is indeed loved, and that so much is made of her in connection to an ideal of love (and hence of emotion and sentiment) distracts from the fact that she claims a central place in the life of a working institution.

7 In their biographies of Dickens, Edgar Johnson and Fred Kaplan make much of his childhood "trauma": his father's bankruptcy, his family's imprisonment in the debtors' prison and his own consequent work experience in the infamous blacking factory.

Jennifer Wicke makes the trauma more interesting by implicitly questioning what precisely was so traumatic about this experience: his father's bankruptcy, his removal from the family, the industrial workplace, or his job there, which often involved his sitting as a human advertisement in what might have passed for a vitrine:

> Not only was the young Dickens assigned to paste the advertising labels on the shoe polish, but he was placed in a niche at the exposed street-level window, embedded as an attractive human pendant to the title "Warren's Blacking" above him, to serve for passers-by as a "working advertisement" for the seriousness and assiduity of the warehouse as a whole.

See Jennifer Wicke, *Advertising Fictions: Literature, Advertisement, and Social Reading* (New York: Columbia University Press, 1988), 25.

8 A perfect example of this occurs in Anthony Trollope's *Framley Parsonage* when Mark Robarts finds himself ruined, his house invaded by creditors and

his professional reputation sullied when a fairly distant acquaintance defaults on some bills.

9 Altick catalogues a myriad of depictions of bankruptcy in the popular media and how they reflected the various financial scandals of the time (*The Presence of the Present*, esp. 609–11 and 647).

10 One of Fernand Braudel's explanations for England's rise as an economic empire focuses on the unprecedented stability of the British pound sterling from the time of Queen Elizabeth through World War I. According to Braudel, the fact that the English government pursued a policy of stabilizing the pound's value regardless of what economic hardships it caused at home allowed the pound sterling to dominate the international market as the primary basis for determining exchange rates and as a virtually universal standard in garnering credit. In other words, the pound's reputation – its trustworthiness in the eyes of other nations – was a significant economic precondition for the rise of the British commercial empire. This history of England's economic policy here is significant in so far as its implicit acknowledgment of an international economic community further evidences the peculiar depth of England's regard for the market of public opinion (*Civilization and Capitalism*, vol. III, 356–365).

11 David Kunzle, "William Hogarth: The Ravaged Child in the Corrupt City," in *Changing Images of the Family*, ed. Virgina Tufte and Barbara Myerhoff (New Haven: Yale University Press, 1979); R.H. Nichols and F.A. Wray, *The History of the Foundling Hospital* (London: Oxford University Press, 1935).

12 Françoise Barret-Ducrocq, *Love in the Time of Victoria: Sexuality and Desire Among Working-Class Men and Women in Nineteenth-Century London*; trans. John Howe (New York: Penguin Books, 1991).

5 PROFESSING RENUNCIATION: DOMESTICITY IN *FELIX HOLT*

1 Charles Reade, *The Cloister and the Hearth* (London: Heron Books, 1968).

2 It is not unreasonable to see in Erasmus' autobiographical association and final break with Martin Luther a representation in condensed form of many of the Protestant Reformation's central conflicts.

3 Although not a best-seller like his previous novel, *It Is Never Too Late to Mend* (1856), which sold 65, 000 copies in seven years, *The Cloister and the Hearth* was popular enough to figure among the first titles Chatto and Windus included in its groundbreaking 1893 experiment in less expensive publishing strategies, the enterprise they called "sixpenny wonderfuls." After having sold in the thousands since its first publication date, *The Cloister and the Hearth* sixpenny edition sold 380,000 copies over the subsequent fifteen years. See Richard Altick, *The English Common Reader: A Social History of the Mass Reading Public, 1800–1900* (Chicago: University of Chicago Press, 1957) and *Sixpenny Wonderfuls* (London: Chatto and Windus, 1985).

Elton Smith notes, however, that *The Cloister and the Hearth* did receive far more critical acclaim than Reade's more mass-market works. Favorably compared to George Eliot as well as to Dickens and Thackeray, Reade was lauded by many intellectuals and artists of the period: William Dean Howells, George Orwell, W. L. Courtney, Sir Walter Besant, Robert Buchanan and Algernon Charles Swinburne counted among his admirers. See Elton Smith, *Charles Reade* (Boston: Twayne Publishers, 1976).

4 George Eliot, *Felix Holt* (New York: Penguin Books, 1984).

5 Alan Mintz articulates the consensus among Victorianists on work: "The enthusiasm for work is a virtual touchstone of Victorian sensibility. As reason had been to the Enlightenment, work was to the Victorians: an overarching term that sanctioned a multitude of diverse, often antagonistic positions" (*George Eliot and The Novel of Vocation*, 1). Walter E. Houghton corroborates this impression in *The Victorian Frame of Mind, 1830–1870* (New Haven and London: Yale University Press, 1985).

6 George Eliot, *Adam Bede* (New York: Viking Penguin, 1987).

7 Stephen Gill, Notes in *ibid.*

8 Bledstein, *Culture of Professionalism*, 38. Mintz joins others in documenting the rise of professionalism in the nineteenth century:

> The realignment of social forces precipitated by the specialization of function is most evident in the rise and establishment of the professions. Although for centuries there had always been the "ancient three plus two" – the clergy, law, and medicine, in addition to the army and the navy – the nineteenth century saw the rise and establishment of the professional status of many other specialized groups, such as accountants, engineers, surveyors, school teachers, journalists, and under a different set of circumstances, politicians. (*George Eliot and the Novel of Vocation*, 14).

For a more detailed history of English and American professionalism, see David Cannadine, *The Decline and Fall of the British Aristocracy*, 391–444; see also the bibliography for Engel, Freedman, Perkin, Reader, Robbins and Rothblatt.

9 Although its English counterpart remained less developed, the American home economics movement offers an interesting instance of how professionalism extended in a very literal way to the home. Victorians on both sides of the Atlantic saw a proliferation of organizations preaching the rationalization of domestic service whereby managing a home was explicitly compared to running a business: a household of apprentices, servants, boarders, visitors, distant relatives and biological familial members were treated no differently than the ranks of men and women comprising a workshop or factory. Late nineteenth-century America, however, appears to have produced a greater variety of official studies on domestic service (168): organizations such as women's clubs, state and federal departments of labor and college alumnae associations financed research, set up conferences and published reports all in an effort to emphasize the parity between the home and the workplace. The same standards used to reform factories thus applied to the domestic household: "The rhetoric of the domestic service reform movement repeated the point incessantly: domestic service must be rational-

ized according to well-developed principles of capitalist industry." See Susan Strasser, *Never Done: A History of American Housework* (New York: Pantheon Books, 1982), 173.

10 Alan Mintz, *George Eliot and the Novel of Vocation*, and Jonathan Freedman both address these aspects of professionalism. Describing the difference between the American and British models of professionalism, Freedman writes:

> It is true that British professionals emphasized the same relation between their social function and an ethic of service as their American counterparts: British and American teachers, bankers, lawyers, and doctors all claimed to be performing a special function in society by using their training, talents, and expertise to aid others . . . But British professionals seem to have been far more intent than their American counterparts to differentiate themselves from what they saw as the acquisitive ethos of mercantile classes or orders, and far more interested in conforming to the codes of behavior appropriate to the "gentleman." (*Professions of Taste* 52)

11 The original line is uttered by Ladislaw in *Middlemarch* when he complains that Dorothea has anachronistic notions of self-sacrifice, of martyrdom, "horrible notions that choose the sweetest of women to devour – like Minotaurs."

12 Felix's role in the riot demonstrates the sense in which he pursues his calling according to what Max Weber has called an "ethic of ultimate ends." According to Weber, the professional who follows an "ethic of ultimate ends," as opposed to an "ethic of responsibility," presumes goodness to reside entirely in intention, in something like character judged according to an ultimate moral scheme, rather than in the specific results of specific deeds. For such careerists, consequences are, ethically speaking, irrelevant:

> The believer in an ethic of ultimate ends feels "responsible" only for seeing to it that the flame of pure intentions is not quelled: for example, the flame of protesting against the injustice of the social order. To rekindle the flame ever anew is the purpose of his quite irrational deeds, judged in view of their possible success. They are acts that can and shall have only exemplary value.

See Max Weber, "Politics as Vocation," in *From Max Weber*, ed. and trans. H. H. Gerth and C. Wright Mills (New York: Oxford University Press, 1958), 120–7.

Favoring work that is exemplary rather than effective in any specific way, the novel seems to construct a system of values around such callings. That the novel allows Felix to remain a righteous man regardless of the consequences of his actions in the riot reveals that it too operates according to an ethic of ultimate ends: although pub-conversing, tea-making and maybe even novel-writing do not allow for tallying the specific goods they produce, the novel registers them all as careers of influence.

13 Certainly this is what remains a question at the end of *Middlemarch*. Although a degree of critical consensus holds that Dorothea must channel her vocational visions into a marriage with Will because she is a woman, the

novel never explains exactly why she abandons her original plans for a philanthropic housing project. It would seem that Dorothea's position as a wealthy widow would have allowed her to join the ranks of other female – not to mention male – philanthropists. That she chooses instead to be a housewife to Will (and also a financial help to Lydgate) perhaps attests to the cultural significance of domestic careers.

14 I take the terms "satellite" and "kernel function" from Roland Barthes' essay, "Introduction to the Structural Analysis of Narratives," *Image-Music-Text* (London: Collins, 1977), 79–124.

6 A PREJUDICE FOR MILK: PROFESSIONALISM, NATIONALISM AND DOMESTICISM IN *DANIEL DERONDA*

1 As discussed in previous chapter.

2 In all of Brontë's works there is a tension between the topos of self-renunciation typical of domestic plots and a sadomasochistic discourse whereby the reader's desires are relentlessly misdirected. In an action plot similar to *Villette*'s, *Shirley* focuses on an isolated and lonely heroine in unrequited and selfless love with a French-born factory-owner in need of moral reform. See Charlotte Brontë, *Shirley* (Oxford and New York: Oxford University Press, 1986).

3 David Cannadine, "Cutting Classes," *New York Review of Books* 17 Dec. 1992: 52. This position is common even among historians who accept a Marxist definition of middle-class culture as central to the Victorian period. Despite some differences from the gentry and the working class, Davidoff and Hall claim "the middle strata cannot be seen as a block. It was criss-crossed by differences of interest and riven with internal dissension" (*Family Fortunes*, 23). Distinctions among professionals and merchants in London, manufacturing families in the north and Midlands, market-town tradesmen and solicitors and their farming clients, Evangelical and traditionalist Anglicans and a host of nonconformist sects, Radicals and Tories, manufacturers and retailers, wage-earners and fee-earners suggest such a perplexing degree of division that it is hard to accept the conviction that all these social Balkans were unified into a capitalistic middle-class nation.

4 Ian P. Watt, *The Rise of the Novel: Studies in Defoe, Richardson, and Fielding* (Berkley: University of California Press, 1964); Georg Lukács *The Theory of the Novel: A Historico-Philosophical Essay on the Forms of Great Epic Literature*, trans. Anna Bostock (Cambridge, Mass.: MIT Press, 1973).

5 I want to suggest here that what looks *prima facie* as an anxiety about manual labor can be seen as the professionalization and aestheticization of work that is done by hand, be it handknit sweaters or handwritten novels. Hence I suspect that much of the hand imagery pervasive in *Great Expectations*, for example, and even in *Villette* (Lucy is first distinguished by M. Paul when he asks her to serve as his "amanuensis") betrays a complicated relationship between the novel's professionalization of storytelling and the boutique's

professionalization of arts and crafts. This explains in part why lawyers are rarely idealized in Victorian novels whereas doctors generally are, the intellectual work that lawyers perform being less manual than that of doctors.

It is possible that these petty professionals borrowed from a well-established tradition among craftsmen whereby skilled labor could be represented as a property whose intellectual borders and derivative rights were determined and protected by guilds. This would suggest that professionals emulated both aristocratic and artisinal classes. See John Rule, "The Property of Skill in the Period of Manufacture" in *The Historical Meanings of Work*, ed. Patrick Joyce (Chicago: Chicago University Press, 1987).

6 The resistance of class categories in the nineteenth century to easy class generalizations is especially obvious whenever a sociological portrait of English religious divisions is under discussion. In its analysis of the Religious Consensus of 1851, David Martin's *A Sociology of English Religion* illustrates what a morass the Victorian class structure was when it arrives at a heuristic catalogue that both relies on and dismisses economic classifications. Thus Martin divides the British population for future discussion in terms of five unparallel "patterns of attitudes": Catholic, Evangelical, Aristocratic, Working Class, Progressive (58–60).

Interestingly enough, he also cites an equivalent to Marx's fourth class which, not unlike Perkin's proto-professionals, reveals a greater degree of potential solidarity:

No class lines in England are strictly maintained; everywhere there is some interchange between class and class, but the uncertainty of the division between lower and upper working class is quite special in character, and may perhaps point to a coming change of great importance, if it should indicate a diversity of status amongst the working classes that is likely to break up their solidarity of sentiment. (32)

According to Perkin, that diversity of status would divide the professional workers from the nonprofessionals. See David Martin, *A Sociology of English Religion* (New York: Basic Books, 1967).

7 George Eliot, *Daniel Deronda* (New York: Penguin Books, 1987).

8 Benedict Anderson, *Imagined Communities* (London and New York: Verso, 1991).

9 Harry G. Frankfurt, *The Importance of What We Care About* (Cambridge: Cambridge University Press, 1988), 12.

10 Henry James, review in *The Nation* 22 (24 February 1876), p.131.

11 *Dublin Review* 28 (1877), p. 545.

12 Jeff Nunokawa, *The Afterlife of Property: Domestic Security and the Victorian Novel* (Princeton: Princeton University Press, 1994).

13 The famous Offendene passage stands in an interesting relation to Burke's description of the nation. As I will argue, Eliot's substitution of a sense of the universal communion for a sense of national identification suggests that once the immediate community of the family is abstracted into that of the

nation, there is no reason why it cannot be abstracted even further, into that of universal mankind. But such a further abstraction risks emptying the imagined nation of its viability. Eliot's rewriting of Burke problematizes what is central to his passage, that is, national identity. Gary Kelly quotes Burke's famous statement:

> We begin our public affections in our families. No cold relation is as zealous a citizen. We pass on to our neighbors, and our habitual provincial connections . . . such divisions of our country as have been formed by habit . . . were so many little images of the great country in which the heart found something which it could fill. The love of the whole is not extinguished by this subordinate partiality. Perhaps it is a sort of elemental training to those higher and more large regards, by which alone men come to be affected, as with their own concern, in the prosperity of a kingdom so extensive as that of France (quoted in Kelly, *Women, Writing and Revolution, 1790–1927* [Oxford: Oxford University Press, 1993], 16).

14 Sharon Marcus, "The Profession of the Author: Abstraction, Advertising, and *Jane Eyre*" *PMLA* 2:206–219.

15 Edwin P. Whipple, *North American Review*, 124 (1877), 42.

16 George Eliot, *Essays and Leaves from a Notebook* (Edinburgh and London: William Blackwood and Sons, 1885), 291.

17 Deirdre David, *Fictions of Resolution in Three Victorian Novels: North and South, Our Mutual Friend, Daniel Deronda* (New York: Columbia University Press, 1981), 142.

18 Catherine Gallagher, "Politics, The Profession, and The Critic," *Diacritics*, Summer 1985: 39.

19 Homi K. Bhabha, ed. *Nation and Narration* (London: Routledge, 1993), 2.

20 Michael Ragussis, *Figures of Conversion: "The Jewish Question" and English National Identity* (Durham and London: Duke University Press, 1995).

21 Mark Crispin Miller, *Boxed In: The Culture of TV* (Evanston: Northwestern University Press, 1989), 14.

22 Whereas Sharon Marcus focuses on abstraction in her discussion of the centrality of advertising techniques in the self-fashioning of the female professional author, I would focus on Miller's concept of preemptive irony and its capacity to accommodate the apparent oppositions of domestic and professional ideology: production and consumption, male and female, professional and amateur, the self-interest of commercial endeavor and the self-renunciation of vocational commitment.

23 On the divergence between the professional and entrepreneurial classes, Perkin writes:

> especially in the reformed public schools and universities which formed the next generation of hardworking gentleman, the professional and entrepreneurial ideals began to diverge. The gentleman came to be defined by his 'fine and governing qualities', his cultured education, intellectual interests and qualities of character, which rose above mere money making, while the work permissible to him was narrowed down to professional or public service to society, the state or the empire, to the exclusion of "money-grabbing" industry and trade. (*The Rise of Professionalism* 121)

24 Eric Hobsbawm, *The Age of Empire: 1875–1914* (New York: Pantheon Books, 1987); Ernest Gellner, *Nations and Nationalism* (Ithaca: Cornell University Press, 1983).

25 Benedict Anderson, *Imagined Communities* (London and New York: Verso, 1991), 12–36.

26 Reviews of *Daniel Deronda* dismissed the importance of the Jewish question in the second half of the novel as unworthy of Eliot's artistry. A writer for the *Fortnightly Review*, for example, complained:

> We find it hard to believe that the gathering of Jews and the promotion of their national destinies, is a cause real and substantial enough to consecrate the love of Deronda and Mirah . . . It is not a question of what may or may not be going on around us, but of what our imagination can effectively realize.

See Sidney Colvin, "*Daniel Deronda*," *Fortnightly Review* 26 (1876), 605.

And so it is no wonder that the 1878 sequel to *Daniel Deronda* rewrites the original in order to better fulfill the fairytale happy ending of an "after all": the sequel features Daniel disillusioned with the grubby Palestinians (Jews and Arabs alike), burying Mirah in Christian ground after she dies during childbirth, returning to England, converting to Christianity and marrying Gwendolen *after all*. See *Reclaimed, or Gwendolen: A Sequel to "Daniel Deronda"* (Boston: Ira Bradley and Co., 1878).

27 George Eliot, "The Modern Hep, Hep, Hep," in *Impressions of Theophrastus Such* (Edinburgh and London: William Blackwood and Sons, 1885), 278.

28 Catherine Gallagher, "George Eliot and *Daniel Deronda*" in *Sex, Politics, and Science in the Nineteenth-Century Novel*, ed. Ruth Bernard Yeazell (Baltimore and London: Johns Hopkins University Press, 1986), 56.

29 Borrowing Bodenheimer's concept of the benevolent "female paternalist" who intervenes in the regional class-conflicts pivotal in novels by Trollope, and especially in industrial novels by Gaskell and Charlotte Brontë, Linehan argues that *Daniel Deronda* imagines "male maternalism" when social unrest takes on a distinctly national significance:

> In this emphasis on love that begins at home we may find an overlap with the Victorian novel's characteristic urging of female-centered private goodness of heart as the sentimental solution to social problems as well as a parallel with the adaptive feminism found in Rosemarie Bodenheimer's "romance of the female paternalist." *Daniel Deronda* goes to special extremes, however, in making the sexual separation of spheres part of a conscious, ambitious program for national political recovery and yet conceptually breaching those spheres through the nurturance-centered fantasy we might call the romance of the male maternalist.

See Katherine Bailey Linehan, "Mixed Politics: The Critique of Imperialism in *Daniel Deronda*," *Texas Studies in Literature and Language* 34 (1992): 342–3.

30 Nancy Chodorow, *Feminism and Psychoanalytic Theory* (New Haven and London: Yale University Press, 1989), 10.

31 Barry Millington, *Wagner* (New York: Vintage Books, 1986), 157; Galit Hasan-Rokem and Alan Dundes, ed., *The Wandering Jew: Essays in the*

Interpretation of a Legend (Bloomington: Indiana University Press, 1986), 78.

32 G. K. Anderson, *The Legend of the Wandering Jew* (Providence: Brown University Press, 1965), 244.

33 Gordon S. Haight, *George Eliot: A Biography* (New York: Penguin Books, 1986), 156.

34 Heinrich Heine, "The Memoirs of Herr Von Schnabelewopski," *The Works of Heinrich Heine*, trans. Charles Godfrey Leyland (12 vols., London:William Heinemann, 1892), vol. 1,132.

35 Richard Wagner, *Der Fleigende Hollander*. With the BBC Chorus and The New Philharmonia Orchestra. Cond. Otto Klemperer. EMI Records Ltd. CMS 7–633442 (1989).

36 The libretto reads:

> Vonach mit Sehnsucht es dick treibt – das Heil,
> wurd'es, du Armster, dir durch mich zuteil! (Wagner, *Der Fleigende Hollander* 55)

37 Alan Blyth, "Wagner's *Flying Dutchman*: An Operatic Revolution Begins," introduction to the libretto, *Der Fleigende Hollander* (1989).

Selected bibliography

Altick, Richard, *The English Common Reader: A Social History of the Mass Reading Public, 1800–1900*. Chicago: University of Chicago Press, 1957.

The Presence of the Present. Columbus: Ohio State University Press, 1991.

Alpers, Svetlana, *The Art of Describing*. Chicago: University of Chicago Press, 1983.

Anderson, Benedict, *Imaginged Commmunities*. London and New York: Verso, 1991.

Anderson, G. K., *The Legend of the Wandering Jew*. Providence: Brown University Press, 1965.

Ariès, Philippe and George Duby, gen. eds., *A History of Private Life*, trans. Arthur Goldhammer, 4 vols. Cambridge and London: The Belknap Press of Harvard University Press, 1990.

Armstrong, Nancy, *Desire and Domestic Fiction: A Political History of the Novel*. New York: Oxford University Press, 1987.

Arnstein, Walter, *Britain Yesterday and Today: 1830 to the Present*. Lexington: D. C. Heath, 1983.

Auerbach, Nina, *Romantic Imprisonment: Women and Other Glorified Outcasts*. New York: Columbia University Press, 1986.

Austen, Jane, *The Novels of –*, ed. R. W. Chapman, 5 vols. Oxford and New York: Oxford University Press, 1983.

Mansfield Park. New York: Signet Classic, 1979.

Persuasion. New York: Penguin Classics, 1985

Pride and Prejudice. Penguin Classics, 1987.

Bakhtin, Mikhail, *The Dialogic Imagination*. Austin: Unversity of Texas Press, 1981.

Barret-Ducrocq, Françoise, *Love in the Time of Victoria: Sexuality and Desire Among Working-Class Men and Women in Nineteenth-Century London*, trans. John Howe. New York: Penguin Books, 1991.

Barthes, Roland, *Image-Music-Text*. London: Collins, 1977.

S/Z. New York: Hill and Wang, 1987.

Benjamin, Walter, *Reflections*, ed. Peter Demetz. New York: Schocken Books, 1986.

Bertholet, Denis, *Le Bourgeois dans tous ses etats: Le Roman Familial de la Belle Epoque*. Paris: Olivier Orban, 1987.

Bhabha, Homi K. ed., *Nation and Narration*. London: Routledge, 1993.

Bledstein, Burton, *The Culture of Profesionailism*. Toronto: Norton, 1976.

Blyth, Alan, "Wagner's *Flying Dutchman*: An Operatic Revolution Begins," libretto, *Der Fleigende Hollander*. By Richard Wagner. With the BBC Chorus and The New Philharmonia Orchestra. Cond. Otto Klemperer. EMI Records Ltd. CMS 7-633442, 1989.

Briggs, Asa, *A Social History of England*. New York: Viking Press, 1983.

Braudel, Fernand, *Civilization and Capitalism*. 3 vols., trans. Sian Reynolds. New York: Harper and Row, 1981.

Brontë, Charlotte, *Jane Eyre*. New York: Penguin Books, 1981.

Shirley. Oxford and New York: Oxford University Press, 1986.

Villette. New York: Viking Penguin, 1987.

Brown, Gillian, *Domestic Individualism: Imagining Self in Nineteenth-Century America*. Berkeley, Los Angeles, Oxford: University of California Press, 1992.

"Anorexia, Humanism and Feminism," *Yale Journal of Criticism* 5:1 (1991).

Butler, Marilyn, *Jane Austen and the War of Ideas*. Oxford: Clarendon Press, 1987.

Cannadine, David, *The Decline and Fall of the British Aristocracy*. New Haven and London: Yale University Press, 1990.

"Cutting Classes," *New York Review of Books*, 17 Dec. 1992: 52–7.

Chodorow, Nancy J., *Feminism and Psychoanalytic Theory*. New Haven and London: Yale University Press, 1989.

Chused, Richard H., "Married Women's Property Law: 1800–1850," *Georgetown Law Review Journal*, 71 (1983) 1359.

Colley, Linda, *Britons: Forging the Nation 1707–1837*. New Haven: Yale University Press, 1992.

Colvin, Sidney, "Daniel Deronda," *The Fortnightly Review*, (1876), vol. 26: 601–16.

David, Deirdre, *Fictions of Resolution in Three Victorian Novels: "North and South," "Our Mutual Friend," "Daniel Deronda."* New York: Columbia University Press, 1981.

Davidoff, Leonore, *Worlds Between: Historical Perspectives on Gender and Class*. New York: Routledge, 1995.

Davidoff, Leonore and Catherine Hall, *Family Fortunes: Men and Women of the English Middle Class, 1780–1850*. Chicago: University of Chicago Press, 1987.

Dickens, Charles, *Bleak House*. London: Penguin, 1982.

Great Expectations. London: Penguin, 1985.

Little Dorrit. Ontario: Meridian Classic, 1986.

Our Mutual Friend. Harmondsworth: Penguin, 1986.

Dolin, Tim, "*Cranford* and the Victorian Collection," *Victorian Studies*, 36: 2 (1993), 179–206.

Dublin Review (1877), vol. 28: 545.

Eden, Emily, *The Semi-attached Couple and The Semi-detached House*. New York: Virago Modern Classics–Penguin Books, 1979.

Eisenstein, Sergei, "Dickens, Griffith, and the Film Today," *Film Forum: Essays in Film Theory.* New York: Harcourt, Brace, Jovanovich, 1977, 195–255.

Eliot, George, *Adam Bede.* New York: Viking Penguin, 1987.

Daniel Deronda. New York: Penguin Books, 1987.

Felix Holt. New York: Penguin Books, 1984.

Essays and Leaves from a Notebook. Edinburgh and London: William Blackwood and Sons, 1885.

Impressions of Theophrastus Such, Edinburgh and London: William Blackwood and Sons, 1885.

Middlemarch. New York: Viking Penguin, 1986.

The Mill on the Floss, ed. Gordon S. Haight. Boston: Houghton Mifflin Company, 1961.

Selections from George Eliot's Letters, ed. Gordon S. Haight. New Haven: Yale University Press, 1985.

The Works of –, Cabinet edition, ed. J. W. Cross, 24 vols. Edinburgh and London: William Blackwood and Sons, 1885.

Ellis, Mrs. Sarah Stickney, *The Women of England: Their Social Duties and Domestic Habits.* Philadelphia: E. L. Carey and A. Hart, 1839.

Engel, A. J., *From Clergyman to Don: The Rise of the Academic Profession in Nineteenth Century Oxford.* New York: Oxford University Press, 1983.

Feltes, N. N., *Modes of Production of Victorian Novels.* Chicago and London: University of Chicago Press, 1989.

Filmer, Robert, "Patriarcha," supplement to *Two Treatises of Government,* by John Locke, ed. Thomas I. Cook. New York: Hafner Publishing Company, 1947, 121–308.

Frankfurt, Harry G., *The Importance of What We Care About.* Cambridge: Cambridge University Press, 1988.

Freedman, Jonathan, *Professions of Taste: Henry James, British Aestheticism and Commodity Culture.* Stanford: Stanford University Press, 1990.

Freud, Sigmund, "Family Romance," in *The Standard Edition of the Complete Psychological Works,* ed. James Strachey, 24 vols. London: The Hogarth Press and the Institute of Psychoanalysis 1953–1973, vol. IX, 263–41.

"The 'Uncanny,'" *Standard Edition,* vol. XVII, 217–52.

Gallagher, Catherine, "George Eliot and *Daniel Deronda,*" in *Sex, Politics, and Science in the Nineteenth-Century Novel,* ed. Ruth Bernard Yeazell. Baltimore and London: Johns Hopkins University Press, 1986.

"Politics, The Profession, and The Critic," *Diacritics* Summer 1985: 37–43.

Gaskell, Elizabeth, *The Life of Charlotte Brontë.* New York: Penguin Books, 1985.

Wives and Daughters. New York: Penguin Books, 1986.

Gellner, Ernest, *Nations and Nationalism.* Ithaca: Cornell University Press, 1983.

Gill, Stephen, Notes to *Adame Bede,* by George Elliot. New York: Viking Penguin, 1987.

Goffman, Erving, *Asylums.* New York: Anchor Books, 1961.

Haight, Gordon S., *George Eliot: A Biography.* New York: Penguin Books, 1986.

ed., *Selections from George Eliot's Letters.* New Haven and London: Yale University Press, 1985.

Hall, Catherine, "The Sweet Delights of Home," in *A History of Private Life, Vol. IV: From the Fires of Revolution to the Great War*, ed. Michelle Perrot, trans. Arthur Goldhammer, gen. eds. Philippe Ariès and George Duby. Cambridge and London: The Belknap Press of Harvard University Press, 1990.

Hannah, Leslie, *Inventing Retirement: The Development of Occupational Pensions in Britain*. Cambridge and New York: University of Cambridge Press, 1986.

Hasan-Rokem, Galit and Alan Dundes, eds., *The Wandering Jew: Essays in the Interpretation of a Legend*. Bloomington: Indiana University Press, 1986.

Heine, Heinrich, "The Memoirs of Herr Von Schnabelewopski," trans. Charles Godfrey Leland in *The Works of Heinrich Heine*, 12 vols. William Heinemann, 1892.

Hirsch, Marianne and Evelyn Fox Keller, eds., *Conflicts in Feminism*. New York and London: Routledge, 1990.

Hobsbawm, Eric, *The Age of Empire: 1875–1914*. New York: Pantheon Books, 1987.

Houghton, Walter E., *The Victorian Frame of Mind, 1830–1870*. New Haven and London: Yale University Press, 1985.

James, Henry, "Preface to *The Wings of the Dove*," *French Writers, European Writers, The Prefaces to the New York Edition*. New York: Library of America, 1984. Review in *The Nation* 22 (24 February 1876).

Jay, Elisabeth, *Mrs Oliphant: A Fiction to Herself*. Oxford: Oxford University Press, 1995.

Johnson, Edgar, *Charles Dickens: His Tragedy and Triumph*. New York: Penguin Books, 1980.

Joyce, James, *Ulysses*, ed. Hans Walter Gabler, Wolfhard Steppe and Claus Melchior. New York: Vintage Books, 1986.

Kahler, Erich, *The Inward Turn of Narrative*, trans. Richard and Clara Winston. Princeton: Princeton University Press, 1973.

Kaplan, Fred, *Dickens: A Biography*. New York: Avon Books, 1988.

Kedourie, Elie, *Nationalism*. London: Hutchinson and Co. 1974.

Kelly, Gary, *Revolutionary Feminism: The Mind and Career of Mary Wollstonecraft*. New York: Macmillan, 1992.
  Women, Writing and Revolution, 1790–1927. Oxford: Oxford University Press, 1993.

Kunzle, David, "William Hogarth: The Ravaged Child in the Corrupt City," *Changing Images of the Family*, ed. Virginia Tufte and Barbara Myerhoff. New Haven: Yale University Press, 1979.

Langland, Elizabeth, *Nobody's Angels: Domestic Ideology and Middle-Class Women In Victorian Culture*. Ithaca: Cornell University Press, 1995.

Laslett, Peter, *Household and Family in Past Time*. Cambridge: Cambridge University Press, 1977.

Lewis, Jane, *Women in England 1870–1950: Sexual Divisions and Social Change*. Bloomington: Indiana University Press, 1984.

Lilly, Mark, Notes to *Villette*, by Charlotte Brontë. New York: Viking Penguin, 1987.

Linehan, Katherine Bailey, "Mixed Politics: The Critique of Imperialism in *Daniel Deronda.*" *Texas Studies in Literature and Language*, 34 (1992): 323–46.

McKeon, Michael, *The Origins of the English Novel 1600–1740*. Johns Hopkins University Press, 1988.

Marcus, Sharon, "The Profesion of the Author: Abstraction, Advertising, and *Jane Eyre*," *PMLA* 2: 206–19.

Martin, David, *A Sociology of English Religion*. New York: Basic Books. 1967.

Millington, Barry, *Wagner*. New York: Vintage Books, 1986.

Miller, D. A., *The Novel and the Police*. Berkeley, Los Angeles, London: University of California Press, 1988.

Miller, Mark Crispin, *Boxed In: The Culture of TV*. Evanston: Northwestern University Press, 1989.

Mintz, Alan, *George Eliot and the Novel of Vocation*. Cambridge and London: Harvard University Press, 1978.

Moretti, Franco, *The Way of the World*. London: Verso, 1987.

Morriss, Roger, *The Royal Dockyards during the Revolutionary and Napoleonic Wars*. Leicester University Press, 1993.

Nichols, R. H. and F. A. Wray, *The History of the Foundling Hospital*. London: Oxford University Press, 1935.

Nunokawa, Jeff, *The Afterlife of Property: Domestic Security and the Victorian Novel*. Princeton: Princeton University Press, 1994.

Oliphant, Margaret, *The Autobiography*, ed. Elisabeth Jay. Oxford and New York: Oxford University Press, 1990.

Phoebe Junior. Virago Modern Classic–Penguin Books, 1989.

Padfield, Peter, *Rule Britannia: The Victorian and Edwardian Navy*. London, Boston, and Henley: Routledge and Kegan Paul, 1981.

Parkinson, C. Northcote, *Britannia Rules: The Classic Age of Naval History 1793–1815*. Gloucester: Alan Sutton, 1987.

Perkin, Harold, *The Rise of Professional Society*. New York: Routledge, 1990.

Perrot, Michelle, "The Family Triumphant," in *A History of Private Life, Vol. IV: From the Fires of Revolution to the Great War*, ed. Michelle Perrot, trans. Arthur Goldhammer, gen. eds. Philippe Ariès and George Duby. Cambridge and London: The Belknap Press of Harvard University Press, 1990.

Poovey, Mary, *Uneven Developments: The Ideological Work of Gender in Mid-Victorian England*. Chicago: University of Chicago Press, 1988.

Pope, Dudley, *Life in Nelson's Navy*. London: Unwin Hyman, 1989.

Ragussis, Michael, *Figures of Conversion: "The Jewish Question" and English National Identity*. Durham and London: Duke University Press, 1995.

Reade, W. J., *Professional Men: The Rise of the Professional Classes in Nineteenth-Century England*. New York: Basic Books 1966.

Reclaimed, or Gwendolyn: A Sequel to Daniel Deronda. Boston: Ira Bradley and Co., 1878.

Riley, Denise, *"Am I That Name?" Feminism and the Category of "Women" in History*. Minneapolis: University of Minnesota, 1988.

Robbins, Bruce, *Secular Vocations: Intellectuals, Professionalism, Culture*. London and New York: Verso, 1993.

Roth, Alan, "He Though He Was Right (But Wasn't): Property Law in Anthony Trollope's *The Eustace Diamonds*," *Stanford Law Review* 44: 891, 1992.

Rothblatt, Sheldon, *The Revolution of the Dons: Cambridge Society in Victorian England*. New York: Basic Books, 1968.

Rubinstein, W. D., *Capitalism, Culture and Decline in Britain 1750–1990*. Routledge, 1993.

Rule, John, "The Property of Skill in The Period of Manufacture," in *The Historical Meanings of Work*, ed. Patrick Joyce. Chicago: Chicago University Press, 1987.

Ruskin, John, *Sesame and Lilies*. New York: Chelsea House Publishers, 1987.

Rybczynski, Witold, *Home: A Short History of an Idea*. New York: Viking Penguin, 1987.

Waiting for the Weekend. New York: Penguin Books, 1992.

Said, Edward, *Culture and Imperialism*. New York: Knopf, 1993.

Schama, Simon, "Homelands," *Social Research* 58.1 (1991), 11–30.

Sennett, Richard, *The Fall of Public Man*. New York: Vintage Books, 1978.

Shanley, Mary Lyndon, *Feminism, Marriage, and the Law in Victorian England, 1850–1895*. Princeton: Princeton University Press, 1989.

Shorter, Edward, *The Making of the Modern Family*. New York: Basic Books, 1977.

Showalter, Elaine, *The Female Malady*. New York: Random House, 1985.

"Family Secrets and Domestic Subversion: Rebellion in the Novels of the 1860s," in *The Victorian Family: Structures and Stresses*, ed. Anthony S. Wohl. London: Croom Helm, 1978.

Siegel, Reva, "Home as Work: The First Woman's Rights Claims Concerning Wives' Household Labor, 1850–1880," *Yale Law Journal* 103: 5 (1994).

Sigwart, E. E., *The Royal Fleet Auxiliary: Its Ancestry and Affiliations 1600–1968*. Adlard Coles Limited, 1969.

Simpson, David, *Romanticism, Nationalism and the Revolt of Theory*. Chicago: University of Chicago Press, 1994.

Sixpenny Wonderfuls. London: Chatto and Windus, 1985.

Smith, Elton, E., *Charles Reade*. Boston: Twayne Publishers, 1976.

Sontag, Susan, "Notes on Camp," in *A Susan Sontag Reader*. New York: Vintage Books, 1983.

Staves, Susan, *Married Women's Separate Property in England, 1660–1833*. Cambridge and London: Harvard University Press, 1990.

Stone, Lawrence, *Family, Sex and Marriage in England 1500–1800*. London: Weidenfeld and Nicolson, 1977.

"The Public and the Private in the Stately Homes of England 1500–1990," *Social Research* 58.1 (1991), 227–51.

Strasser, Susan, *Never Done: A History of American Housework*. New York: Pantheon Books, 1982.

Sutherland, J. A., *Victorian Novelists and Publishers*. Chicago: University of

Chicago Press, 1978.

Tanner, Tony, Introduction to *Villette*, by Charlotte Brontë. New York: Viking Penguin, 1987, 7–51.

Thompson, F. M. L., ed., *The Cambridge Social History of Britain, 1750–1950*. 3 vols. Cambridge: Cambridge University Press, 1990.

The Rise of Respectable Society: A Social History of Victorian Britain, 1830–1900. Cambridge: Harvard University Press, 1988.

Vicinus, Martha, *Independent Women: Work and Community for Single Women, 1850–1920*. Chicago: University of Chicago Press, 1985.

Wagner, Richard, *Der Fleigende Hollander*. With the BBC Chorus and The New Philharmonia Orhestra. Cond. Otto Klemperer. EMI Records Ltd. CMS 7-633442. 1989.

Weber, Max, *The Protestant Ethic and the Spirit of Capitalism*. New York: Charles Scribner's Sons, 1958.

"Politics as Vocation," in *From Max Weber*, ed. and trans. H. H. Gerth and C. Wright Mills. New York: Oxford University Press, 1958.

Welsh, Alexander, *The City of Dickens*. Cambridge, Mass., and London: Harvard University Press, 1986.

West, Robin, "Jurisprudence and Gender," *University of Chicago Law Review* 55.1 (1988) 1–249.

Whipple, Edwin, "Review of *Daniel Deronda*," *North American Review*, vol. 124 (1877), 31–52

Wicke, Jennifer, *Advertising Fictions: Literature, Advertisement, and Social Reading*. New York: Columbia University Press, 1988.

Wilson, Angus, *The World of Charles Dickens*. New York: Viking Press, 1970.

Index

CAMBRIDGE STUDIES IN NINETEENTH-CENTURY
LITERATURE AND CULTURE

General editors
Gillian Beer, *University of Cambridge*
Catherine Gallagher, *University of California, Berkeley*

Titles published

1. The Sickroom in Victorian Fiction: The Art of Being Ill
   by Miriam Bailin, *Washington University*

2. Muscular Christianity: Embodying the Victorian Age
   edited by Donald E. Hall, *California State University, Northridge*

3. Victorian Masculinites: Manhood and Masculine Poetics
   in Early Victorian Literature and Art
   by Herbert Sussman, *Northeastern University*

4. Byron and the Victorians
   by Andrew Elfenbein, *University of Minnesota*

5. Literature in the Marketplace: Nineteenth-Century British
   Publishing and the Circulation of Books
   edited by John O. Jordon, *University of California, Santa Cruz*
   and Robert L. Patten, *Rice University*

6. Victorian Photography, Painting and Poetry:
   The Enigma of Visibility in Ruskin, Morris and the Pre-Raphaelites
   by Lindsay Smith, *University of Sussex*

7. Charlotte Brontë and Victorian Psychology
   by Sally Shuttleworth, *University of Sheffield*

8. The Gothic Body
   Sexuality, Materialism, and Degeneration at the *Fin de Siècle*
   Kelly Hurley, *University of Colorado at Boulder*

9. Rereading Walter Pater
   by William F. Shuter, *Eastern Michigan University*